Border Bodies

BERNADINE MARIE HERNÁNDEZ

Border Bodies
Racialized Sexuality, Sexual Capital, and Violence in the Nineteenth-Century Borderlands

The University of North Carolina Press *Chapel Hill*

This book was published with the assistance of the Authors Fund of the University of North Carolina Press.

© 2022 Bernadine Marie Hernández
All rights reserved
Set in Arno Pro by Westchester Publishing Services
Manufactured in the United States of America

The University of North Carolina Press has been a member of the Green Press Initiative since 2003.

Library of Congress Cataloging-in-Publication Data
Names: Hernández, Bernadine Marie, author.
Title: Border bodies : racialized sexuality, sexual capital, and violence in the nineteenth-century borderlands / Bernadine Marie Hernández.
Description: Chapel Hill : University of North Carolina Press, [2022] | Includes bibliographical references and index.
Identifiers: LCCN 2021052599 | ISBN 9781469667881 (cloth) | ISBN 9781469667898 (paperback) | ISBN 9781469667904 (ebook)
Subjects: LCSH: Sex role—Southwest, New—History. | Women—Southwest, New—History. | Mexican American women—Southwest, New—History. | Sex crimes—Southwest, New—History. | Sexual abuse victims—Southwest, New—History. | Capitalism—Southwest, New—History.
Classification: LCC HQ1075.5.U6 H47 2022 | DDC 305.30979—dc23/eng/20211108
LC record available at https://lccn.loc.gov/2021052599

Cover illustration: Woman identified as "Carmen" (colorized version of monochrome photo). Arizona Historical Society, Gustave van Hemert Schneider Archive, 1912.

Chapter 4 was previously published in a different form as "Productive Racialized Sex: The Sexual Economy of the Southwest Borderlands, the Nuevomexicana Body Politic, and Memory Archives," in *Querencia: Reflections on the New Mexico Homeland*, eds. Vanessa Fonseca-Chávez, Levi Romero, and Spencer R. Herrera (Albuquerque: University of New Mexico Press, 2020).

*For Eleanor Tapía Barreras and Guadalupe María Hernández,
my first examples of what it meant to be a fierce mujer.*

Contents

Acknowledgments xi

Introduction: Sexual Frontiers, Racialized Bodies, and Sexual Capital 1

CHAPTER ONE
The Oikopolitic: The Father of All, Brokering of the Californiana Body, and the "Natural Order of Things" in Alta California 25

CHAPTER TWO
Circuits of Brown, Black, and Red: The Politics of Racialized Gender and Sexuality in the Nineteenth-Century Borderlands 48

CHAPTER THREE
Absent Presence: The Ghost of the "Only Woman Hanged" in Texas and the Abstract Labor of Gender Racial Formations 79

CHAPTER FOUR
Productive Racialized Sex: The Sexual Economy of the Southwest Borderlands, the Nuevomexicana Body Politic, and Memory Archives 105

CHAPTER FIVE
Technology of "Unproductive" Brown Bodies: The Political Economy of Prostitution and Racialized Sexual Pathology in Arizona at the Turn of the Century 139

Coda 176

Notes 181

Bibliography 203

Index 219

Illustrations and Map

ILLUSTRATIONS
Anita de la Guerra de Thompson 46
Map of San Patricio County 82
"Chipita," by Iris Guthrie 97
Bettie 166
Unnamed woman 167
Carmen[?] 170
Molly 1 172
Molly 2 173
Molly 3 173
Women's Memorial Park cross 180

MAP
The Cotton Trail to the Rio Grande 92

Acknowledgments

This project began while I was a student in the Department of Literature at the University of California, San Diego. My committee members, Rosaura Sánchez, Shelley Streeby, Gloría Chacón, Fatima El-Tayeb, and David Gutiérrez, were exponentially supportive of my half-baked ideas to think sex and capital together. However, it was my advisor, Rosaura Sánchez, who introduced me to Marxist thought, and I have never turned back. Doña Rosaura Sánchez supported my academic curiosities and flooded me with Marx, Engels, Jameson, Harvey, and Callinicos. I remember her tough love until this day, as she was instrumental in pushing me to think about literature, history, and capital together. Her work in the archives modeled for me what I wanted my own work to look like. I am completely indebted to her for being one of the first Chicanas to pave the way for me in academia. I also found lifelong friends who just happened to be scholars with me while at UCSD. Ren Heintz, Jade Hidle, Anthony Kim, Melissa Martinez, Chris Perriera, and Lekeisha Hughes all created an intellectual community that felt more like family to me.

The staffs at various archives throughout the United States made this project possible. Elizabeth Zepeda at the Arizona Historical Society in Tucson introduced me to the prostitution photographs that are part of the Gustav Schneider archive. Theresa Salazar at the Bancroft Library at the University of California, Berkeley, helped me with finding everything I could about the de la Guerra daughters. Nancy Brown Martinez at the Center for Southwest Research at the University of New Mexico was so helpful in pulling guia records for me from the Mexican Archives of New Mexico. The staff at the Santa Barbara Mission Archive Library, the Corpus Christi Public Libraries, and the San Patricio County District Court were all invaluable in finishing this project. Thank you to my mapmaker and dear friend Martín Wannam. Your digital genius always impresses me. Many of these archives were written in Spanish, and Sonia Mariscal-Domínguez translated the formal nineteenth-century Spanish that I could neither make out in penmanship nor linguistically. She was fast and dexterous and I thank her for her expertise.

This project had financial backing from the beginning, and many people and institutes believed in it. A Feminist Research Institute Faculty Grant at

UNM gave me the initial resources I needed to start my archival research for this project that extended beyond the dissertation. After, the Center for Regional Studies at UNM gave me funding for the second chapter of this book that I wrote from scratch. A visiting scholar position in the Institute of American Cultures and the Chicano Studies Research Center at the University of California, Los Angeles, allowed me the time and space to write the first half of the book. David Yoo, Chon Noriega, Rebecca Epstein, and Marissa López welcomed me with open arms and provided not only administrative support but intellectual support throughout my tenure at UCLA.

I would be remiss not to thank the University of North Carolina Press. Lucas Church has been instrumental in pushing this project forward and has been the most helpful, knowledgeable, attentive, and communicative editor I have ever worked with. His assistant, Dylan White, was equally helpful and made this process very smooth.

After I left UCSD as a graduate student, I secured a tenure track position at the University of New Mexico, my home state. Coming home felt heavy. But all the work I was invested in was happening on the U.S.–Mexico border, where my father was born. Coming home was necessary. There will never be enough words to thank my mentor of fifteen-plus years and intellectual hero, Jesse Alemán. I first met "the Professor," as I so affectionately call him, when I walked in to his undergraduate Chicano Literature class in 2005. I had never heard the term "Chicano" before, but I left his class with fists raised and politicized. Quite honestly, he changed my life. By believing in my intellectual abilities, the Professor fought tooth and nail to secure me a job in the department that had raised me. I received the New Mexico Higher Education Minority Doctoral Fellowship, which funded me for four years at UCSD with the promise of bringing me back home as a newly minted PhD. Since coming back, I have cultivated a community of friends, first and foremost. Lucky for me, they are all the smartest people I know. Thank you, Szu Han Ho, Jorge López-McKnight, Ana Alonso Minutti, Kency Cornejo, and Erin Lebacqz for the long nights thinking, talking, and dancing. Thank you especially to Amy Brandzel, who makes me laugh until I cry, knows all my deepest secrets, and commiserates with me over the long days of academia. My colleagues in the English Department at UNM have always been supportive: Marissa Greenberg, Bethany Davila, Scarlett Higgins, Sarah Hernandez, and Nahir Otaño Garcia.

My brilliant students at the University of New Mexico gave me the intellectual power to continue growing as a scholar, especially Tania Balderas, Laurie Lowrance, Lauren Perry, Chrysta Carson, Austin Tyra, Katherine Walker, and Mario Montoya. I am especially indebted to Oliver Baker, a former graduate student in the Department of English at UNM and now an assistant professor at Penn State. Our conversations my first year as a junior professor at UNM sustained me, and our continued dialogue on racial capitalism brings new insights to my work every time we talk.

There have been many Chicanas by my side throughout this crazy journey: Emma Peréz, Adela Licona, Viviana MacManus, Anita Huizar-Hernández, and Vanessa Fonseca showed me kindness, brilliance, and friendship all at once. Karen Roybal and Melina Vizcaíno-Alemán are both my familia. Karen and I coedited a collection together, but our connection runs deep, and I would be lost without her to call and get advice on everything from life to writing. Words fail me in attempting to express the impact Melina has had on my life. She is by far my biggest supporter, my strongest defender, and my smartest hermana. We are a gang of two at UNM, and I wouldn't have it any other way.

One day during my first year as an assistant professor at UNM, I met Szu Han Ho. We were both working on the Race and Social Justice graduate certificate. Little did I know then that Szu Han and the rest of the community organizers I met thereafter would hold such an important space in my life today. I love teaching. And I love researching. But I love fighting for justice even more. Szu Han and I cofounded an artist and writer's collective called fronteristxs. Since 2018, we have been on the ground organizing in New Mexico for abolition. We have had many amazing successes together and have also felt the burden of injustice so deeply that we lean on each other for support to continue. hazel batrezchavez and Martín Wannam joined our collective soon after, and we have become a known organizing force in New Mexico. Thank you to the fronteristxs for giving me the space to love, learn, abolish, cry, laugh, fight, scream, and find peace. Thank you to all the organizers I have met along the way; Prison Divest NM, Anti-War Coalition, Free Them All NM Coalition, White Coats for Black and Indigenous Lives, Teachers Against Childhood Detention, La Raza Unida, ABQ Mutual Aid, Asian American Association New Mexico (AAANM), Millions for Prisoners NM, Albuquerque SURJ, Free Them All NM, National Asian Pacific American Women's Forum (NAPAWF), Save the Kids from Incarceration, Bend the Arc Jewish Action New Mexico, and No Border Wall Coalition. You all are the real MVPs of the world because you are on the ground every day fighting for social justice.

This book would not be the project it turned out to be without the rigorous workshops it went through. The Bancroft Seminar on Interdisciplinary Latina/o History was a huge opportunity for me to sit in a room and talk about my manuscript with senior Latino scholars who work in Northern California. Thank you, Raúl Coronado, Grace Delgado, Lisbeth Haas, Christian

Paiz, Robert Irwin, Desiree Martin, Marcial Gonzalez, and Lorena Oropeza for all your wonderful and kind feedback. Adela Licona and Jamie Lee hosted me at a Salon through the University of Arizona to give me feedback on chapter 4. It was amazing to be around so many fierce and strong mujeres who understood what I was trying to do in my work. Lastly, the UCLA Latinx Literary Reading group gave me brilliant feedback on chapter 3 of this book. I am indebted to all those who sat in rooms with me for hours to talk about my work. You will see all your comments in this final form.

Francisco Galarte, my partner in love, life, and letters, there are volumes of books that could be written about our love. You came in to my life during a transformative period, and you quite literally transformed the way I think about everything. You are caring, understanding, vast, gentle, and divine. You are everything that I have looked for in a partner and more. Your love never tires. You helped me do research in the archives, get all the permissions for the images in this book, and formatted all my notes and bibliography. Your love and support have never wavered. We are the best team I know. Thank you for pushing me lovingly but firmly to realize my full potential. Here is to many more life-changing events we are sure to experience together.

My family endured the most while I was writing this book. My grandmother, Eleanor Tapia Barreras, passed away one month before I defended my dissertation, which would eventually become this book. A modest cafeteria worker who kept the community kids fed, she never made it past the eighth grade. However, she was the smartest woman I have ever known. She taught me algebra in high school when every other teacher failed to do so. She would have screamed it from the rooftops that her granddaughter wrote a book. My other grandmother, Guadalupe Hernández, raised her family on the U.S.-Mexico border before moving to New Mexico. I am indebted to both of them for their strength, their wisdom, and their love. Ericka Baca, Jessica Castillo, and Toni Hernández are my prima-hermanas, and we have been through everything in life together. They never took it personally when I missed a family party or milestone because I was writing or in the archive.

My father, Antonio Hernández Jr., is an unwavering force in my life. I cannot remember a time where I needed him and he failed to be there. He worked as a teacher in El Paso, Texas, when he was young, went back to Albuquerque to marry my mother, worked for over forty years as an educator and coach in the Albuquerque Public School system, and changed so many students' lives. As we are all aware, teachers don't make millions, so he laid tile, cleaned car washes, and coached Little League to keep our family comfortable. He taught me the value of education wholeheartedly. Te amo mucho,

Daddy. And finally, Bernadine Ann Hernández, my mother and my namesake, this book is for you. My mother, the beautician, I was raised right beside you in the beauty salon. I have many times looked up at you and admired your resilience (standing on your feet for over ten hours a day), your friendships (all your customers love you and confide in you), and your discipline (you've woken up every day for forty-seven years and counting to go make people beautiful). I quickly learned what feminism meant to me in your beauty salon. And not the type of feminism that you learn in the classroom, that hood type of feminism. The type of feminism that understands winged eyeliner and acrylic nails. The type of feminism that takes care of family and community, because community is family. The type of feminism that allows all the beautician's children to stay all day in the beauty shop, running wild because all the moms needed to work but also wanted to spend time with their children. That is my feminism, and it all started with you.

Border Bodies

Introduction
Sexual Frontiers, Racialized Bodies, and Sexual Capital

In 2009, a woman walking her dog on the West Mesa in Albuquerque found a human bone and called the police.[1] Further investigation revealed a shallow mass gravesite containing the remains of eleven women's bodies and a fetus. The desolate area, then owned by the developer KB Home, once housed a municipal shooting range and the Bernalillo County Metropolitan Detention Center. KB Home, at the time, planned to build swaths of housing on the land but halted production due to the housing collapse in 2008. As other new development encroached on the land, the developer built a retaining wall to channel stormwater, inadvertently exposing the women's bones.[2] Today the neighborhood is known as Anderson Heights, where track homes sell for $140,000 to $250,000. It took the Albuquerque Police Department weeks to uncover all the bodies, which were scattered around the ninety-two acres of land. After the prolonged excavation, it took almost a year to identify all the victims: Jamie Barela, Monica Candelaria, Victoria Chavez, Virginia Cloven, Syllania Edwards, Cinnamon Elks, Doreen Marquez, Julie Nieto, Veronica Romero, Evelyn Salazar, and Michelle Valdez. They all went missing between 2001 and 2005, and the Albuquerque Police Department made it a point to publicly portray the victims as prostitutes and sex workers involved with drugs. Michelle Valdez was four months pregnant when she was killed. The youngest victim, Jamie Barela, was fifteen years old. Eight of the victims were "Hispanic" women, two were white women, and one was a Black woman from out of state. However, the Albuquerque Police Department publicly racialized *all* eleven women as non-white due to their occupation and class. To this day, no one has been arrested for the murders, and the Albuquerque Police Department's first culprit was dead by the time they officially announced the prime suspects, a list that has now grown to twenty people. The police continue to publicly depict the women as prostitutes and sex workers to justify their deaths.[3]

This act of gendered and sexual violence in the Southwest borderlands is no modern phenomenon, but rather illustrates how poor Mexicanas in the region are and have historically been racialized through their gender, sex, and sexuality and their bodies utilized for capital gain.[4] I focus on the formation of racialized gender and sexuality in the nineteenth-century borderlands, and how they became inextricably linked to capital during the rise of U.S. empire into the early twentieth century as they contributed to the American Southwest's economic development. A history of violence against poor Mexicanas during this time remains largely absent from the archive, but, as I reveal, some Californio, Tejana, and Hispana women do appear. Sex, sexuality, and sexual pairing have always been naturalized as noneconomic, but I argue that these "identity categories" have material consequences on the economy. To tell this history of economic struggle tied to gender and sexual violence in the borderlands, I read American literary and cultural history to develop a theory of *sexual capital* that is inextricable from race. This history remains relevant today, as made clear by the eleven women's bodies found in the Albuquerque desert in 2009.

When the people of Albuquerque and surrounding communities heard about the mass gravesite, it reminded many of the uncannily similar instances of mass feminicides happening across the border in Ciudad Juárez.[5] Just four hours away, poor Mexican women were being killed and left in the desert as well. And while Albuquerque is not a border town, I examine the Southwest borderlands as a region that informs the historical gender and sexual codes that create border discourse and law—a place that has shifted many times between colonial and imperial powers but has a long historical lineage in the changes of borders and boundary making.[6] Cross-border feminicides, as Julia Fragoso Monárrez and Cynthia Bejarano label them, illustrate how gender-based violence on one side of the border "inspires" gender violence on the other.[7] This side, *el otro lado*, participates in the long-standing objectification of poor women of color and racial, gender, class, and sexual normativity.[8]

However, for the purposes of this book, these acts of gender and sexual violence reveal the intersections of race, capital, and sex that are disarticulated throughout history. The eleven women were found in a mass gravesite where KB Home, the seventh-highest-grossing residential home builder in the United States, later built swaths of track homes. The bones were only exposed because the home developer built a retaining wall to prevent flooding on the land. KB Home represents monopoly capitalism, and the women are connected to capital not only through the location of their bodies, but also through their occupations—sex work. In the first year of excavation and identification, every press conference and news article made a point of labeling the women "prostitutes" and "sex workers," all living a "high-risk lifestyle."[9] And while their occupational labels might have been accurate, it is unclear why the Albuquerque Police Department felt it necessary to pathologize the women as culpable for their own murders, thereby rendering them disposable. Why were sex and sexual excess at the forefront of this conversation?

And how were they tied up with capital? The victims' nonproductive occupation became a key component in grouping them together and racializing them. These women engaged in sex work, but they did not produce anything monetarily for the city, state, or nation in which they lived. They used sex only to sustain themselves, according to the Albuquerque Police Department. And through this sexually excessive non-occupation, they got caught up in the "wrong" lifestyle because, as nation-state logic goes, if you are not producing anything for the nation-state, then you have time to get in to trouble. They did not live a "proper" lifestyle, so obviously, as the Albuquerque Police Department's line of thought went, they were deserving of violence. Couple this discourse about their nonproductive (for the nation-state), non-occupation lifestyle with the fact that these women's bodies were found on land owned by a wealthy developer, and the connection between these eleven women and capital through racialized sex, gender, and sexuality becomes clear.

The purpose of this study is not to understand how poor Mexicanas in the borderlands are connected *to* capital but how they are connected *through* capital. By *through* capital, I argue that women's bodies in the borderlands are lynchpins in the capitalist transformation of the West and Southwest. I argue that racialized sex, gender, and sexuality are very much tied to the ways capital is able to function through what I call *sexual capital*.[10] The feminicide of the women on the border and in the borderlands suggests an ongoing process of gender and sexual violence. However, this violence is enunciated differently throughout history, and that historical *difference* is the crux of this study. I do not begin with this contemporary example to suggest that there is a monolithic continuation of sexual and gender violence against women of color in the borderlands and that nineteenth-century U.S. empire is the loci or beginning of that violence. Rather, I begin with this example as a way to explore "systematic patterns of violence," as Nicole Guidotti-Hernández states, which illustrate varied relationships to colonialism and imperialism and provide a roadmap to unveil how racialized sex, gender and sexuality are inextricably tied to sexual capital and how the relationship between sex and capital produce cases of violence.[11] I examine, interrogate, and make clear how sexual capital is mobilized at different historical moments for different projects on the U.S.–Mexico border and in the Southwest borderlands before and after annexation. Whether tied to racist colonial ideology, economic interests, or nation-building projects, racialized sex, gender, and sexuality utilize the extraction of sexual capital in violent ways.

This study is multi-genre and interdisciplinary at its core. I investigate moments of gender and sexual violence in the U.S. borderlands from 1834 to

1912. To do so, I rely on a range of previously unconnected archival materials—court cases, testimonies, letters, narratives, photographs, maps, newspapers, editorials, and other historical documents—to reveal a discourse of violence toward certain poor, racialized, female bodies in the borderlands that has become normalized in dominant histories, literary narratives, and imaginaries. The abstraction of the cultural artifacts that I utilize in this study (many of them out of print, newly uncovered, or on the edge of annihilation) mirrors the abstraction of labor and the materiality of the flesh for poor Mexicanas in the borderlands. I begin during a time when an influx of white settlers were migrating west and conducting business with elite landholding Californios, Hispanos, and Tejanos. This starting point is also twelve years before the beginning of the Mexican-American War, which resulted in the annexation of northern Mexico; during this time, gender and sex were closely linked to wealth in the borderlands. I end in 1912, a year that signified major shifts in economics, immigration law, and moral reform before the Progressive Era. I utilize four distinct case studies as examples of how racialized sex, sexuality, and, by extension, gender were inextricably tied to capital and how these historical instances often led to violence. The archival materials and primary sources I use are interdisciplinary, mostly unexamined, and robust. I circumvent the oppressive telos of period divisions by extracting moments that radiate backward, forward, and outward, demanding that they be read nonlinearly. In short, I tell a revisionist teleology of Latina/o history and build upon the foundational and field-defining work of Chicana feminists.[12]

I make the case for racialized sex and sexuality for brown female bodies in the borderlands, a term coined by Abdul R. JanMohamed but extended by Chicana/Latina, Black, and Asian feminists. I maintain that sexual capital, as I define it, utilizes racialized sex, gender, and sexuality to build capital. While capital is most often recognized solely as the exploitation of labor, I foreground the exploitation of *the body*. Therefore, I build on Chicana feminist Antonia Casteñeda's use of racialized gender and sexuality, where she defines gender as denoting the social construction and performativity of masculinity, as well as of femininity—and thus the social construction of distinctions between male and female.[13] Gender gives sex (both biological and the "act" of heteronormative sex) its coherence, and gender and sexuality are dimensions of "subjectivity that are both an effect of power and a technology of rule, that analyze colonial and settler colonial domination in relation to the construction of subjectivities—meaning forms of personhood, power, and social positioning."[14] Therefore, I argue, racialized sexuality is linked to historical sexual economies and processes of sexualization that situate the utility of bodies to a particular historical moment and maintenance of racialized gendered and sexual social roles.

In conjunction with Chicana feminists in my consideration of racialized sex and sexuality, I also expand on Abdul R. JanMohamed's work where sex and sexuality fall outside of discursive normativity and are maintained and regulated by law, prohibition, and production.[15] Within the U.S. nation-state, racialized sexuality exists at the point where powerlessness of racialized subjects intersects with prohibitive power.[16] For JanMohamed, racialized sexuality is more than Foucault's "incitement to discourse"; Foucault's discursive polymorphous power is actually centralized in the juridico-discursive, where power acts as law. Thus, for this book, racialized sex and sexuality fall outside of the discursive power of normative "sexuality" because they are maintained and regulated by law, prohibition, and the violent miscegenation of racialization. In contradistinction to white sexuality, where the women (many of whom were ethnic minorities—i.e., white Mexicanas or white Mexican Americans) were seen as the center and boundary of the home and, by extension, the nation, women of color had already failed as proper feminine figures, and their sex and sexuality were written into debt peonage, prostitution, and lynching laws.[17] Utilizing the colonial and imperial history of sexual violence in the Southwest that pathologizes poor, brown female bodies, their sexual politics, and their sexual relations as excessive and hypersexual, I construct my notion of racialized sex and sexuality.

The intersection of race, sex, gender, capital, and labor constitutes the main contention in this study; this intersection goes "unseen" historically in a multitude of ways that solidify the poor, racialized Mexicana's position in society. While I did not coin the term "sexual capital," I make a rather different intervention than sociologists who have conventionally theorized it. I take cues from scholars in the humanities who are involved in the discussion of racial capitalism, like Lisa Lowe, Cedric Robinson, Iyko Day, and Nikhil Pal Singh. Let me briefly explain my definition of sexual capital by first laying out what it is not. Early Marx had a hard time identifying what sex actually *did* in a capitalist society. His musings on sexual labor began with the prostitute in the *Economic and Philosophic Manuscripts of 1844*. In one instance he states that the prostitute "becomes a piece of *communal* and *common* property."[18] Just below this, in a footnote, Marx states, "Prostitution is only a *specific* expression of the *general* prostitution of the *labourer*, and since it is a relationship in which one falls on not the prostitute alone, but also the one who prostitutes—and the latter's abomination is still greater—the capitalist etc., also comes under head."[19] In one instance, the prostitute's body belongs to the community and is therefore the most degraded commodity. In another instance, people can buy the labor of the prostitute because she is like the worker—degraded. Either way, she is degraded and an exception to the labor theory of value. However, there is a big difference between being owned and selling your labor. The first part of my concept of sexual capital intervenes here and states that sex itself is not an exception to the labor theory of value. Quite the opposite, when sex intersects with race, which it most oftentimes does within empire, that labor goes unseen and contributes to the flows of capital in violent ways. Labor is not, as Marx states, "homogenous human labor," and the wage laborer is not the only person who produces for capital. Whether through economic systems like debt peonage, where racialized sex maintains an entire economic system, or through immigration laws like the Page Act in 1875, where the unlikely relationship between Chinese deportation aligned with the decreasing political and economic power of Mexican prostitutes in Arizona, racialized sex (and by extension racialized gender) in the U.S.–Mexico borderlands is labor power that upholds violent institutions.

In other musings on sexual labor, both Marx and Engels discuss how private property is fundamental to capitalism and how monogamy is situated at the center of private property. The wife is private property and "expected to . . . remain strictly chaste and faithful."[20] This ensures that private property passes on through the fidelity of the woman. Because the woman in the monogamous family does not produce commodities as the wage-laborer, but rather produces children who transform into labor power, Marx and Engels do not consider her reproductive labor of value. Out of this come Marx's notions of productive and reproductive labor.[21] Marxist feminists, like Leopoldina Fortunati, began rewriting reproductive labor as the mystified form of capitalist labor, a type of labor that produces labor power as a commodity.[22] However, what Marx and Marxist feminists overlook is how racialized sex, and by extension gender, produces labor power and commodities simultaneously through sexual capital. The second part of my concept of sexual capital considers how poor Mexicanas in the borderlands in the nineteenth century engage in highly differentiated gendered and sexual practices, which are abstracted labor in order to create value. This is most evident within the economic systems that were running before industrial capitalism entered the Southwest borderlands. Economic systems, such as the hacienda system, the communal land system, and debt peonage, enunciate the ways in which the brown female body was utilized for her sex in order to create value not only in those spaces, but also through transnational trading relations. The brown female body is not seen as producing value, but her sex not only produces value (like commodities that were traded) but also reproduces the entire workforce through her children. Sexual capital interrogates how different bodies are signified differently through race, gender, and sex that depend upon different geospatial environments and are made spatially competitive through the circulation of capital.[23] Therefore, the third way I define sexual capital centers on how the needs of capital in the cultural construction of racialized sex and gender go unseen in the conversation of labor and come to signify a much different meaning against normative femininity. This look at how different bodily qualities that are codified in relation to the circulation of capital, the myriad ways in which sex is not an exception to the labor theory of value, and the ways racialized gender and sexual practices are abstracted labor in order to create value all work to unveil sexual capital in this study.

The unproblematized history of racialized gendered violence central to the discourse of proper femininity, the same discourse adopted by the Albuquerque Police Department, is an important part of the history of the borderlands. I unsettle this history by uncovering *why* gender and sexual violence are tied to race and capital. I examine how sexual and gendered power and intimacies are first and foremost sites of intrusive interventions, and how problems of empire and its related forms of racialization are shaped against gender, sex, and sexuality. In other words, how are gender and sexual order/power, which are regulated through private and public life, inextricable from other regulatory schematics of property holding, labor, and citizenship?[24] I interrogate the notion of modern sexuality as it emerges through sexual, colonial, and expansionist conquest and violence in the Southwest and how these material and discursive processes work to pathologize women in the borderlands as "disposable" or "proper" in the nineteenth and early twentieth centuries. Simultaneously, I study the relationship and slippage in normalized discourse that renders certain poor Mexicanas, Nuevomexicanas, and Tejanas only visible through brutal gendered and sexual violence, in contrast to the elite landholding Mexicanos, Californios, Tejanos, Hispanos, and Mexican American women who represent themselves as "proper" and "civil" citizens propelling the nation forward during a time when the rhetoric of "civility" was at its peak at the height of the U.S. empire. I trace the transformation of racialized female bodies from productive under different colonial and imperial regimes to unproductive at the turn of the century in the United States through racialized sexuality.

In doing so, I make clear how racialized sexuality and, by extension, gender affect the different classes of the Southwest borderlands through sexual capital in the nineteenth and early twentieth centuries. While the Southwest borderlands in the nineteenth century were a contested zone, the area's inhabitants fought against empire and subscribed to it, held political power and were excluded from it, and functioned within different economic systems that led to our current global capitalist moment. Many of the women in the nineteenth-century borderlands were of mixed Spanish-Mexican or Spanish-Indian ethnicity, and the making over of this racialized population depended on class, skin color, and the accession to whiteness. While Mexicanos, Californios, Hispanos, and Tejanos were displaced from their land, class, and cultural positions, they were not exempt from attempting to establish their whiteness and/or take part in reproducing violence against lower classes of Mexicanas, as well as Black and Indigenous peoples. I approach this clash of hierarchy by making clear how sex was prescribed to different women and how some functioned as the "proper" feminine, while others were cemented as less than "proper" through violence and discourses of excess due to the forced enunciation of their sex and sexuality.

I must briefly explain how I use the terms "sex," "sexuality," and "gender" in this study. These terms are not interchangeable, and I do not always use them in the same manner as contemporary scholars of critical gender and sexuality studies. Much work has been done on the performativity of gender, and there has been equal work done to undo the biological understanding of anatomical sex.[25] However, I focus on the act of sex and how power over sex leads to, many times, forced heterosexuality within empire. The sexuality of the racialized female body is tied to heteronormative power, which utilizes racial subjects to build and contend with capital and empire. I am interested in sexuality, not because of the psychic desire behind the sexual choice, which is a whole other interesting and needed book, but because sexual difference for the racialized female in the nineteenth century affected material, lived experience that constituted subjectivity.

The Latino nineteenth-century archive is at odds with forms of U.S. literary history because many of the narratives are written in Spanish and based on the writer's travel inside and outside of U.S. national boundaries; more importantly, the archive also does not contain the narratives of poor racialized women in the borderlands. I reckon with subjects in what Rodrigo Lazo has coined "migrant" archives—those that "reside in obscurity and are always at the edge of annihilation."[26] Though not included in the archive "proper," I read racialized female subjects who reside in the Southwest borderlands in the silences of that archive. Racialized sex and sexuality have been neglected, yet important, historical concepts for the racialized female subject on the borderlands through colonialism and imperialism. I argue that racialized sex, sexuality, and gender fall outside of the discursive power of their normative constructions because these differentiations are maintained and regulated by law, prohibition, and the violent miscegenation of racialization. I intervene in many historical and contemporary discussions of sex, gender, and capital to elucidate how racialized bodies, which are central to economic growth, fall out of the theorization, but, more importantly, how sexual capital—through racialized gender and sex—accumulates capital. Race, sex, gender, and capital produce an intersection of bodily violence for racialized Mexicanas in the borderlands that extracts value from their bodies but goes completely unseen.

Uncovering the Sexual and Gendered Borderlands Archive

While I wanted this study to be a reading of material "textual imperial power," that proved to be extremely difficult.[27] "Racialized sexuality" and "sexual capital" are not search terms that appear in library catalogs, making it an investigative journey from the beginning. The historical record favored upper-class, elite, landholding Californianas, Tejanas, and Hispanas, which said a great deal about power struggles through the discursive absences and presences. The correlation between elite landholding Californianas, Tejanas, and Hispanas and poor, dark-skinned, racialized women on the borderlands during the same period unveils how pathology is mapped onto certain bodies with intersections of race and class. I begin this study with the discursive production of "proper" femininity and how it functions on the borderlands in relation to racialized sex, sexuality, and gender through the brokering of elite Californiana women. In examining the de la Guerra archive located at the Santa Bárbara Mission Archive-Library, I recovered letters between the de la Guerra daughters (four daughters in total) and their family members discussing the onus of married life to white eastern male settlers and separation from their culture and their families in order to assuage their father, Don José de la Guerra y Noriega, one of the richest men in Alta California. These letters (and the other materials from Latino print culture I uncovered) are part of a dynamic multilingual culture on the borderlands that required linguistic dexterity. Written in Spanish, these letters unveil the aristocratic condition of sexual capital; they are one of the earliest examples of how women, sex, and bodies made the West and Southwest a capitalist region *before* capitalist transformation took hold in the United States during the industrial revolution as an outwork system of labor shifted toward a factory system of labor in the North and South. By the logic of sexual capital, the West was operating on capitalist principles by brokering the reproductive labor of women long before the transfer to U.S. rule. I look at how the de la Guerra estate functioned at the interstices of the household and political economy, allowing the patriarch to broker his daughters for economic gain but under the guise of private life, which would later become the province of biological reproduction and what is natural and proper about affective and domestic labor. The archive of the de la Guerra daughters began to merge the discourse of racialized sexuality with the material effects of sexual capital. The de la Guerra daughters' letters served as a window into how certain bodies were worthy of brokering and others were not. But, most importantly, the letters laid out quite clearly how males in the borderlands extracted value from female bodies, with very distinct differences in how value was assigned to those bodies. For the elite landholding Don José de la Guerra y Noriega, brokering his daughters' bodies and sex added to his fortune.

To understand how elite landholding Californios and poor, racialized Mexicanas were inextricable from each other, I needed to look at what *was* archived, like the de la Guerra daughters' letters, and I needed to know the rich economic history of California. California—a maritime trade focal point, a key site for the cattle industry, and, of course, home to the Gold Rush—began dealing with land disputes when the U.S. Congress passed the Land Law Act in 1851, establishing a commission to review land grants from the Spanish crown and Mexican government.[28] However, before 1851, Don José de la Guerra y Noriega was already one of the richest men in northern California. He garnered his wealth by shaping trade and profit in the military outposts, which he was able to do because of his "noble" Spanish blood. De la Guerra had no shame in "economizing" the female bodies of his daughters because it held in tact his household, political power, and wealth. And as Erika Pérez uncovers in her astute study of gender and sexual relations in California, the de la Guerra daughters remained monogamous to their white Yankee and European husbands in a melding of religious beliefs and respect for the family name.[29] The de la Guerra daughters were "properly" feminine, and even as Californios, they were not racialized in the same manner as their peons and workers because of their Spanish nobility and wealth. Along with their archival letters, I also examine the de la Guerra Family Photograph Archive, Teresa de la Guerra's *testimonio* in the Bancroft Library, and the rare text *The California Recollections of Angustias de la Guerra Ord*.

The palpable undertone of anti-Indigeneity and anti-Blackness in the de la Guerra letters led me to wonder how discourses circulated and inform(ed) racialized sexuality in the Americas. I then turned to the discursive construction of racialized sex, sexuality, and gender by examining how race is nation-bound, pushed through Mexican discourse that reveals hemispheric (Mexican) racial trajectories. Before I was even able to connect how racialized sex produces capital, I had to examine the discourses around racialized sex, sexuality, and gender in the nineteenth-century borderlands. By mapping how gendered racialization and racialized sexuality took form in the U.S.–Mexico borderlands through discursive ideology, I interrogate racial hierarchies that are attached to gender and sex through hemispheric anti-Black and anti-Indigenous discourses. One of the most popular cultural artifacts examining the intersection of anti-Indigeneity, anti-Blackness, and *mexicanidad* is María Ruiz de Burton's English novel, *Who Would Have Thought It?*, published in 1872. While there is no lack of scholarship on Ruiz de Burton or her writings, I began examining the relationship between Mexico and the newly acquired northern part of Mexico in relation to racialization in the Americas. The tropes of *los indios (bárbaros)* and *la cautiva*, used by Ruiz de Burton with her characters Lola and Doña Theresa, and of *la mulata*, which Ruiz de Burton reworks in her construction of Lola as dyed Black, all point to discourses that were prevalent at the time in Mexico.[30] In thinking about the locales of the book, I researched nineteenth-century newspapers from Sonora, Mexico, which brought me to the archive of the Mexican, Spanish-language newspaper *La Estrella de Occidente* (later published as *Boletín Oficial* and *La Constitución*) and the legends of La Mulata de Córdoba. Together, the novel, archival documents, and folklore tell a story of the construction of white *mexicanidad* in relation to the discursive ideology of racialized gender and sexuality in the Americas and unveil how racial discourses move throughout space. It is not enough to read Ruiz be Burton from a U.S.-centric racial ideology. I read her through a Mexican racial discourse that becomes hemispheric and influential on racialized gender, sex, and sexuality in the newly acquired U.S.–Mexico borderlands.

The next three chapters and their respective archives all reveal the material consequences of how sexual capital produces racialized gender and sex and then produces violence. I first turn to the slim archive of Josefa (Chipita) Rodríguez, who was executed by hanging in San Patricio, Texas, in 1863. I was struck by the ghostly presence of Chipita, not only through the absence of most of her archive, but also through the cultural production that ensued after her death, mostly in the 1970s and '80s. Rodríguez is invisible through her labor and capital accumulation for the Confederacy, and only visible through violence, which is her hanging. Because gender is always inextricable from sex, the third chapter and thin archive is a bridge chapter that examines the gendered racial formation of Mexicanas in the borderlands that leads to violence. Josefa Chipita Rodríguez was sixty-three years old when she was executed by hanging in San Patricio County on November 13, 1863. Most of the archival records that documented her hanging are gone due to natural occurrences like fire and flooding, but also due to the lack of archival preservation even after these events. The remaining court transcripts of her trial, housed at the San Patricio County District Court Records Office, the legislative bill exonerating her, which passed in 1985 as Senate Concurrent Resolution 14, and the cultural artifacts produced after her execution tell a story that constructs racialized gender and sexuality in the nineteenth century for Mexicanas in the borderlands. This chapter marks a turn in the discussion to examine what happens when gender racial formations are only visible through violence. Rodríguez's body is fraught, her labor is invisible throughout her life, and her body is only visible through violence after her death. The archival gap renders the numerous narratives surrounding her story fraught as well. Her slim archive and the cultural production produced after her death grapple with the overlay of racialized sexual difference, as witnessed in Rodríguez's already castrated body, as the ultimate denouncement of her position in society. Racialized sexuality functions differently in this instance, in that it has less to do with the actual act of sex and more to do with the violence of the already racially sexed and gendered body. This archive connects the discursive construction of racialized gender and sexuality with the material consequences of those constructions on Mexicana lives.

The materiality of how sex and gender affected Mexicanas in the borderlands is a tangible way to read the archives. There were many different economic systems in the Southwest borderlands before and after U.S. annexation. I challenge the historical understanding that the nineteenth-century Southwest borderlands were absent from burgeoning capitalist relations in the United States and instead only utilized agrarian and mercantile relations in their "backward" land. Just as the circulation of ideas and texts spilled over national boundaries in the Latino archive, so did trade in the Southwest borderlands. According to early European modern economic thought, wealth in the nineteenth century was measured by how much a nation produced and traded. Before, in the eighteenth century, wealth was measured by the amount of gold or silver a nation held.[31] This line of thinking that Adam Smith revolutionized favored free trade over trade restrictions, which focused on the well-being of the nation-state and vacillated between the power of the monarch and that of the monarch's vassals.[32] However, the economic situation in the Southwest borderlands was a bit different. Elite landholding Spanish-speaking subjects "sought reform as members of the aristocracy *becoming* bourgeoisie (many *letrados* were involved in extensive private business ventures that suffered because of the lack of free trade) who had witnessed the impoverished living conditions of the [Spanish]."³³ Many "nobles" wanted free trade, but they stopped short of economic reform that provided for the well-being of the masses. This shift from mercantile capitalism to free trade was a hard one for those in the Southwest borderlands because these Californios, Tejanos, and Hispanos wanted to stay at the top of the hierarchy. As evidenced by their accumulation of wealth before annexation, they stayed at the top, but their wealth dwindled when Anglo settlers began migrating into their geopolitical locations. Still, the Southwest borderlands were involved in intricate free-trade capitalism.

I also examine how sex informs social production in the borderlands and the intersection of the political economy of sex and race. My study begins in 1834, twelve years after the opening of the Santa Fe Trail and fourteen years before the United States annexed the northern Mexican frontier—a time that many historians would say is anachronistic to capitalism. I argue that elite Californios, Tejanos, Hispanos, and white settlers utilized racialized sexuality for the expansion of their wealth and were deeply involved in transnational trading and commerce. While merchants from Missouri and the eastern states "had gained the upper hand over the local merchants in the trade itself, if not in local governance," the elite landholding families in the Southwest played a pivotal role in the economic system that was developing in the territory as a result of the Santa Fe Trail.³⁴ From "large land holdings to extensive involvement in mercantile and livestock trade," the role that *ricos* played in the continued economic and geographic growth of commercial networks significantly impacted the shift from mercantilism to the saturated market of the production of goods, industrialization (the railroad), and commercial finance even as Hispanos, Californios, Mexicanos, and Tejanos were in a precarious political and economic position during Euro-Anglo encroachment.³⁵ This is all to say that racialized sex subsidized capitalist relations in the Southwest borderlands.

One of the economic systems that thrived in the Southwest borderlands before and after annexation was debt peonage. In the Center for Southwest Research at the University of New Mexico, I uncovered New Mexico Territorial Supreme Court cases that exemplified the role racialized sex had in keeping the system of debt peonage alive. The case of *Marcellina Bustamento v. Juana Analla* in 1857 solidified debt peonage as a sexual economy that built capital. These archival court cases illuminate the material consequences of technologies like sex and gender. Where Marxist feminists uncover reproductive labor as the mystified form of capitalist labor, breaking down the distinction between that which is a condition of labor and that which is labor (and they state that both are forms of labor), they cannot consider how racialization is mapped onto certain bodies in the Southwest borderlands and tied to sexual capital. Being at this juncture means we can read their labor both as productive and reproductive within debt peonage. The dual capacity occupied by poor, brown female bodies in the borderlands produced for the family, because the male was indebted to his patrón and did not bring home enough to sustain a family, and also reproduced the labor force that enabled the patrón to build up his economic system and participate in transnational exchange. However, with the interests in capital changing, her body moves from being productive for capital in the nineteenth century to unproductive at the turn of the twentieth century. This means that her body became sexually excessive in the eyes of the U.S. nation-state, and her body failed to produce for the nation in the "proper" ways or even in the concealed and invisible ways as it was before. In New Mexico, prior to industrialization, communal and land grants allowed part agrarian economy (agriculture) and part pastoral economy (the sheep and cattle industries) to exist, along with mercantile capital after the creation of the Santa Fe Trail in 1822. The economic opportunities were not vast for Nuevomexicans, and debt peonage was a stable source of income.

The last archive I consult in this study takes seriously this shift from productive bodies to unproductive at the turn of the twentieth century. Arizona had small mining towns that sustained the sparse settler populations after the Gadsden Purchase in 1854. The Southwest borderlands experienced economic growth quite violently and late in the game, and the economic background of the region was vast and shifting. Where debt peonage was a Southwest sexual economic system that built capital, prostitution on the borderlands was a sexual economy that was willful for otherwise poor Mexicanas at the turn of the century. However, once prostitution became tied to immigration and racialization for Mexicans, the pathology of brown women became palpable and worthy of deportation. I uncover an expansive archive of territorial journalism in Arizona from the Arizona Historical Society in Tucson that tells the story of prostitution on the border. This, coupled with immigration reports filed for Arizona and Gustav Schneider's prostitution photography, allow me to illustrate how racialized sex and sexuality were a technology of power on the borderlands and shifted racialized sex and sexuality from productive to unproductive.

La Traidora: When Racialized Pathology Meets "Civility" in the Borderlands

When the historian Frederick Jackson Turner addressed the American Historical Association in 1893 with his paper "The Significance of the Frontier in

American History," which claimed that American identity and democracy were formed by the American frontier, there was already an ideology of American exceptionalism that celebrated the discourse of white settler "superiority" and the notion that Euro-Americans had "civilized" the rugged, "open" frontier.[36] This mythology grossly misconstrues how space was "open" in the Southwest borderlands, but more importantly it ignores the instrumental roles played by Black, Indigenous, and Mexican peoples in the construction of American empire. By this time in American history, there were already stereotypes of the racialized female cemented in the popular discourse. While there were Mexicanas who "passed" for white because of their light skin or their connection to elite, landholding Mexican families—women who subscribed to the notion of "proper" (white)—this was not the case across the board in the Southwest borderlands.

Elite Spanish-speaking women and white femininity meet within American empire through the domestic sphere. Whiteness, femininity, and domesticity together have been the center of U.S. national discourse since its inception.[37] The "domestic" is seen as the home of the nation, making the home and femininity central to the construction of the nation.[38] Domesticity follows the logic of heteronormative relations and in turn constructs what becomes "proper" feminine behavior up against racialized others.[39] As Amanda Zink tells us, nineteenth-century femininity constructed the dialectical relationship of whiteness (interior, private, domestic) in opposition to the racialized (exterior, public, foreign).[40] Anything from manner of dress, grooming, and even breeding went into the makeup of "proper" femininity. Elite classes had enough cultural and economic capital to assuage this dialectic.

The regulation of brown women's sexuality dates back to the early days of colonialism, but during westward expansion and at the height of U.S. empire, Deena Gonzalez states, "Euro-Americans—white, non-immigrant Americans of the United States—practiced a dehumanization campaign against people [in the present-day U.S. Southwest], especially [Mexican] women."[41] Nineteenth-century travel diaries, narratives, letters, editorials, and memoirs cement the racist, nativist impulses of colonialism, Manifest Destiny, U.S. imperialism, and control of sex and sexuality over poor, brown female bodies in the Southwest. Euro-Americans migrating to and settling the "west" during this time constantly referred to the racialized women in their writings as witches, whores, subservient to their husbands, treacherous, flirtatious, and seductive.[42] These portrayals can be tied to sexual violence and brutal attacks on women in California (mostly Indo-mestizo and Afro-mestizo) as early as 1769, when the first *entrada* (incursion) of soldiers and priests arrived in California to begin their campaign of colonial domination.⁴³ Meanwhile, the Spanish-speaking women from elite, landholding California families distinguished themselves as "good" Spanish women, who were chaste, modest, virtuous, and beautiful, in contrast to "bad" Mexican women, who lacked virtue and morality.⁴⁴ The good (Spanish) / bad (Mexican) binary mirrors the virgin/whore dichotomy, which appears in the story of La Malinche / Malintzín and becomes a flashpoint for this book, as La Malinche / Malintzín is the historical figure that cements racialized sexuality for Mexicanas in the Americas.

La Malinche is known by many names, including Malintzín and Doña Marina, and she was a key figure in the struggle between the Aztec and Spanish empires in Mesoamerica for almost three years. Malintzín's mother sold her into enslavement, and she lived as a slave among the Maya, near Coatzacoalcos, when Spanish conquistadors arrived in Tenochtitlán in 1519. One of fifteen slaves offered to the conquistadors, Malintzín was taken as the personal slave and mistress of Hernán Cortés. Her knowledge of Mayan, Nahuatl, several regional dialects, and Spanish made her instrumental to the Spanish as a translator, negotiator, and cultural mediator. She mothered a son with Cortés and then a daughter with her husband, the conquistador Juan de Jaramillo, in 1524, symbolically giving birth to the first generation of mestizos (people of Spanish and Indigenous ancestry).⁴⁵ The Mexican philosopher Octavio Paz positions her as the "mother of mestizo Mexico" or the Mexican Eve.⁴⁶ She became a trope for a type of Chicana sexuality that is dishonorable and tarnished with *malinchismo*—the choice to marry a foreigner, the enemy, instead of another native.⁴⁷ Because of her sexual relations, many uncritically see her as a traitor and the cause of much of the destruction in the Americas. One of the first large-scale Indigenous massacres in Cholula is attributed to Malintzín, or as she is called now Malinche, because she warned Cortés of impending Indigenous insurrection.

However, Chicana and Mexican transnational feminist scholars have reclaimed the power of Malintzín as the embodiment of a different type of Chicana sexuality, one in which Malintzín became the mother of the new race ("la raza") and empowered herself with her own agency, thereby subverting masculine and nationalist portrayals of her as dependent and disenfranchised. She switched between multiple languages to challenge and manipulate men who did nothing but abuse her. She became, as Norma Alarcón states, "Guadalupe's monstrous double," which meant that she was in contradistinction to the national patroness and purity of Guadalupe.⁴⁸ In their re-envisioning of Malintzín, Chicana scholars such as Adelaida del Castillo, Adalijiza Sosa Riddel, and Carmen Tafolla have upset the concept of the virgin/whore dichotomy and point to her productive role—not in the sense of producing commodities, but in terms of creating a new race. Using the narrative of Malintzín to lay the theoretical framework for the sexual economies I deploy, I expand on these analyses, focusing on a much later time, to reveal the productive and reproductive capacities of racialized female bodies.[49]

The racial hierarchy in the Southwest borderlands, based on class and color, originated in the Spanish ideological framework of social and racial inequality placing *gente decente, gente de razón,* or *criollos* at the top, mestizas/os in the middle, and Indians (both Mexican and North American) and African Americans at the bottom.[50] Coupled with U.S. imperial discourse on race and social station, this construction historically tended to coincide with the notion of "civility," and the elite landholding Spanish-Mexicans in the nineteenth century upheld this ideology. Castañeda reminds us that "women from more recently arrived or non-elite families were called 'Mexican.' 'Spanish' women were morally, sexually, and racially pure; 'Mexican' women were immoral and sexually and racially impure. These sexual stereotypes not only reveal the convergence of contemporary political and social ideological currents but also underscore the centrality of the politics of sex to the ideological justification of expansion, war, and conquest."[51]

Racialized gender, sex, and sexuality were structured during Spanish colonial times and by the Mexican national government. They both enacted restrictive and protective provisions that dictated how women were to act and what rights were afforded to them. As Omar Valerio-Jiménez reminds us, the laws under Spanish and Mexican rule excluded women from voting, holding elected office, and serving as lawyers or judges.[52] However, women in the Southwest were protected from economic or social destitution, and laws guaranteed that daughters and sons alike received equal amounts of their inheritance. When their husbands encountered financial difficulties or died, they maintained legal ownership of their dowries and *arras* (wedding gifts from husbands).[53] Women could also take men to court for infidelity or sexual assault because a woman's sexual virtue protected her family name and allowed for wealth to remain within the family through inheritances. Monogamy and the accumulation of wealth were a Mexicana's main functions in an elite family, which made family prestige and proper civil femininity critical to her future. The term "civility" equated to colonial and national power along the U.S.–Mexico border. On the U.S. side, the sexual pathology of brown female bodies threatened the nation-state, and the government managed this threat by using immigration laws to practice what was essentially ethnic cleaning.[54] "Civility" extended into the idea of Manifest Destiny, where the U.S. imperial government saw itself as the god-chosen people tasked with "civilizing" brown female bodies in the borderlands. On the Mexican side, Spanish colonizers utilized the term to subdue the Indigenous community through missionization and Catholicism. But more important for this study, "civility" was used in travel diaries to express discontent with the Indigenous female population in the nineteenth century.

What's Sex Got to Do with It?

I am often asked, why center sex? How does capital produce race and sex as an intersection of violences that at once extracts value from brown, poor, feminized bodies while simultaneously rendering them worthless before the law? There has been a recent trend in academia toward what is known as surface reading, which decenters historical materialism and centers instead the foreground (as opposed to the background) of a text. It is a way of studying a piece of cultural production by staying inside of the text without worrying that we are "missing" something in the reading.[55] Bruno Latour made the case against Fredric Jameson's symptomatic reading (or the political unconscious), an interpretive method arguing that the most interesting aspect of a text lies in what it represses and that interpretation should seek "a latent meaning behind a manifest one."[56] With surface reading rising to the forefront of literary scholarship, it is critical to examine material and discursive practices that arise out of violence on the border and in the borderlands. An episteme of violence exists in the disparities of the United States and the applicability of Western philosophies that inform economic, social, political, and cultural conditions.[57] This episteme of violence is rooted in the historical violence at the intersection of race, sex, gender, and capital. Sex, and by extension gender, is a technology of power that produces capital and racialization. While contemporary scholars have theorized sex, sexuality, and gender as identity categories, I destabilize that line of thought by exploring the material consequences of these categories in society.

The industrial boom of the U.S. nation-state was made possible through the accumulation of wealth from territories in westward expansion, slavery, and Indigenous genocide and displacement. "The development of monopoly capitalism . . . depended on finding sources of raw materials and expanding markets in far-flung colonial territories."[58] The sexual and gendered capital invested in the bodies of racialized women allowed Euro-Anglos and those elite Hispanos, Tejanos, Californios, and Mexicanos to position themselves on the path toward capitalism. In the nineteenth century, the basic material inequality that permeates the capitalist model of creating commodities was the same method that came to fruition in processes of categorizing social differentiation in the forms of race, sex, and gender. We cannot view sex, and by extension sexuality, as monolithic or universal.[59] Sexual identity is and has been fundamentally impacted by race, class, and (re)production. Historically positioning these racialized women exemplifies how the base-superstructure metaphor, which explains society in the limited terms between the base (economics) and the superstructure (cultural ideology), only takes into account exploitative tactics "without denying either the determining effects of this organization or the historically specific way it is lived."[60]

Marxist feminists developed a feminist critique of capital, but since the late nineteenth century, they have been more concerned with developing an analysis of gender oppression than with a materialist approach to sexuality and how sex informs sexuality. Few have examined the inextricability of race and class. Alexandra Kollontai was one of the earliest Marxist thinkers to address sexuality in the class struggle.[61] She did not speak to sexual identity per se, and was inherently heteronormative in her conception of the bourgeois family and relations, but she led the way in thinking about sexuality in the private and political realms.[62] After this, Wilhelm Reich and Herbet Marcuse did substantial work on sexuality, but it focused on the identity of sexuality and not how sex is a function of capitalism. In attempting to materialize psychoanalysis, they localized sexuality in the body and therefore contended that sexuality originates in "innate instinctual drives."[63] Reich's main objective in his work on sexuality and class was to connect sexuality and the varied demands of social production. He stated that sexual repression secures the existing class structure and uses psychoanalysis to help us understand the psychic effects of life under capitalism.[64] Marcuse theorized that the changes in the organization of sexuality and libidinal pleasure are connected to divisions of labor. Marcuse stated that capitalist societies have made sex a commodity and that this commodification averts different sexual possibilities that would prompt a sexual revolution.[65] While these leading thinkers fail to historicize sexuality or connect race inextricably to class, they come close to considering how sex and sexuality lead the social arrangements through which sexuality has historically been organized.[66]

Although I am in conversation with contemporary Marxist critics, there is no other book-length study on the intersection of race, sex, gender, and capital in the borderlands in the nineteenth century. Where Michael Szalay coined the term "new deal Modernism," which reads modernist avant-garde writers as being able to take risks and enjoy success because of a public insurance (the welfare state), I read different political moments in the history of the borderlands and utilize the term "sexual capital." In a recent account of the relationship between debt, sociality, and political subjectivity, Annie McClanahan argues that credit is the means through which capital extends itself in periods of growth and renews itself in moments of crisis. She exemplifies this through Marx and argues that credit allowed seventeenth-century merchant capitalists to create a vast export market, which made possible some of the "primitive accumulations" that led to duly developed capitalism. Following this same logic, *Border Bodies* argues that sexual capital had export potential, but through unseen productive labor, and led to a fully developed capitalism.[67] I examine the ways that sex leads to the reproduction of subjects that then produce commodities for transnational exchange. I also interrogate how sexual capital cements racialized sexuality through the brokering of "proper" Mexicana bodies.

Also a contemporary Marxist, Jasper Bernes utilizes Marx to think about the uncanny and alienating nature of labor and asks us to consider "dead labor with past (or accumulated, or stored, or 'remembered') labor, and living labor with present labor.... [When we do,] we see that what Marx is really describing is a complex temporality, where the past remains present in an objective form, in the form of material accumulation that makes demands on, limits, and fates the course of the present."[68] I expand on Bernes's work and examine labor and how Mexicanas in the borderlands fall outside of wage labor while still producing. Wage labor produces "dead labor," as Bernes states, but I look at the ways that Mexicanas accumulate capital *outside* of wage labor, a violent and exploitative process formed through racialization. Bernes makes clear that neither compelled work nor wage labor is unique to capitalist societies; however, on the border there is a "spatial fix" that happens where unseen racialized gender and sex are central to the development of capitalism.[69] I am in line with Bernes where he theorizes about the unwaged laborer, unwork, dispossession, and wage-lessness as "bare life, wasted life, disposable life, precarious life, superfluous life, through informal economy supplied by those without access to formal employment."[70] I decenter wage labor, and I ask you to think about what counts as labor and capital accumulation. And how do race, sex, and gender abstract the labor that produces capital?

In thinking about what Cedric Robinson calls "racial capitalism," we must examine the economic trends from the nineteenth century that, as Lisa Lowe states, profited from labor not by "rendering it abstract but by *producing* racialized difference."[71] However, I build off this conception of abstract labor as racialized labor, and concrete labor as white, wage labor. I take cues from Iyko Day in her complete rethinking of Marx and Lowe, where she states that abstract labor already erases highly differentiated gendered and racialized labor *in order to create value*. Therefore, value is created by obscuring racialized and gendered difference, and abstract labor is not necessarily hidden from society. Forced masculine labor within agrarian and mercantile economies also forced poor, racialized female bodies in the Southwest borderlands to use sex to subsidize capital through the (re)production of a labor force involved in international, global, and transnational trade. We see the beginnings of U.S. imperialism in the sexual economic system of debt peonage while the patrones grew their fortunes through imports and exports of American and European products. With capitalism on the rise and westward expansion in full effect in the North, I examine racialized women's bodies as a lens to understand how difference functioned, similar to Marx's *labor theory of value*. Where *differentiation* and *hierarchy* took form in the Southwest borderlands through colonialism and imperialism, abstract labor was taking form through burgeoning capitalist relations. Marx defines abstract capitalism as "disregard[ing] the use-value of commodities only [where] one property remains, that of being products of labor."[72] For Marx, the difference between abstract labor and concrete labor is *pure and simple* labor in comparison to labor that produces commodities for use-value. While ethnic studies scholars have studied racial capitalism as *abstract labor*, I argue that gendered and racialized labor *create and give value* to concrete labor. Marx argues that capitalism maximizes profit by rendering labor abstract; however, I concentrate on the juncture between what scholars have distinguished as mercantile/monopoly capitalism and global/transnational capitalism and how modes of production within this juncture relied on socially produced differences marked by "race, nation, geographical origin, and gender."[73] So while this is not a reading of capital in the nineteenth-century borderlands, it undertakes *how* bodies are utilized for capital through sex and race.[74] In paying attention to the nucleus of human relations through difference, we come to know what makes the "bosses" money, otherwise known as surplus labor. By looking at the way different bodies were used in different capacities in the Southwest borderlands, I push back against the metaphor of the base-superstructure model (to consider the intersections of race and sex) of Marx while taking seriously how class organized the methods of how and when bodies were used.

Chapter Overview

Capital (in all its formulations) draws on the racial, sexual, and gendered ideology at key flash points in the nineteenth century and the turn of the twentieth century in the borderlands: marriage within elite landholding Californio families before 1848, the economy of gendered violence through lynching in the 1860s, the sexual economic system of debt peonage in the 1860s and 1870s, and prostitution on the borderlands at the turn of the century (1911). Drawing on literary and visual history, I aim to reveal how classed, racialized women in the borderlands are portrayed in the archive and in cultural production as either pious or sexually excessive. The first three chapters unravel the national imaginary of the sexually excessive and the discursive construction of racialized gender and sexuality through newspapers, novels, legislative reports, and other forms of popular culture. The last two chapters draw on legal cases, ordinances, and immigration law to examine and interrogate the material effects of racialized gender and sexuality on some women through different forms of sexual economies in the Southwest borderlands.

Chapter 1, "The Oikopolitic: The Father of All, Brokering of the Californiana Body, and the 'Natural Order of Things' in Alta California," argues that the trading of elite Californiana female bodies made possible a political economy and capitalist expansion in the nineteenth-century borderlands. I draw on letters written by the daughters of wealthy Don José de la Guerra y Noriega, as well as testimonios and photographic collections from members of his family and those connected to him. I utilize the Greek understanding of *oikonomia*, which distinguishes the management of the household (or the domestic) from that of the state. De la Guerra's *oikonomia* rests at the intersection of household management and political economy because of the ways in which he was able to use his daughters' bodies (mostly through marriage) to gain economic leverage and political power. This meaning of the domestic and the political depended on biological reproduction and defined what were natural and proper forms of domestic labor. The de la Guerra household created the basis for racialized sexuality, which has always gone unseen and been abstract, but has also been both productive and reproductive. This precedent set the stage for constructions of "proper" femininity in opposition to racialized women who fell outside of these constructions.

Extending from the movement of racialized gender and sexuality throughout Mexican racial discourse, chapter 2, "Circuits of Brown, Black, and Red: The Politics of Racialized Gender and Sexuality in the Nineteenth-Century Borderlands," relies on the 1872 novel *Who Would Have Thought It?* by María Amparo Ruiz de Burton, the first Mexican American author to write in English, to examine constructions of and lay the groundwork for racialized gender and sexuality on the U.S.–Mexico border. Because Ruiz de Burton defines whiteness and femininity in opposition to U.S. imperialism (blaming the United States for the problems facing Mexico at the time), her perspective crosses national boundaries and discourses. Ruiz de Burton merges U.S. and Mexican racial hierarchies by relying on racist feminine tropes circulating in the Americas during the colonial period, including *la mulata, los indios,* and *la cautiva,* all of which speak to notions of colorism, Blackness, and Indigeneity. Considering Ruiz de Burton's novel in conversation with Mexican newspaper accounts of these same tropes at the time, I provide an ideological foundation for problematic perceptions of utopian white femininity and the sexualization of racialized Mexicana, Indigenous, and Black female bodies in Mexico and how these notions circulated across the border in the United States.

Continuing my discussion of racialized sex and gendered racial formations, chapter 3, "Absent Presence: The Ghost of the 'Only Woman Hanged' in Texas and the Abstract Labor of Gender Racial Formations," examines the archive of Josefa (Chipita) Rodríguez, hung by execution in San Patricio, Texas, in 1863. Rodríguez is largely absent from the historical archive, and her ghost, but never her actual body, is pursued in cultural productions after her death. Drawing on two books (the Texas Syndicated Press's *A Noose for Chipita* and Eakin Press's *The Legend of Chipita: The One Woman Hanged in Texas,* which left more gaps than they filled), as well as poetry and opera, I argue that Chipita is only visible through the economy of racially gendered violence she endured and invisible through her labor and capital accumulation.

Chapter 4 marks a turn in this study and focuses on the material consequences of racialized sexuality in the Southwest borderlands. "Productive Racialized Sex: The Sexual Economy of the Southwest Borderlands, the Nuevomexicana Body Politic, and Memory Archives" relies on court cases, short stories, and memoir to expose debt peonage as a sexual economy that built racialized civility and *sexual capital,* where idealized femininity and its counterpart, the fraught figure of poor and racialized Nuevomexicana and Hispana women—required not just to produce for their families but also the economic system of debt peonage—were tied to land and inheritance. While the first three chapters focus on the social history of sex and sexuality in the borderlands, this chapter marks a shift in this study to material effects of racialized sexuality in the court system and in the eyes of the law. The sexual economy produced by this system built both civility and capital, many times on the backs of lower-class Nuevomexicana bodies as opposed to the elite landholding Hispana body.

The final chapter, "Technology of 'Unproductive' Brown Bodies: The Political Economy of Prostitution and Racialized Sexual Pathology in Arizona at the Turn of the Century," tells the story of how prostitutes' local political and economic power in Tucson and throughout the state dwindled and became racially pathologized and dangerous within the first decade of the twentieth century. Because Arizona was seen as too Mexican, too Indigenous, and too sexually excessive, it was denied statehood in 1902. At the same time, immigration laws made prostitution a dangerous endeavor for many Mexican women in Arizona, which racially sexualized them and made them prone to deportation in the borderlands. Drawing on newspaper accounts, I uncover the thriving sexual economy of prostitution in Arizona at the time in relation to discussions of statehood, an economy hampered by moral reform laws introduced by one of the biggest anti-prostitution proponents of the time, Tucson's Josephine Hughes. Later, immigration reports from Arizona dating from around 1909 reveal the increasingly dangerous and violent nature of sex work in the region. These reports focus on male procurers, but they also incidentally deport only the Mexican prostitutes; men seemed to escape unscathed. I connect this pathology of prostitution with the photography of Gustav Schneider, which was used as a technology of power to target Mexican sex workers on the border. The turn of the century on the border provided the legal and social contract that shifted racialized sexuality from productive racialized sex to unproductive racialized sex during the U.S. Progressive Era and the rise of the welfare state.

The coda offers a reflection on how the "systematic patterns of violences" in this study reflect and inform our contemporary moment. To explore this contemporary moment, I turn to where the West Mesa Murders are now. The coda is concerned with thinking about sexual capital in our current moment and how our transnational economic context is central to the gender and sexual violence toward brown females in the borderlands. However, while this study is concerned with the abstract labor of racialized sex, gender, and sexuality, I attempt to imagine a world beyond the value of labor seen and unseen. The coda imagines a world of transfeminist connections that unravel a violent world for the brown feminine on the borderlands.

CHAPTER ONE

The Oikopolitic
The Father of All, Brokering of the Californiana Body, and the "Natural Order of Things" in Alta California

Alfred Robinson always addressed his father-in-law, Don José de la Guerra y Noriega, as "Mi Querido Padre" (My Dear Father) in his letters. The letters ended with "Sus Querido Hijos" (Your Dear Children).[1] But there are three exceptions to these warm salutations in Robinson's letters where he uses the less affectionate "Mi Suegro" (My Father-in-Law). The first time we see this more detached correspondence is in a letter he wrote to Don José de la Guerra y Noriega from New York on October 21, 1847, a little more than a year after the start of the Mexican-American War (April 25, 1846). He plainly relayed the news "Que Acabo de recibir noticia de Washington que mi conocido el Comodoro Jones, de antiqua memoria, sale pronto, para el fiar de tomar el mando de las fuerzas navales que por lo presente ocupan la costa de las Alta California" ("I just received the news from Washington that my friend, Comodore Jones, of ancient memory, is soon leaving to take charge of the naval forces that at present occupy the coast of Upper California").[2] In one letter to de la Guerra from New York on November 22, 1846, Robinson decried the "injusto" against his beloved Californios. But Robinson had a different tune in a September 20, 1846, letter to his brother-in-law Pablo de la Guerra (Don José de la Guerra y Noriega's fourth son); here, he was more optimistic about the war, claiming that since the war was well underway and the Americanos looked toward a victory, money would not be lacking in California, and in place of hides and tallow, there would be coins in all parts of California.[3] The road would indeed be paved in golden coins now that the United States had come to civilize the West. At the end of Robinson's letter to his brother-in-law Pablo, he told him that he should wait to marry until a "gringa" came with the expedition.[4] This was in stark contrast to his own love for Californianas (or Californio women) before the outbreak of the war; indeed, Robinson married de la Guerra's third daughter Ana María Antonia de la Guerra (also known as Anita) when he saw Californios on the road to wealth and success.[5]

Robinson's character and respectful demeanor toward the de la Guerras shifted as the war progressed. No longer the dutiful "son" of de la Guerra, as represented by his harsh shift in tone toward his father-in-law and his salutation of "Suegro," Robinson anticipated significant political and economic changes in the borderlands. The U.S. invasion threatened the de la Guerra estate, and the economic system in California was transforming at a fast pace. Robinson's slip of the tongue could easily go unnoticed, but it signifies two things. First and most obvious, it signifies the specter of defeat for the Californios from the vantage point of an American. Robinson no longer needs to honor de la Guerra in the same manner as he did before the U.S. invasion—although he still does—because de la Guerra is no longer of political or economic benefit to him. Second, it exemplifies this economic shift; Robinson no longer has a need for such affections as "Querido Padre" because he no longer benefits from his wealth in the form of his marriage to Anita. This slip of the tongue reveals the shift in the sexual economic structure of the Southwest through the brokering of Californiana bodies.

The change in familial salutations shows a pivotal shift in the management of the household under de la Guerra's authority. The wealthy, elite landholding, and patriarchal de la Guerra ran a tight ship in terms of his family's spirituality and religion, their political reputation, and their engagement in economic ventures. When Robinson married Anita de la Guerra, both Robinson and de la Guerra saw great economic, social, and cultural potential in teaming up together through the marriage to Anita. However, once the United States invaded California, everything shifted. Before the U.S. invasion, one way de la Guerra maintained control of his estate was by brokering off his daughters to *extranjeros* (Anglo-Americans and Europeans) who could potentially expand his wealth. The reproductive and sexual labor that the de la Guerra daughters performed not only affected de la Guerra's economics, but it also bridged the household sphere (*oikos*) with state relations (*polis*). The oikopolitic that de la Guerra creates through his daughters' bodies exemplifies the limited notion of Marx's "natural" reproductive labor and the unseen and violent nature of racialized subjects' sexual labor, as I explain in later chapters. The importance of Californiana bodies in keeping economic systems afloat demonstrates the centrality of women, gender, patriarchy, and sexuality in imperial expansion, and it also reveals the ways in which culture and class informed the policies and practices of capitalism and expansion.[6] Scholars have long been interested in discussions of nineteenth-century Californio elites, their never-ending critique of U.S. invasion, and their displacement after the war. However, that analysis tends to miss how many elite landholding Californios invested in and endorsed the free market. Clearly de la Guerra was not the only man to broker his daughters' bodies off to *extran-*

jeros, nor was elite Californio culture the only place this practice existed. However, the de la Guerra women are foundational female figures at the center of a free-trade economy in the West. This chapter begins my study not only because it chronologically makes sense (the de la Guerra family were operating on capitalist principles long before the West was considered a capitalist region), but also because the de la Guerra estate functioned at the interstices of the household and political economy, allowing the patriarch to broker his daughters for economic gain but under the guise of private life, which would later become the province of biological reproduction and what is natural and proper about affective and domestic labor. The de la Guerra daughters perfectly encapsulate how sexual capital functions in the West, but they also exemplify how bodily qualities (sex, sexuality, heteronormativity) become codified in relation to the circulation of capital and the accumulation of wealth.

This chapter unveils the value-laden body of the Californiana as it becomes the basis for an economy of sex regulated by hierarchies of race and class. I center the female Californiana body to explore the political economy of Alta California and reveal a history of the sexual and gendered economic systems of elite landholding Californios. Scholars have defined these practices as the brokering of classes between Californios and Euro-Americans and Europeans, but I argue that household management for the de la Guerra estate meant access to the bodies of their "proper" daughters, which opened up social capital for de la Guerra himself. To do so, I rely on the 1878 *Californnia Recollections of Angustias de la Guerra Ord* dictated by Mariá de las Angustias de la Guerra Ord; letters written to Don José de la Guerra y Noriega by his daughter Ana Maria Antonia de la Guerra, better known as Anita de la Guerra; and Teresa de la Guerra de Hartnell's testimonio dictated on March 12, 1875, to Henry Cerritu. I utilize the Greek understanding of *oikonomia*, which distinguishes the management of the household (*oikos*) from that of the state (*polis*), to suggest that the de la Guerra estate functioned at the interstices of the household and political economy, allowing the patriarch to broker his daughters for economic gain but under the guise of private life. I label this intersection the oikopolitic. For Aristotle, *oikonomia* was the foundation of politics, but it was also a completely different realm because "it was composed not by the hierarchal logics deemed proper to the *oikos* but conditioned by the premise of equality between free, adult men."[7] *Oikos*, which is synonymous with "household," spoke to the natural way households were supposed to function, but *oikonomia* extended beyond the familial space because it included unrelated servants and slaves.[8] While the de la Guerra estate was most definitely a household in that it housed the servants and peons on the hacienda, de la Guerra's *oikonomia* existed in the ways he used the Californio female bodies of his family for economic leverage and political power, which "turns on a series of architectural, affective, geopolitical and not least, contractual shifts in what have been simultaneously intimate and global reorganizations of divisions of labor."[9] Through the brokering off of his daughters, de la Guerra merged the loci of the household and political economy, which would later become the province of biological reproduction and what is natural and proper about affective and domestic labor. These household economics are then "poised analogous to the processes of socio-economic reproduction existing at the level of the nation-state."[10] Marx takes the Aristotelian philosophy of the *oikos* and uses the concept to critique the political economy of capitalism, making use of the *oikos* (household) and *nomos* (governing law), to iterate the labor theory of value. Said differently, Marx uses the same construction of Aristotelian philosophy to interrogate the differences between productive labor, that which produces value, and reproductive labor, that which does not. I build off Marx on Aristotle first to claim that the de la Guerras crafted an oikopolitical realm for themselves, and second to examine Marx's "naturalized" reproductive labor within the household that lies in stark contrast to racialized subjectivity. The de la Guerra estate was advanced in merging the two, while pointedly contrasting with racialized sex, which has always been unseen, abstract, and both productive and reproductive. I build off Angela Mitropoulos's work to term this merging as *oikopolitics*: "an attentiveness to personal comportment in a simultaneously political and oikonomic register."[11] This chapter is not so much concerned with the agency of the de la Guerra daughters in their marriage arrangements, as that word has lost much of its meaning in recent years, but rather with what happens within the mitigated relationships of the oikopolitics.

While marriage arrangements for economic gain were common in different geopolitical spaces and places, scholars of the Southwest borderlands are divided into two main camps on the significance of interethnic marriages in nineteenth-century California. One astute suggestion interrogates the brokering of classes between *extranjeros* and Californio elite landholding families that eventually led to acculturation and assimilation of the Californiana bride. The other, a more feminist reading, views the Californianas as the negotiators of exchange for their own bodies by *choosing* to marry these outsiders.[12] But as Deena Gonzalez states, rather than "write about these relationships in terms that imply that women, worth nothing, married men worth something, and that Spanish-Mexican women gained mobility as their

Euro-American men in turn gained entrance into Spanish-American society," this chapter rests at the intersection of these two popular arguments by examining how their bodies, whether volitionally or not, merge through the oikopolitical.[13] Rather than thinking of these interethnic marriages as ushering Californios into a modern future because of the white male counterpart, I contend that this was a mode of political economy actually centered on the power of the Californios. This chapter reads these Californiana elite bodies as surplus value, not in the Marxist sense, but rather containing an excessive amount of value for cultural, social, and economic capital.

Aristotle, Marx, Race, and Sex

The meaning of *oikos*, the etymological root of the word "economics," has shifted over time, but we must understand its meaning in order to historicize and interrogate the naturalized configuration of sex, intimacy, and reproductive work. The crux of *oikonomia* centers hierarchy that rests on the management of others. While the debate continues among economic historians on whether or not the Greek understanding of *oikonomia* is akin to the current understanding of economics, it is an instructive placeholder for the shifting relationships between economics, politics, sexuality, class, and race.[14] The *oikos*, in its classical Greek understanding, was not a synonym for the family but a word for the household.[15] For Aristotle, *oikonomia* was the study of household management. Within politics, there is a clear distinction for Aristotle between the management of a household and the management of the state. For Aristotle, the *oikos* (household) is juxtaposed to the *polis* (city/state); however, the *oikos* is the foundation of the *polis* in that the *oikos* produced the bare necessities of life; with the generation of surplus, the *oikos* was to be spent on noneconomic activities and a leisurely life.[16] Where Aristotle gives us a formal distinction between the *oikos* and the *polis*, Xenophon in the "The Estate-Manager [Oeconomicus]," one of the earliest iterations of *oikonomia*, "was concerned with a highly stylised managerialism, one premised on self-discipline, and capable of moving between city (and battlefield) and household with ease."[17] Xenophon's discussion of household economy and the division of labor (management) is central to the formulation of political economy. For Xenophon the *oikos* was "whatever is useful to an individual," meaning all that went into managing wealthy agrarian estates, handing out punishments and rewards, the management of slaves, and the relationship between husband and wife, focused on increasing the estate's wealth and assets.[18]

Oikonomia has become the normative disposition of political economy, and it structures Marx's thinking on the labor theory of value, where the value of each commodity is equal to the total amount of labor required in its production and reproduction. For Aristotle, there is a distinction between the presumably natural and artificial ways of acquiring wealth, where one is the "acquisition . . . in the order of nature [that] is a part of the household art," and the other, "[which] is specially called wealth-getting, and that is so called with justice [or equity and just price]; and to this kind it is due that there is thought to be no limit to riches and property."[19] This becomes the basis for his argument regarding "natural slavery."[20]

How does this philosophy provide the foundation for legal and economic norms? Angela Mitropoulos reminds us, "There and since then, the vaulted antiquarianism of *oikos* has marked an appeal to a rhetorical archaism, its nostalgic iteration through the selective retrieval of a natural philosophy of classical properties, categorical logic, and nascent scientific concepts of biological heritability and "organic society," all of which aimed to anchor laws and norms of proper generation, possession, and the transfer of property in circumstances where the question of property right was both highly uncertain and increasingly contested."[21] The norms constructing family relations through heteronormativity, genealogy, and monogamy appear throughout time in different iterations. Thus, the *oikos* becomes an important way to understand "the proper" way of developing race, sex, and gender. Marx's critique of political economy reflects an understanding of Aristotle's "natural law" and the advent of capitalism. In *Capital*, Marx explains why Aristotle cannot proceed beyond a certain point in his discussion of exchange because "Greek society was founded upon slavery, and had, therefore, for its natural basis, the inequality of men and of their labor powers."[22] For years, scholars have proved Marx's inability to fit slavery into his critique of political economy, understanding labor as hegemonic and erasing anything outside the bounds of wage labor. Marx also downplays the presumable natural qualifiers such as race, gender, and sexuality and, like many other scholars, considers slavery a natural condition. Marx underestimates the oikonomic implications, which, as Mitropoulos tells us, "imbue property ownership and the extended extraction of surplus value with a natural or divine qualification—and therefore the meaning of gender and race in quantifying and qualifying both the division of labor and in validating the extraction of surplus value at the threshold of its contractual, measurable, and anthropological terms."[23] By "naturalizing" slavery through Aristotelian thought, Marx speaks to the exploitation and unjustness of wage labor, while simultaneously creating a labor theory of value that establishes a norm of value. This, in turn, allows

Marx to diminish Aristotle's natural philosophy in favor of the economic. While Marx utilizes the "natural" forms of life to think about production and reproduction, he sees production from labor power as the only form of value, and reproduction as everything that does not produce value, including domestic work, which is the natural order and part of the *oikos*.[24] Marx fails to "make explicit that these measures concern not just the quantities of useful things (property) but the very qualification that defines some things, or people, as property and others as owners of property, seemingly by their nature—and that this concept is one of Aristotelian substances."[25]

This chapter unveils the limits of Marx's conceptualization of the natural order of things. Where Marx centers the "natural" configuration of sex and intimacy of the household through reproductive labor and, vis-à-vis Aristotle, the demarcations of the domestic space as "natural" and crucial to the concept of the nation, I apply the intersections of race, gender, sex, and class to the space of the household and go beyond Marx to unveil that there is not a "natural" order to the household space. This, as Mitropoulos states, "amplifies the perception of the household as the foundation of an ostensibly natural economy founded on a similarly naturalized sexual difference that, in turn, becomes the premise which links sex to the reproduction of race, nation and (conceived as an identity) class."[26] This natural and "proper" construction of the household, combined with the political influence of the state, allows de la Guerra to broker his daughters' bodies off to *extranjeros* who promised economic opportunity, all while remaining within the "natural" order of things. The de la Guerra daughters participate in the sexual labor that bridges the *oikos* with the *polis*. Meanwhile, the labor of poor, racialized women is abstract and unseen. The oikopolitics blurs the lines between household management, economics, and politics. For the de la Guerra daughters, this distinguished their labor as productive, as opposed to unproductive, because it gained wealth for the estate.

This practice of brokering female bodies in a family was not unheard of in the circles of wealthy Californios, and de la Guerra was among the wealthiest. Don José de la Guerra y Noriega was born in 1779 in Novales, a valley town in Santander, Spain. Born of noble blood dating back to a war hero in the armies of Ferdinand and Isabella, de la Guerra set out for New Spain in 1792, at the age of thirteen, with other Spaniards who "governed the largest and richest of Spain's colonial holdings in the world."[27] Throughout his teens, he shadowed his uncle, Pedro González de Noriega, as a merchant, but in 1798 he entered the officer corps of the newly created Habilitado General for the Californians at the Presidio of San Diego.[28] It was his "noble" blood that got him appointed as a cadet. At this time, the Bourbon Reforms were gaining traction in the New

World, where peninsular Spaniards enjoyed legal privileges in "international commerce, government, administration, the Church, and the judiciary" and ousted native-born Mexicans from high positions because of purer blood.[29] As he quickly climbed ranks on the military ladder, eventually becoming comandante of the Santa Barbara Presidio where he retired, de la Guerra also gained the opportunity to shape trade and profit in the military outposts, where mercantile restrictions had otherwise made it difficult. Through his acquired swaths of land (over five hundred thousand acres) and his investment in the political sphere, de la Guerra became one of the wealthiest and most influential men in California.

In 1804, José de la Guerra y Noriega married María Antonia Carrillo y Lugo, the daughter of a frontier officer and granddaughter of a solider, and they had eight children under the Spanish flag (including Anita) and four after Mexican Independence in 1822. As was the case, the "marriage was serious business in late colonial Mexico. It represented an indissoluble link between two families ... [which joined] interests and fortunes."[30] As racial hierarchy became linked with wealth in what is now the Southwest borderlands, the union of two elite racial and wealth classes made clear that the actual body of the female was worth just as much, if not more, in cultural and economic capital, as that of the male she married. But more importantly, it reveals how this construction of social and economic activities, anchored to the upkeep of the household, meant "economizing" the female body. During the early years of California's colonization, Bourbon bureaucrats did not allow marriages among new arrivals, but they soon realized that land accumulated wealth, and they encouraged soldiers to marry Christianized California Indian women.[31] This arrangement quickly ended because the elite status of the colonizers in California became synonymous with the military officer class; the crown swiftly reversed its policy of awarding land as a result of these marriages because the racial mixing was disrupting social order. By the time de la Guerra married María Antonia Carrillo y Lugo, the 1776 Royal Pragmatic of Marriage was amended to give parents the ability to prevent marriages of sons under twenty-five, and daughters under twenty-three, for any reason.[32] Because de la Guerra was over the age of consent but still ensigned, he had to apply for royal permission to marry Carrillo y Lugo. Carrillo y Lugo still had a certain amount of prestige because her father could reward de la Guerra through military advancement, but de la Guerra was ultimately "forfeiting his title and inheritance."[33] His permit to marry Carrillo y Lugo arrived in March 1804 and represents the official documentation Californios needed to enact elite status.[34] Through marriages like this one, other soldiers in California came to respect the hierarchal order and attempted, through marriage, to emulate the accession to elite status and rise through the *casta* system.

Oikopolitic: Bridging the Household with the Californiana Body

Five de la Guerra daughters (one daughter died in 1811) were brokered off to different sectors of European or Euro-American males. Angustias de la Guerra Ord is the most famous and most studied of the de la Guerra daughters. She watched over children in the presidio that her father commanded and in 1833 married Manuel Jimeno Casarín, who had come to Alta California from Mexico in the 1820s. She gave birth to thirteen children, lived in Monterey, and in 1853 separated from Casarín, who died the same year. In 1856, she married Dr. James L. Ord, a U.S. army surgeon. They later divorced because of his infidelity in 1875. She vocally protested the U.S. invasion of Alta California, and in the testimonio she gave to Thomas Savage for Hubert Howe Bancroft from 1877 to 1878, she states, "La tristeza que he tenido, tiene algo de trajico parece que es la agonia, con todos sus dolores, de una época que se acaba, que se muere!" ("There is something tragic about the sadness that I have been feeling. It seems like the sorrowful death of an era!").[35] Instead of revealing the customs of Californianas, which Savage wanted to hear and document, Angustias de la Guerra was overtly political in the 156 pages of her testimonio. By the time of her death, she was a fallen woman in her brother's eyes because her marriages failed and because she remained an active agent of her own life through two divorces.

Angustias de la Guerra Ord (María de las Angustias de la Guerra) was born in San Diego on June 11, 1815, and was forty days old when her parents moved to Santa Barbara so her father could take command of the presidio there. She was the sixth child and second daughter of the prestigious and wealthy de la Guerras and dictated her recollections of events that occurred during the years preceding the statehood of California (1850) to Thomas Savage in 1878. Although fluent in English, she gave her testimonio in her native Spanish. In 1956 the Academy of American Franciscan History published María de las Angustias de la Guerra Ord's *Occurrences in California*, an English translation of the original Spanish version. Doña Angustias's recollections begin with the Hipólito Bouchard episode in 1818 and take us through the Indian Revolt of 1824, Mexican Independence, the secularization of the mission system, and the U.S. invasion of California. No better recollection from a Californiana exemplifies the oikopolitic that de la Guerra possessed not only over his daughters, but also over the entire community. Naming him the "father of all," Doña Angustias paints a protective picture of her father, who is distant yet authoritative.

While her testimonio includes autobiographical elements, Doña Angustias's is a mediated testimonio of the de la Guerra family history and not necessarily an autobiographical text. The autobiography and testimonio scholar Rosaura Sánchez defines autobiography according to Gusdorf Georges and states it is a "self-generated/agential discursive construction of 'self' within particular social spaces. This agency, this awareness of the singularity of self, and the structural capacity to construct a 'self' textually, that is, to textualize the various discourses structuring this identity, clearly defines and constitutes an autobiography."[36] Autobiography differs greatly from testimonio because "collaborative efforts of the type generated under 'sponsorship of members of the dominant culture' would not then enter within this definition of autobiography, as their production is mediated and filtered through a second, more powerful agency, that of the interviewer/editor.... In its very production the mediated testimonials introduce a disjuncture, a doubling, a split voice, an overlay of subaltern and hegemonic narrative spaces, perceptible in its dual modality: oral and written."[37] The construction of the "self" in testimonios is textually removed and replaced with a mediated narration of a *collective identity*. However, as Marissa López cautions us, many elite landholding Californios were not necessarily narrating a collective identity forged out of loss. López states of Californio testimonio that the text itself, "inaugurates a textual mode of Chicana/o nationalism, defined as a set of economic relations to self and history articulated within the nexus of national institutions structuring class and racial identities."[38] Doña Angustias is set on revealing the grandiose figure that is her father and by extension narrates her family's—the de la Guerras'—history. There is not a collective loss that gets expressed in her 1878 *California Recollections of Angustias de la Guerra Ord* but a familial trajectory of historical and economic influence on Northern California's region. And while this chapter is not about testimonio, I would be remiss to gloss over this important literary genre and how it works to create the oikopolitic through the construction of de la Guerra's subjectivity. The politics of testimonio in Doña Angustias's recollections work to establish a familial history and then pivot to construct her father as leading the community through a paternalistic ethics, one that bridges the household with the political.

Doña Angustias establishes a network of not only familial relations with important politico through *compadrazgo* (godparents), but also through what the *oikos* took seriously: servantry. This was the major reason why the household was not called a "family" space but a space of household management.

She tells the story of privateer Hipólito Bouchard, who intended to harass commercial Spanish interests to hinder trade and communications between distinct colonies and Spain. Bouchard took prisoners captive and attempted to forge deals with de la Guerra to release the captives. Doña Angustias states, "The insurgents did not commit any outrages in Santa Barbara. A boat came in under a flag of truce, and a man leaped from it to the beach and left there a paper and departed immediately. I do not know what the paper contained, but I have an idea that Bouchard proposed an exchange of prisoners. The one was put ashore was the said Molina, a Peruvian whom they had captured at Monterey. Molina, years later, was a servant to my father and died in his service."[39] De la Guerra exchanged his three prisoners for Molina, even though he was a drunk, and legend states that he walked aboard the privateer boat of his own volition because he was incapacitated. In 1830, the "father of all" received a ship from Mexico that brought seventy-seven to eighty-three male convicts. Doña Angustias stated that the "majority [were convicted] of very grave offenses."[40] The secretary of justice of Mexico issued a circular urging the justices to sentence criminals to California presidios instead of Veracruz. The ship to which Doña Angustias refers was the *María Ester*, sailing from Acapulco to San Diego in February 1830. It was not allowed to land in San Diego, so it went to Santa Barbara. Doña Angustias exaggerates the number of men when she says that "a ship from Mexico [brought] 200 or more men all convicts."[41] Doña Angustias's father begged Don Romualdo Pacheco to have them "bathed and dressed" before they came to the pueblo, and he "sent them shirts and trousers and blankets."[42] The men asked to go by the de la Guerra estate to give thanks to him. Doña Angustias's father "went out to receive them" and told them he would see to it that they had an honorable way of making a living.[43] Doña Angustias then states, "He assured them that he would be a father in every way conducive to their welfare; that is [if] any of them came to be in need, he should come to him for assistance."[44] Ten of those men were assigned to the de la Guerra household as servants. There are two things happening in Doña Angustias's recollection of her father and the convicts. First, we see how Doña Angustias rhetorically uses de la Guerra's hiring of convicts as servants and his willingness to serve as their "father" to distract us from his paternalistic actions and convince us he is acting charitably. Second, in this rhetorical turn, readers do not question the "natural" condition of these convicts as servants. Why did they have to work for de la Guerra? This is rooted in the *oikos*, which naturalizes hierarchy, where the head of the household controls all. If this was the only way de la Guerra controlled the *oikos*, it would be a traditional iteration of the idea. But that is not the case. He utilizes his daughters' bodies to bridge the household with the political and economic realms, therefore naturalizing reproductive and sexual labor through the oikopolitics.

After California ports opened to foreign trade and Eastern Euro-American traders and businessmen in 1821, they came in droves to Alta California and caused a boom in the local economy. Each year the number of ships that docked increased, and by the 1830s, "the ships were taking on an average of 285,000 hides and 570,000 arrobas of tallow annually."[45] Compared to the economy of Mexico, Alta California was booming. Shifts were happening all over the present-day U.S. Southwest, and these new connections opened the market up to transnational trade, which eventually reoriented Mexico's economy. Before 1821, Mexico was dependent on colonial Spain and the markets in Chihuahua, Durango, San Bals, and Mexico City.[46] After Mexican Independence, Alta California forged close ties with the United States because it was geographically closer. Tallow, hide, and sea otter were profitable industries, but around the 1830s, land and what could be produced off the land were commodified. With the influx of foreign and Eastern Euro-American traders, many newcomers needed de la Guerra's authority to trade and exchange. De la Guerra profited from the merchants selling goods to the mission by taking a cut because of the close relationships he had with the mission fathers. And after Mexican Independence he continued to profit by buying and selling goods and libranzas (a bill of exchange or a written order for payment) from merchant vessels and holding the accounts of missionaries, soldiers, and townspeople. De la Guerra had his hands in *all* trade happening on the coast. However, it should be noted that this chapter is very careful *not* to proclaim de la Guerra's wealth, trading, and estate as pre-capitalist, which for many means premodern. While this chapter understands that much of the wealth de la Guerra made came from trading goods, he also traded for coins and could use stores of coin to acquire more wealth by lending out "money" to foreign merchants.[47]

Many great books have been written about de la Guerra and his wealth, trading relations, and business practices, but this chapter explores how de la Guerra utilized his daughters' bodies to secure wealth and social and cultural capital.[48] As Pubols states, "Every level of trade [on the coast] depended on him."[49] But how could de la Guerra balance merchant and business transactions while actively forging relationships to help him acquire wealth for the long term? His daughters' bodies and their sexual labor merged his household and political economy. He invested in their bodies to create political connections that would keep his wealth ahead of the curve. De la Guerra was a gambler.

He did not know whether the European and Euro-American spouses of his daughters would garner him overwhelming wealth or not, but he was speculative in his mission.

Ana María Antonia de la Guerra Robinson, also known as Anita, was de la Guerra's third daughter. Anita was born in 1821, the first de la Guerra born in independent Mexico. She married Alfred Robinson in 1836 at the Santa Barbara Mission church when she was just fourteen years old. Their wedding was immortalized in Richard Henry Dana's book *Two Years before the Mast* in 1840, where he recalls the white plume of smoke from the guns aboard the *Alert* when the church bells rang and the bride entered the mission church. Alfred Robinson was born in Massachusetts in 1807. He first came to Alta California in 1829 on the ship *Brookline*, employed by Bryant, Sturgis and Company, when he visited Hartnell and other politically and economically influential men in Monterey. Robinson was employed by the largest merchant ship on the coast, and he set up a stockroom, showroom, and home in Santa Barbara in 1830. In 1831, de la Guerra took notice of Robinson's success and began to foster a relationship with him. Once de la Guerra saw how successful Bryant and Sturgis had become, he set up his own personal accounts with them. In 1833, Robinson decided to become a permanent resident of California and was baptized in the Catholic Church. He quickly embedded himself in the everyday life of the de la Guerras. He served as de la Guerra's agent in Monterey, and in May 1834, he wrote a letter to María Antonia, Anita's mother, stating that he was sending Anita a silk rebozo through the administrator Angel Ramírez.[50] On December 28, 1834, de la Guerra's "obedient servant, who kisses your hand," also known as Alfred Robinson, wrote him a letter stating that Anita and "her attractions have persuaded me without her I cannot live or be happy in this world," and "consequently I am begging for her hand."[51] De la Guerra quickly agreed, and in 1835 Robinson borrowed $5,000 in silver and doubloons from de la Guerra to cover his debt and new tax impositions.[52]

After Anita and Robinson wed, they had eight children. In 1837, he and Anita sailed for Boston, but they left their eldest daughter, Elena, in California with her grandparents because she was too young to endure the long trip to the East Coast. Once they arrived, Robinson left Anita in Boston to learn English while he returned to Alta California to work until 1842. In 1846, Robinson anonymously published the book *Life in California*, where he gave an account of his first voyage to California. After the U.S. invasion, Robinson became the first agent of the Pacific Steamship Company and served in that role until 1849. Anita was "dutifully" stranded in Boston and New York for thirteen years and only spent about three years back in California before her untimely death in 1854.

Anita learned English as best she could and wrote infrequently to her parents and family, always in Spanish, from the East Coast. But in the few letters Anita did write back home, she laments leaving California and the time away from her family. A grieving tone is present in all of her letters, but Anita often proclaims that she is "doing what is best" for her parents by remaining in Boston. The first letter Anita writes to her parents is from Boston on June 11, 1838. She tells them bluntly, "Voy a hacer un esfuerzo para escribir una carta para decir que mucho me he acordado de la casa y que siempre pensando de vmos. [ustedes] y de la niña." ("I am going to make an effort to write you a letter to tell you how much I remember the house and that I [will] always think of you and the child.")[53] Anita's tone is disturbed yet honorable in all of her letters. Anita attempts to fulfill her household duty of being a good wife and mother, but she also follows her father's wishes in order to maintain her status as a respectable and proper Californiana. This includes remaining faithful to the Catholic religion and learning English. Writing from New York on February 24, 1839, Anita tells her parents, "Voy a ponerme unos singulars para tal de mostrar de q [que] todavía me acuerdo de u.u. [ustedes], y también para ensenar q [que] si he estado entreteniéndome osiosa." ("I will show you how much I still remember you, and also show you that I have had idle entertainment.")[54] This is one of Anita's longest letters, and it is hard to comprehend. She tries very hard to make clear that she is getting a good education and even jokes around with her father when she states, "¿Qué hace la bocona de Angustias q [que] no hace una carta con los demás?" ("What has happened to loudmouth Angustias that [she] does not make a letter like everyone else?")[55] Her "duties" to learn English, remain a faithful Catholic, and remain on the East Coast while Robinson conducted business in her family home in California exemplify two moves. The first is that de la Guerra solidified the connection of his own household (where Anita did not live anymore) and his political and cultural capital. The second exemplifies the naturalization around reproductive labor. If de la Guerra's merging of his different interests can be portrayed as natural, Anita's duties are also natural in that they do not produce value. However, as the Marxist feminist Leopoldina Fortunati clearly states, reproductive labor is the unseen form of capitalist labor. She explains the distinction between that which is the condition of labor and that which is labor. For Fortunati, both forms are labor. As Marxist feminists theorize, Anita's position and role in the household are "labor" because reproductive labor does indeed produce value.[56] However, to break it down one level further, Anita also exemplifies how racialized sex and gender can *never* be seen as labor. If we cannot see reproductive and sexual labor as actual labor, then we can never see racialized sex and gender as labor adding value.

Anita is most concerned with her daughter, Elena, whom she left behind in order to appease her husband and her father. She asks her father unusual questions, like "Esta bonita?" ("Is she pretty?").[57] Such questions reveal how Anita was already thinking about Elena's potential to fulfill the needs of the *oikos*. How valuable would Elena be to her father (and her grandfather, of course)? The *oikos* is concerned with the "natural" order of the house and how it functions. The house's hierarchy was not necessarily explicit but rather was silently understood by everyone in the household as the natural arrangement of things. The ancient Greeks thought nature, meaning the *oikos*, "possessed excessive *means* that can supply people's natural needs."[58] This is where the de la Guerra family departs from the ancient understanding of the *oikos* and merges the political, economic, and household management with investment of their daughters' bodies. While there was a "natural" order to the de la Guerra household, the *ends* for the de la Guerras were not enough through the *oikos* alone; through savvy business practices and the leveraging of his daughters' bodies, de la Guerra increased his wealth and political power. Anita tells her father,

> ¡Don Alfredo ha pasado algo en hacer un viaje solo a California! Pues, para mi seria vergonzoso regresarme otra vez sin haberme primero adelantado algo en mis estudios. . . . Tambien conosco que para u.u. [ustedes] seria gustosos de tener una hija educada como las muchachas que ves aquí todos los días. No crean mis idolatrados Padres que no lo hare / si acabo que lo hago / por falta de amor a u.u. [ustedes].
>
> (Don Alfredo has passed sometime to make a trip alone to California! Well, for me it would be embarrassing to return again without first making headways into my studies. . . . I also know that for you it would be pleasurable to have an educated daughter like those girls (young women) that you see here every day. My adoring parents, don't think I will not finish/I finish what I start /not due to lack of love for you.)[59]

As an investment for her family, Anita realigns the de la Guerra name through *oikos* and *polis* by immersing herself in her education and becoming a proper subject of the estate. This transformation of the de la Guerra daughter from loyal servant to the patriarch to a political subject perfectly exemplifies the oikopolitic. She tells her father that she "quedarme más perfecta" (will stay perfect). She is not only an asset to the de la Guerra estate through her marriage but also in her position as the "perfect daughter."[60]

Anita also makes clear that she remains faithful to the Catholic religion in addition to her education. She states, "Diga a su hijita que su mama con el casarme de Dios vendrá un dia estos y que la tendrá algunas cositas." ("Please tell my daughter with her mom getting married with God, there will come a day when she will have some nice things.")[61] Even in the unknown territory of the United States, as she puts it, Anita performs her household duty as a proper Catholic. Anita is "consciente q [que] no descuide de la obligaciones Catolica" ("conscious that I am not abandoning my Catholic obligations"), but she tells her parents that she cannot make it to confession often because "de no tener perfecto conocimiento del idioma Ingles" ("I do not have a perfect knowledge of the English language").[62] Away from home, Anita bemoans her lack of community, but she establishes her proper femininity through her disciplined practice of Catholicism, even when she is among other religions. And while she obediently performs all the duties asked of a wife, she also educates herself and invests in religion. Her circulation within society is the hidden site of production for her father and Robinson—what Jasper Bernes calls "social reproduction."[63] Bernes considers "social reproduction" in terms of contemporary industries involved in the circulation of commodities, but Anita's "naturalized" female body affords her father trading and commodity options in much the same way.

Surplus within Bodies: Civility, Respectability, and the Dialectical Relationship to Racialized Gender and Sex

Ideas of nationalism, and its implications for racialized gender and sexuality, were nothing new in the discourse of Manifest Destiny and westward expansion in the nineteenth century. A close examination of nationalist notions reveals the ways in which a nation is constructed not only in terms of domestic metaphors (i.e., "home" as nation and "family" as the people who occupy the nation), but also in terms of placing women at the center of the domestic unit, keeping everything together though heteronormative relations. Deniz Kandiyoti, following Benedict Anderson, explores the conflation of "women," "home," "family," and "nation" by stating that "nationalism describes its object using either the vocabulary of kinship (motherland, *patria*) or home (*heimat*) in order to denote something to which one is 'naturally' tied."[64] Proper femininity is tied to the home and therefore to nationalism. To be properly feminine is to align with a heteronormative hierarchy that naturalizes patriarchy and the gender binary system, to be the center and boundary of the home. To be a proper feminine figure in California meant having a certain amount of surplus value.

Spanish colonization set the stage for gender and sexual relations throughout Alta California in the eighteenth century. As Miroslava Chávez-García reminds us, there was a long and brutal history of rape and sexual assault against Indigenous women during the imperial invasion of New Spain that shaped relations based on gender, patriarchy, and culture rooted in conquering and violence.[65] The crown of Spain and the church were deeply embedded in each other, and the crown served as the secular head of the church when it came to managing people, converting the Indigenous population, and ecclesiastical taxation.[66] The church felt the urgent need to bring "proper" people to colonize Alta California to stop the Spanish rape of and violence against the Indigenous populations. They embarked on three different colonization projects with sex and gender relations at the forefront. First, Junípero Serra y Ferrer urged the viceroy to promote marriages between Spanish-speaking soldiers and *neófitas* (Christian native women), with livestock and mission lands promised to them.[67] This resulted in the *Echeveste Reglamento*, the first regulatory code in California.[68] The second key effort encouraged the civilian settlement of families to serve as the basis for the establishment of agrarian communities, or *pueblos*.[69] The third project aimed to recruit artisan families from Mexico with Spanish-speaking wives so they could teach the neófitas how to cook and clean, but also about monogamy and sexual purity.[70]

Spanish gender and sexual norms permeated the nineteenth century, where women were expected to maintain their sexual purity before marriage and fidelity during marriage.[71] A father or husband dishonored by sexual indiscretion was a stain on the entire family. But monogamy on the wife's part guaranteed that the family wealth would continue to grow and be passed on within the family. Thus, where elite landholding Spanish-speaking women in the Southwest borderlands and white femininity meet within American empire is through the household. Whiteness, femininity, and domesticity are always in contradistinction to the foreign. When we think about how the U.S. nation-state legitimizes wars and imperial interference, "domestic policy" and protection of the nation are often at the forefront. So "domestic" not only means the home, a private space where the woman is the center, but it also consolidates the white male and female against the "outsider." Domesticity follows the logic of heteronormative relations and in turn constructs what becomes "proper" feminine behavior against racialized others. As Amanda Zink tells us, the construction of femininity in the nineteenth century shaped the dialectical relationship between whiteness (interior, private, domestic) and the racialized (exterior, public, foreign).[72] Anything from manner of dress to grooming and even breeding went into the makeup of "proper" femininity, and elite classes had the cultural and economic capital to assuage this dialectic.

Throughout Alta California, access to land was the key to wealth. The Spanish government issued fewer than twenty land grants during colonization, but when Mexico won its independence from Spain, land grants became much more abundant. The Mexican government secularized the missions, and Governor Figueroa's 1834 manifesto of secularization codified into law "a policy of land grants for settlers' benefit that initiated the rancho era."[73] While many Californios underwent a significant class transformation, de la Guerra was already marked for success as a Spaniard of pure blood. As Erika Pérez reminds us, "Californios benefited economically from the Mexican government's new secularization policy as well as a liberalization in trade which introduced new consumer goods and intimately affected California families through the arrival of foreign merchants."[74] This meant that in order to retain their economic capital, families needed social capital as well. For de la Guerra, this came in the form of bridging wealth alliances through the marriage of his daughters to *extranjero* (foreign) traders. These types of marriages represented approximately 15 percent of all marriages in Mexican California.[75] While this percentage may seem small, in reality these unions gave a disproportionate amount of economic wealth to a small number of people living in California because they allowed Californios to diversify their financial holdings.

In addition to Anita, Teresa de la Guerra Hartnell was another de la Guerra daughter who married an *extranjero*. Born in 1809, Teresa was the eldest daughter of Don José de la Guerra y Noriega. Shortly after Mexican Independence, Euro-Anglos arrived in Alta California to trade on the new liberal market. One of the first businessmen to arrive was an Englishman named William Edward Petty Hartnell. He moved from South America to start his own business with his former colleague Hugh McCullough. He married Teresa around her sixteenth birthday. When Hartnell arrived in Alta California, he negotiated contracts with de la Guerra and the missions. As a merchant and habilitado (presidio quartermaster), de la Guerra "made *his* money under Spanish rule as a commercial agent for the missions, and as shopkeeper for the soldiers under his command."[76] After Mexican Independence, he was the middleman for the expanding hide and tallow trade. De la Guerra saw great potential in the European businessman who sold him hides and tallows and arranged the marriage with Teresa to connect his business with the opening of California ports to foreign trade. On December 13, 1821, "newly independent

Mexico decreed that the ports of Monterey and San Diego were open to foreign trade."[77] However, Hartnell's business and other endeavors were not successful. After their marriage, Teresa and Hartnell moved to Monterey and had twenty boys and five girls, some of them adopted. Rose Marie Beebe and Robert M. Senkewicz note that Hartnell, who was supposed to be an asset to the de la Guerra family, "quickly became a liability."[78] In 1829, the wreck of the *Danube*, which held his merchandise, was the last straw for his business. He garnered land in Alisal and opened a school there, but it also went out of business. Hartnell performed other jobs, such as inspector of missions and translator after the Mexican-American War, but never with much success. After Hartnell's death, Teresa remarried Manuel Maturano but had trouble paying Hartnell's remaining taxes and debts.

Teresa de la Guerra Hartnell's testimonio, narrated to Enrique Cerruti in 1875, provides historical accounts of the California she remembered but little information about her husband's failures. Instead, she discusses her sisters'—Angustias de la Guerra Ord's and Anita de la Guerra Robinson's—husbands and their successes for the family. She spends much of the testimonio establishing that the reverend fathers of the missions were "good people" because they made her "native land" civilized and safe for the foreign traders who came to California. She states, "When the foreigners came here, they found the land free of its primitive ways because the Indians had already disappeared."[79] Teresa's mediated testimonio does express the ways in which she was brokered, but her anti-native rhetoric in the testimonio is very telling of how she saw herself in relation to them. Teresa was learning how to be a proper Californiana long before she married. The de la Guerra daughters represent the merging of household management and political economy through their different marriage arrangements.

Teresa tells Cerruti that the Indians were always "conspiring against the lives, property, and interests of California."[80] In fact, in Doña Angustias's *California Recollections of Angustias de la Guerra Ord*, she addresses the secularization of the missions after Mexican Independence and remembers how José María de Echeandía, governor of Alta California, espoused republican and liberal principals that did not sit well with de la Guerra. This man of "advanced ideas" made the Indians of the missions "know that they were free and citizens."[81] Doña Angustias says, "My father counseled moderation in his enthusiasm and that he should try to curb the Indians because many of them were treacherous and any day might uprise and kill the whites, including Echeandía himself who was giving them their wings."[82] The Indians stopped listening to de la Guerra as a paternal father figure, and he began to lose control.

In talking about the Mexican politicos who came to Alta California after Mexican Independence, Teresa states that they were all "very bad individuals."[83] For much of both testimonios, the two de la Guerra daughters carefully construct an insular white family in Alta California through the direction of their father but against other racialized subjects in the region. Through their bodies, their whiteness, their sex, and their wealth, as constructed through the oikopolitics, the de la Guerra daughters establish what is "proper" and feminine.

The Pastness of the Present: The de la Guerra Feminized Photograph Archive

While documentation of Californio history was mostly centered on male voices, it is significant that three of the five de la Guerra daughters have a written history attributed to them. Along the same spectrum of visibility, of all the photographs in the de la Guerra Family Photography archive at the Bancroft Library at UC Berkeley, thirty-six of the forty-nine photographs are of women in the family. What the feminine-rich archive tells me is that women were important in the de la Guerra family, in whatever capacity, but there are also hidden discourses in those photographs that reveal and conceal. Why were so many de la Guerra women professionally photographed in the studio? In nineteenth-century California, "the public imagination was consumed with a photographic nostalgia predicated on rendering Mexicans things of the past rather than the future by naturalizing them into a racialized landscape."[84] Lopez reminds us that Mexicans are read as romantic relics of the Spanish heritage past or resistant figures that are the precursors to oppositional politics.[85] By the end of the nineteenth century, photography was used to classify people into "types" extending from Victorian phrenology and physiognomy.[86] The way the subjects are posed, represented, arranged, and placed is all part of the discipline of photography.[87] If we examine the de la Guerra "family" archive, we recognize the wealthy positionality they occupied and the large female presence the photograph archive represents. However, as Laura Wexler reminds us, the signification that sitting portrait represents maps onto domestication. The de la Guerra women have to be represented as proper and pacified, so there is no photography scene more fitting for them than the sitting portrait. Only a handful of the photographs are candid; otherwise, all of the women are intricately posed. However, as Wexler goes on, she also reminds us that "domestication" comes to mean "pacification," and underneath the intricate posing of the sitting portrait is the entire history of female brokering that came to represent the de la Guerra oikopolitics.

Anita de la Guerra Robinson poses for a photograph taken in 1872 by Tuttle & Fitzgerald, showing her donned in a black lace coat and a black mantilla on her head to match. The mantilla was very popular among Spanish women at the end of the sixteenth century. It is situated on the crown of her head with a large braid wrapped around the front of her forehead. She wears a large pearl necklace and pearl earrings. At first glance, she seems to be looking at the camera, but upon further investigation she is looking off slightly to her right. Anita's demeanor and dress speak to the official "knowledge" of the time, when Spanish gender and sexual norms dominated social and cultural spaces and women were expected to maintain their sexual purity before marriage and fidelity during marriage. While this portrait tells us almost nothing about sex, it was clearly constructed for the male gaze. Anita is covered up modestly, she dons expensive jewelry, she wears the traditional cloth of Spanish women on her head, and she is not looking straight into the camera. She seems unhappy with the portrait, but she persists, nonetheless, because she is aware of her "natural" role as a woman in the de la Guerra family. The fact that the de la Guerra family photograph archive contains thirty-six photographs of women says nothing about representation and agency. Rather, it suggests that the dominant de la Guerra men thought it proper for these de la Guerra women to pose for portraits. We cannot see the reproductive labor that stabilizes the de la Guerra estate in any of these female portraits, particularly in Anita's photo, revealing just how difficult it is to see unseen labor and how ideology fixes itself through historical, social, and political life.

The de la Guerra photography archive occludes more than it unveils. In the most literal sense, Jay Prosser tells us that "photographs contain a realization of loss in the fundamental sense that every photograph represents a past real moment that actually happened but is no longer."[88] In a more theoretical sense, the photograph only brings up the pastness of the present, which brings to our attention everything that we cannot see in the photograph. We are all constructed through this loss. The disciplinary interpellation of the gendered sitting portrait of Anita—donning femininized dress, orderly, expensive jewelry—is indicative of what Laura Wexler calls the sentimentality of the domestic space.[89] This means that American domesticity's ideal optic, like Anita sitting completely properly and femininely, cancels out the social effects of other Mexicanas having their sex used violently and unattached to wealth.[90] Wexler also calls this optics, which Prosser states is the construction of the invisible made visible through photographs, "tender violence."[91] This means that there is a coded discourse of American domesticity that flirts with the mechanics of racialized terror "that kept a firm hold throughout the

Anita de la Guerra de Thompson, daughter of José de la Guerra y Noriega. This is a sitting portrait where Anita was posed by the photographers. Note that her correct name was Anita de la Guerra Robinson; however, she is listed as Anita de la Guerra de Thompson in the Bancroft Library archives. De la Guerra Family Photographs, the Bancroft Library, 1872, Tuttle & Fitzgerald, Photographer, call number, BANC PIC 1984.062:04—PIC, filename: cubanc_1_2_00004792a.tif.

entire course of the nineteenth century."[92] If we think about how the photograph of Anita makes invisible the actual terror of racialized sexual violence, we can see just how complex the sitting portrait really is in the nineteenth century. There is not very much to the sitting portrait besides the human body that is centralized. Aside from their dress and their jewelry, there is nothing in the background or on the body that would indicate that racial terror surrounds the bodies of Mexicanas. The frame around the portrait takes up a little less than half the circumference of the actual photo. However, with a critical eye to historical materialism in the nineteenth century, this chapter has unveiled the complicated positionality within the hierarchy of racialized sex. This is not to say that only women sat for studio portraits. Quite the opposite. Nineteenth-century photography is filled with images of war heroes and wealthy men sitting for studio portraits. What becomes interesting in the photograph archive of the de la Guerras is the noticeable feminine presence in the collection.

De la Guerra was able to control his estate by brokering off his daughters to *extranjeros* to potentially expand his wealth. This chapter centers the female Californiana body and the de la Guerras' expansive archives to explore the political economy of Alta California and reveal a history of the sexual and gendered economic systems of elite landholding Californios. De la Guerra had his daughters marry *extranjeros* who could potentially grow his economic wealth; however, this chapter is not about the brokering of classes between Californios and Euro-Americans and Europeans, but rather about the brokering of gendered bodies for household management. De la Guerra's access to the "proper" bodies of his daughters opened up social capital for de la Guerra himself. The reproductive and sexual labor of the de la Guerra daughters not only affected de la Guerra's economics but also bridged the household sphere (*oikos*) with state relations (*polis*) by connecting him with traders in the region. The oikopolitic that de la Guerra created through his daughters' bodies makes clear the limited notion of Marx's "natural" reproductive labor but solidifies the discursive construction of racialized sex, sexuality, and gender by extracting value from female bodies, with very distinct differences in how value was assigned to those bodies in the first place. The next chapter takes a deep dive into the discursive construction of racialized gender, sex, and sexuality by examining how Mexican racial discourse circulated through the U.S.–Mexico borderlands in María Amparo Ruiz de Burton's *Who Would Have Thought It?*

CHAPTER TWO

Circuits of Brown, Black, and Red
The Politics of Racialized Gender and Sexuality in the Nineteenth-Century Borderlands

Whose voices and what ideas have been silenced in and excluded from the archive? There is no shortage of experiences from Protestant northern Europe and British America, but how did information circulate for those who spoke Spanish, for example? In this chapter, I examine these questions, particularly how they relate to the ways that ideas of racialization travel across borders and the implications for white, female Mexican bodies in the nineteenth century. The value of Mexicanas, which I examined in chapter 1, emerged from the complex discourses of the time surrounding Black and Indigenous peoples in Mexico, discourses that inform the concept of *mexicanidad* for the U.S.–Mexico borderlands region. Following the work of Raul Coronado, I explore how racial ideologies flowed through circuits of Spanish America's own intellectual heritage and landed on U.S. imperial soil.[1] Although not visible in the archive, we must understand the genealogies, in the Foucauldian sense, of certain ideas.[2] This chapter challenges the notion of a "universal femininity" that structures daily life and nation-building in the present-day U.S.–Mexico borderlands. Rather than telling the story of how certain elite Californios became U.S. citizens after annexation and immediately adopted U.S. ideas of gender and sexuality, I focus on how circuits of gendered and sexual discourses traveled through literary and cultural spaces between Mexico and the United States. This story, as Coronado astutely states, "traces a circulation of ideas and texts ... it is a history that spills over national boundaries."[3]

THIS CHAPTER RECKONS WITH all the ways that *mexicanidad* establishes itself as relationally disengaged from Black and Indigenous peoples through nineteenth-century tropes of *la mulata, los indios,* and *la cautiva* in the borderlands and Mexico. By mapping how gendered racialization and racialized sexuality took form in this region through discursive ideology, I interrogate racial hierarchies that are attached to gender and sex through Mexican racial discourses of anti-Blackness and anti-Indigeneity in the writing of María Amparo Ruiz de Burton. I argue that Ruiz de Burton takes an anti-U.S. imperialist stance in her writings while employing racist ideas of *mexicanidad* in her construction of racialized gender and sexuality. This chapter lays more of the discursive foundations of racialized gender and sex, like chapter 1, which examines how gendered racialization and gendered sexuality exist materially in different geopolitical spaces in the borderlands. I ask how *mexicanidad* becomes a "panethnic logic of narrow identities assuming an 'epistemically shallow sense of coalition based on coincidence of interests.'"[4] This chapter adopts a hemispheric perspective of María Amparo Ruiz de Burton, the first Mexican American author to write in English, and reveals how she merges a U.S. racial hierarchy with a Mexican racial hierarchy through hemispheric feminine tropes of racist ideology in her 1872 novel *Who Would Have Thought It?* Put differently, this chapter examines how racialized gender and sexuality in the nineteenth-century borderlands is constructed through Mexican racial discourse in the Americas that situates *mexicanidad* as a homogenous category of whiteness that sees itself working within and against U.S. exceptionalism— a U.S. exceptionalism endemic to hypocrisy, forced invasion, and pseudo-democracy. This chapter decenters U.S. racial ideology and also the ways in which Mexicans are racialized in the United States and instead focuses on race through Mexican racialization. This perspective is necessary to understand how Ruiz de Burton attempts to expand the U.S. definition of whiteness to include the Mexican elite, otherwise her historical novel does not make much sense in her critique of whiteness in America. Whereas Julie Ruiz argues that "the unification of Lola's Mexican family as a coalescence of the Mexican nation represents Mexico's repossession of its Spanish borderlands," this chapter argues that Ruiz de Burton defines whiteness and femininity in opposition to U.S. imperialism and racialized discourse in Mexico by attempting to position Mexico and idyllic Mexicanas as prominent players in New World history.[5]

While this chapter offers a discursive look at racialized gender and sexuality in the borderlands through cultural production and print culture in the nineteenth century, it informs the closing chapters, which make clear the materiality of racialized gender, sex, and sexuality. How are poor, dark Mexicanas (oftentimes problematically mapped onto Indigenous women in Mexico) incorporated into the U.S. imperial imaginary before and after the annexation of northern Mexico? How are they imagined in Mexico? This hemispheric rethinking of relationality across geopolitical space treads an important yet slippery slope, because these locations were very regional until the end of the nineteenth century, when the intercontinental railroad became a way to link regions that had never before been linked. However, I reveal important circuits of connections that occurred through print culture. The uncovering of ideological discourse is never straightforward, even while we have a teleological desire to construct a clear linear timeline and narrative of how ideas come to be. This chapter looks closely at the cultural and print production from three key (hemispheric) sites in the novel *Who Would Have Thought It?* (1872) and makes an argument that these sites in Mexico tell an alternative history of racialized gender and sexuality in the borderlands.

First, in a climactic scene at the end of *Who Would Have Thought It?* John Hackwell scolds his clandestine wife, Jemima Norval, a white abolitionist who supposedly serves as the symbol of "proper" white femininity. Hackwell and Mrs. Norval marry secretly after Norval's husband, Dr. Norval, leaves the country and is presumed dead. Before leaving, Dr. Norval rescues Lola, a young woman of Spanish descent who was captured by Native Americans and whose skin is dyed black by her captors, and brings her back to his home in New England. Mrs. Norval is angered that her husband has contaminated their home with the presence of a Black body until she learns of Lola's extreme wealth. After the departure of Dr. Norval, Mrs. Norval and the Reverend Hackwell marry and plot to control Lola's wealth. In the scene in question, Hackwell is upset because Mrs. Norval has failed to separate Lola from her son, Julian Norval, after the two declare their love for one another, thereby threatening Norval and Hackwell's access to Lola's wealth. When Hackwell threatens to leave Mrs. Norval because Lola is slipping out of his control, Mrs. Norval cries out. Though noticeably upset, she simultaneously feels "a thrill through her entire frame, just as might have felt one of those creatures—whom she so abhorred—who go to parties in low necks and short sleeves, and go to theatres, and, in their wild chase after worldly pleasures, do court such thrills. She, a strict hater of popery, a pious, proper churchwoman, felt just the same."[6] Even as she abhors the excessive rogues and declares herself above them, she simultaneously yearns for something that is "off-limits" within her social circle. Mrs. Norval is almost unaware of her fall from a "proper" type of white femininity because she is so consumed with the destruction she causes. In truth, she was never a pious and God-fearing woman, considering all the problematics of those terms in the first place. Her affair and secret marriage to Hackwell, a Protestant minister, illustrate this. In Ruiz de Burton's eyes, both of these characters are emblematic of everything that is wrong with the ideology of American exceptionalism. However, this does not solely represent the failure of white femininity or, as Rosaura Sánchez and Beatrice Pita state, "the fall of Republican Motherhood"; it also constructs the ideological foundation of a "proper" Mexican white femininity, represented by Lola, in contrast to the racialized gender and sexuality of Indigenous and Black bodies.[7]

Second, just five chapters after Mrs. Norval's symbolic cry, symbolizing that rather than falling from white proper femininity, she is endemic to the problem of American democracy in the first place, Mrs. Norval's brother Isaac reaches the coast of Veracruz, Mexico. Here he seeks out Don Felipe Almenera, Lola's grandfather, and Don Luis Medina, her father, to give them the written testimonio of Doña Theresa, Lola's mother. In 1640, as a colony of New Spain, Veracruz had the second-largest population of enslaved Africans; by 1810, there were approximately 634,000 free Black people, or 10 percent of the total population. Veracruz is also the home of Don Luis Medina, from where he finances resistance to French, English, and Spanish military forces attempting to occupy Mexico. And while support for a French monarchy becomes apparent *after* these facts are established, we first experience Don Felipe and Don Luis through the geopolitical locale of Veracruz—the point of entry for the nation's first invaders and the last place from which the exiles depart, making it a very historically political location in itself. It is not clear whether Ruiz de Burton was speaking through her characters in support of a Mexican monarchy or in condemnation of U.S. imperialist actions, but this scene begins an uncanny mirroring of the tale of La Mulata de Córdoba, the legend of a Mexican *mulata* from the coastal region of Veracruz who entranced men with her beauty and sexuality. In the novel, Veracruz figures prominently as a focal point in not only establishing Mexico as a place of esteem in the New World, but also in constructing racialized gender and sexuality through *mexicanidad* that privileges whiteness against excessive Black female sexuality.

Blackness plays a large role in *Who Would Have Thought It?* in the ways in which Lola is able to move in and out of Blackness and is therefore able to escape sexually excessive depictions of racialized gender and sexuality inherited by the Black female figure in Mexico. The legend of La Mulata de Córdoba is an emblematic figure of "eroticized otherness."[8] There is no factual evidence that La Mulata de Córdoba actually existed during the Inquisition in Mexico (1571), but the earliest written accounts of her life were published in nineteenth-century Mexico. Legend goes that this unnamed *mulata* was beautiful and lived on the edge of town making potions for the sick. She was imprisoned for turning down first the mayor of the city of Córdoba and later a solider in the Inquisition, but she used her magic to draw a boat on the side of her prison wall and sail away into the sunset. While she was a natural healer by trade, she is marked as a witch in the national imaginary. We first see La Mulata de Córdoba in an 1837 article titled "Historia de un peso," written by José Bernardo Couto and published in the literary newspaper *El Mosaico Mexicano*.[9] Couto states that La Mulata de Córdoba "could, at her desire, make strange shapes, command the elements, and disturb the laws established by nature."[10] The same story appears four years later in *Calendario de las señoritas mejicanas* and is one of the only versions that does not comment on La Mulata de Córdoba's racial makeup but instead calls her an "herchicera" (witch). Every literary instance of the woman after this first story was published mentioned La Mulata de Córdoba's race. Manuel Ramírez Aparicio was the first author to construct La Mulata de Córdoba as *mulata*. Forty-seven years after Couto, and twenty-three years after Ramírez Aparicio, Vicente Riva Palacio reintroduced la *mulata* in *Tradiciones y leyendas mexicanas* in 1884. While La Mulata de Córdoba was present in nineteenth-century literary and cultural production, she was also used as a homogenizing tool to erase the large population of Black subjects in Mexico. Blackness in nineteenth-century Mexico lacked any prestige and was therefore excluded from the national narrative of Mexico.[11]

Third, and simultaneously in this same scene, readers finally witness Don Felipe and Don Luis read the testimonio of Doña Theresa Almernara de Medina's life after her capture by the Apache Indians in Sonora in 1846, when she was brought north of the Colorado River area, sold to the Mohave Indians, and made the wife of the Indian chief. As Don Luis reads the testimonio, he begins "weeping like a child, like a weak woman. But he was not ashamed of his tears."[12] The two men discuss the horror of Doña Theresa's life in native captivity and how "pure and beautiful and accomplished Theresa" was before her capture.[13] Don Luis says of Doña Theresa, "She, the pure, the high-minded, refined, and delicate Theresa, to meet such a fate!"[14] The novel clearly uplifts Doña Theresa as the ideal Mexican female martyr in contradistinction to the "savage Indians." But more than this, Ruiz de Burton advances a hemispheric understanding of white *mexicanidad* by blaming U.S. imperial forces for destabilizing Mexico and for Doña Theresa's capture by the "savage" Apache Indians. In blaming U.S. imperialism for Doña Theresa and Lola's capture and subsequent life in captivity, Ruiz de Burton utilizes racist tropes of "*los indios*" and "*la cautiva*" that appear in the Mexican national imaginary in mid-nineteenth-century Sonoran newspapers to solidify the white gendered Mexican constructions of femininity. The Sonoran newspaper *La Estrella de Occidente*, later published as *Boletín Oficial and La Constitución*, comes out of the same exact place where Doña Theresa was captured and evokes the same anti-Indigenous (*indios barbaros*) sentiments as Ruiz de Burton; this is due to the constant invasion by Apache Indians on wealthy Mexican families because of weakened and informal diplomatic zones on the border. The three categories of racialized female subjects in the United States and in the borderlands (New England white, Black, and Native) can never be superior to Mexican gender, sexuality, and femininity. Through the tropes of the *la mulata, los indios,* and *la cautiva,* Ruiz de Burton mobilizes a *mexicanidad* superiority utilizing hemispheric racialized gendered and sexual discourse.

The concept of *la cautiva* has a double meaning in *La Estrella de Occidente*. The first is the actual captivity of Mexican women and families by *los indios*. The second, seemingly contradictory, is how, in 1863 when the French captured Mexico, *cautiva* represented the feminized nation of Mexico. *La Estrella de Occidente* was a state-run newspaper in Sonora, Mexico, that ran from 1855 to 1876. Ignacio Pesqueira, the governor of Sonora, established the newspaper, and Francisco Ramirez later served as editor from 1860 to 1862. Ramirez was a transnational Latino who lived in Los Angeles, where he published *El Clamor Público* (1855–1859). The newspaper covered important issues like Mexican migration to the United States, which it widely criticized, even publishing a list of *sonorenses americanizados,* or individuals who changed their nationality.[15] Thus, *El Clamor Público* criticized U.S. imperial intervention in the same ways as Ruiz de Burton. The most notable fact about this newspaper is that it ran stories about *los indios* almost daily and spoke candidly about the ideal Mexican woman in relation to the nation that was taken *cautiva*.

This chapter is concerned with what Ruiz de Burton both shuts out and opens up in her construction of gender, sex, sexualization, and femininity within U.S. empire through *mexicanidad*. As shown in the previous example, Mrs. Norval is a very clear construction of the hypocrisies of white abolitionist females; however, her position can only be seen as failed up and against Black sexual female excess and the *indio* figure in the Mexican national imaginary. Robert Irwin examines gender in Mexico during the nineteenth century and reminds us of the necessity to establish a masculine and virile culture in the newly independent Mexico to counter the feminized history of national icons like the Virgin of Guadalupe (symbol of independence) and La Malinche (symbol of conquest and *mestizaje*).[16] This masculinizing tension in Mexican nation-building reinforces the racialized gender and sexual constructions of the sexually excessive females and "savage" Native "Indians" who are identified against feminine properness on one end of the spectrum and masculine subordination on the other. Irwin states that "gender, as a main element of the Mexican national *habitus,* goes unquestioned even as it becomes entangled in blatantly racist stereotypes."[17] This, coupled with discourses of Black female "grotesqueness" in chattel slavery and the untamable "Indian" in the United States, complicates Ruiz de Burton's construction of her perfect Mexicana. This is precisely how racialized gender and sexuality enunciate themselves in social, political, and historical discourses in the borderlands and how this book documents these moments of violence, dispossession, or merely rendering invisible certain racialized subjects.

How did Ruiz de Burton create Mexican female characters that were so resistant to other forms of *mexicanidad*, such as the black Mexican or the indigenous Mexican subjectivity? Why did she feel so comfortable reinforcing a racial hierarchy that created the same displacement she experienced, but only through white Anglo-Americans? The circuits of discourse in Mexico that simplified *la mulata* as a stereotype of sexual excess and *los indios* as violent "savages" are consolidated in a conquered subject, Ruiz de Burton, who constructs an allegory of modernization in the United States and Mexico. She portrays racialized gender and sexuality through white failed American femininity by evoking an anti–U.S. imperialist stance through gender (encompassing all of the white American women characters, particularly Mrs. Norval) and through racist discourses of *mexicanidad*. Examining tropes of *la mulata, los indios,* and *la cautiva* throughout Mexico in the nineteenth century, this chapter interrogates the racialized sexual discourse in *Who Would Have Thought It?* in relation to hierarchies of racialization between the United States and Mexico. Thus, *Who Would Have Thought It?* delivers the "failed white female" but evokes an ideological turn of racialized gender and sexuality that is supported by colonial logics of anti-Black and anti-Indigenous discourses in Mexico to construct a perfect white Mexican female figure in the United States.

The Multiple Circuits of María Amparo Ruiz de Burton

There is no lack of scholarship focusing on María Amparo Ruiz de Burton. I really wish I could meet her and simultaneously really wish I could forget about her. She is the thorn in every nineteenth-century Latino/a scholar's side. She is not a subaltern figure, yet she never fully assimilated into U.S. imperial culture. She is not a women's rights advocate, yet she knows what her position in society as a woman does and does not afford her. She was not always "elite," yet she was not always subjugated. She fits into our recovery agenda to a certain extent because of her criticism of U.S. imperialism, yet she deploys racist tropes throughout her novels. Her biography, persona, and novels have been the center of numerous scholarly books, academic journal articles, and edited collections since the recovery of her novel *Who Would Have Thought It?* in 1995. There are many circuits of study that make Ruiz de Burton whole in our contemporary moment. Rosaura Sánchez and Beatrice Pita call her a "subordinated and marginalized national minority" by 1860, but she is always a contradictory and fissured subject.[18] José F. Aranda makes the controversial yet astute claim that Ruiz de Burton is a paradoxical figure who politically aligns herself with her Anglo-American constituencies.[19] Jesse Alemán maintains that Ruiz de Burton relies on cultural rather than biological notions of race to place Californios within the category of whiteness, while very much distinguishing them from Indigenous and Black subjects in the United States.[20] Julie Ruiz expands on these ruminations on Ruiz de Burton's contradictory impulses by arguing that she creates a white gendered criolla identity post–Mexican Independence to salvage her pure lineages—a restoration of Mexico's fractured borders.[21] Clearly, Ruiz de Burton makes us work to make connections. She leaves much to be desired, but also offers much substantial information with which to work. It is within those connections, those circuits, that discursive formations appear.

Born María Amparo Maytorena to Jesús Maytorena (also spelled Maitorena) and Isabel Ruiz in Loreto, Baja California, Mexico, in 1831, she used her maternal last name because it carried the most "prestige and influence."[22] There is much speculation as to why she did not use her paternal last name, but one theory is that "[her grandfather] was not a propertied man and held no influential position."[23] Her grandfather, Captain Ruiz, was an attendant responsible for patrolling the Northern Baja area and was later appointed governor of Baja California while being *teniente de fronteras*. The title of *teniente de fronteras* may sound prestigious, but the frontera, at that moment, was nothing more than a ranch. As Sánchez and Pita remind us in *Conflicts of Interest*, there was a mission on the ranch, and Ruiz de Burton's grandfather captured Native runaways from the mission. As a result of his service, the king gave him land in Ensenada. Ruiz left this land to his son-in-law and retired poor and tired in Loreto. In October 1822, he was appointed interim governor of Baja California.[24] Her grandfather's brief stint as governor and his position as a Spanish soldier and criollo[25] gave Ruiz de Burton the prestige she needed to move along in the world, even though she possessed no money, land, or wealth. She witnessed the 1846 U.S. invasion of La Paz, Baja California, at the start of the Mexican-American War and three years later married the captain of the invading army, Henry S. Burton, a West Point graduate and native of Connecticut. When the 1848 Treaty of Guadalupe Hidalgo ended the war, the United States gained upper California, along with other Southwestern states, but left lower California to Mexico. Captain Burton arranged to have over four hundred "friendly" Mexicans transported to Monterey, California, granting them full citizenship rights guaranteed by the treaty. Among them was María Amparo Ruiz de Burton. Her husband later purchased property on Rancho Jamul (in California) with three other people, but the family moved when the military transferred Burton to New York. Ruiz de Burton returned to California in 1869 after the death of her husband to find some parts of Rancho Jamul sold off and squatters sitting on the remaining land. The Land Act of 1851, contrary to the 1848 treaty, required all Mexican land grants to be validated by the Land Commission or the state courts. Ruiz de Burton, although not an original Californio landholder, would in time, after much litigation, gain her Jamul property as land that she mortgaged several times before she died in Chicago in 1895. She hired a lawyer to take care of her Ensenada land claim case after she died, and he gained an award from the Mexican government for her children years after her death. The historical persona and legacy that she left behind as an "elite" landholding Mexicana/Californio was not dependent as much on her access to old money as it was on her keen sense of networking and positioning herself as something other than a "mongrel Mexicana." Thus, Ruiz de Burton is not unproblematic in any sense of the word. She was a Mexicana in the nineteenth century, negotiating and mediating her position within the geohistorical and geopolitical space of the Americas. Ruiz de Burton could never obtain the position within U.S. democracy she thought she morally deserved because the United States was predicated on the foundational ideology of white supremacy and the ungovernability of difference camouflaged under the guise of disseminating civility and order.

What becomes so interesting in the circuits of information we have about Ruiz de Burton is the absence of actual women in her life archive. Her cultural production centers feminine subjectivity at its core. Even so, her life revolves around her correspondences with powerful men in California and racialized males who shared the same sense of frustration of being displaced by U.S. imperialism. While in New York, she states in a letter to Mariano Guadalupe Vallejo on February 15, 1869, "¡Ah! Si yo fuera hombre! ¡Qué miserable cosa es una mujer! [Ah, if I were a man! What a sorry thing it is to be a woman!]."[26] In her letters to powerful men in California, Ruiz de Burton discusses women in relation to men. She is well aware of the gender dynamics and sexism that flow not only through Mexican society but also in the United States. There is an absence of a definition of the feminine subject in Ruiz de Burton's letters, yet she clearly assigns features, characteristics, and personality to the female characters in her novels. The only time we see her correspond with a female in the archive is in brief notes to Matías Moreno's wife, Prudenciana Moreno. In those letters she is almost unrecognizable, as she asks Prudenciana Moreno to send her cape or ruffles from her trunk.[27] Matías Moreno was a great friend of Ruiz de Burton; she wrote to him frequently and even stayed with him and his wife while her husband was in Yuma. She found common ground with Moreno because he, too, was from Baja, California, and both had disdain for the Californios who sided with U.S. invaders in San Diego. She and Moreno were passionate about La Frontera (the border), a region they both knew well and that was experiencing critical changes. Her letters to him, in contrast to the simplistic correspondence with his wife, are very political in nature, and they mostly deal with matters related to the border. However, there are times when their friendship seems rocky, and Ruiz de Burton tries to assuage the situation by commiserating on their similar political situations. She states, "Comprendo bien la desconfianza con que Ud. mira al mundo; yo tengo motivos para sentir lo mimso." (I well understand the distrust with which you look at the world; I have reasons to feel the same.)[28]

This is not to say that Ruiz de Burton did not have female friends, but we know women weren't deemed important enough to archive, as Ruiz de Burton notes throughout many of her correspondences. She was not interested in fighting for women's rights; she was most interested in the Spanish land grants in Ensenada, on La Frontera. But as she says to Vallejo about her potential as a wealthy Mexicana in California, "¿Para qué? Ni mi raza ni mi sexo van a sacar mejora alguna." (What for? Neither my race nor my sex will allow me to gain anything from it.)[29] Ruiz de Burton is astutely aware of the negative effects of her racialized gender and sexuality from the beginning and therefore must rewrite the history of the Californio female in her novels. But her letters reveal a person navigating "Alta and Baja—capitalist Anglo-Saxons dominat[ing in] California, and underdeveloped-and-defeated Mexican California."[30] She was a product of Mexico but evolved with the United States at the same time. She merged a Mexican consciousness with a U.S. capitalist Californian sensibility. Ruiz de Burton was ever concerned with La Frontera, and when she left for the East Coast with her husband, she wrote a letter to Moreno that stated,

> Le agradezco las noticas que me da de San Diego, etc., y espero que cada vez que me escribe no omintirá cosa alguna de interés, en particular de la Frontera y del resto de la Baja California con sus luchas, sus desgracias y su poca esperanza. No importa en dónde ni qué tan lejos yo me halle, siempre sentiré el mismo interés po mi pobre país natal.

> (I appreciate the news you give me from San Diego, etc., and I hope that every time you write to me you will not miss anything of interest, in particular from the Border and the rest of Baja California with its struggles, its misfortunes and its little hope. No matter where or how far I am, I will always feel the same interest in my poor native country.)[31]

The nation of Mexico becomes intertwined with the region of Baja California for Ruiz de Burton. It is impossible to imagine that she was not invested and interested in the discourses of *mexicandiad* circulating in Mexico.

Contemporarily *mexicanidad* lies at the interstices of two political antecedents: the institutionalization of the *casta* system that flourished in New Spain and the institutionalization of *mestizaje* during the post-revolutionary period.[32] While the *casta* system continued to marginalize Black subjects in Mexico long after Spanish colonial presence, *mestizaje* made *afromexicanos* ultimately invisible in the national imaginary of Mexico by evoking a Spanish and Indian bicultural fantasy where even most Indigenous people in Mexico fell outside of the definition. Ultimately, it was a discourse of ethnic cleansing. Nineteenth-century notions of *mexicanidad* had much to do with questions about how Mexico would move forward with modernization after the Mexican Revolution and the Mexican-American War and how Mexico would retain its culture while doing so. During the nineteenth century, modernization projects in Mexico attempted to move away from the ideologically embedded *casta* system of the colonial days.[33] However, in many instances, Mexico continued to reinforce it. Mexico abolished slavery and tried to "incorporate black subjects into the masses of their national fabric. Simultaneously, Mexican liberal ideology expected *indios* to cease being Indian and accede to the status of 'citizens.'"[34] Mexico claimed that the different values and life systems of Indigenous populations could not be sustained in a modern nation-state. As Claudio Lomnitz-Adler states, "If the 'members of the Aztec race' were to progress, they would have to be considered as (poor) citizens who could then aspire to climb the economic ladder through their work."[35] Nineteenth-century politics in Mexico brought the issue of racialization to the forefront in order to establish *mexicanidad* at the expense of Black and Indigenous subjects. In attempts to abolish Black and Indigenous populations, Mexican laws eliminated the distinguishing of these populations from the rest of society. This was the beginning of the dissolution of the *casta* system and the formation of the "mestizo race."[36] Whiteness assumed a role front and center in Mexican liberal ideology. Lomnitz-Adler reminds us, "With the dissolution of Indianness as a legal category that guaranteed a caste position, the use of the term 'Indian' became synonymous with a combination of material poverty and cultural 'backwardness.'"[37] Class distinction was also framed in racial terms during this time period, where the term *indio* became synonymous with poverty. Racialization became tied to class, and this intersection created what the nineteenth century considered an identity of *mexicanidad*. As a person who existed in both Mexico and the United States, Ruiz de Burton came to detest Yankee imperialism and the subservice of

Latin America to the United States. Therefore, it only makes sense for Ruiz de Burton to consolidate Mexican national discourse and U.S. jingoism steeped in toxic American exceptionalism.

Ruiz de Burton's work can be better understood as part of a broader hemispheric discourse reemphasizing a racial hierarchy that attempts to elevate Mexican American–ness (e.g., whiteness) above articulated white femininity, Blackness, and Indigeneity through the notion of *mexicanidad*. Utilizing tropes of *los indios* and *la mulata*, Ruiz de Burton conceptualizes gender and sexual norms for Mexicans in the newly annexed Southwest through Doña Theresa and Lola. Through the historical romance and Lola's inevitable marriage to a white New Englander (as she herself becomes white by the end of the novel), Ruiz de Burton uses major historical events as the background to invoke her own disapproval of the changing social fabric of the Americas. In thinking about Ruiz de Burton's use of blackface through Lola's character, Anne Goldman indicates that "when the Norval ladies cast (and cast off) Lola as black, they allow the writer . . . to exploit the value of abolitionism as a social currency."[38] I extend this U.S.-centric criticism of Ruiz de Burton utilizing a Black Lola to unveil the hypocrisy of the New England white woman to examine how she engages a Mexican discourse of *la mulata* to cement her positionality as a Mexicana in the United States. Simultaneously, as Jesse Alemán likens Doña Theresa to the Spanish category of *gente de razón* (as opposed to the Natives who captured her from her Sonoran hacienda as *gente sin razón*), I extend this logic to Sonoran literary production that categorizes *los indios* in contradistinction to Doña Theresa's Mexicana martyrdom.[39]

"Magnified into a Very Tall [Black] Woman": Anti-Blackness, Veracruz, and the Fungibility of Excessive Racialized Sexuality

When Isaac lands in Veracruz, he finds Don Felipe Almenera and Don Luis Medina in their country home just outside of Mexico City. Before Isaac locates Don Felipe Almenera and Don Luis Medina, readers are introduced to the two Mexican men's clear "transatlantic" conversation about the possibility of Austrian archduke Maximilian accepting the "newly reestablished Mexican throne, a historical event that marked Mexico's brief reversion from democracy to monarchy."[40] Lola's grandfather, Don Felipe Almenera, says that while he is "liberal," he "will be happy to be the most loyal of subjects" to Maximilian.[41] Lola's father, Don Luis Medina, states, "Whilst the question is of repelling the French, or any other nation that comes to Mexico as a hostile invader, I shall not hesitate in giving my all in the defense of our country. But, though I am Mexican at heart as well as by adoption, I shall find it too difficult to make up my mind to fight against an Austrian prince and above all Prince Maximilian. My Austrian blood rebels against fighting him."[42] Latino/a/x nineteenth-century scholars have long read this moment of conversation between Lola's wealthy Mexican grandfather and her wealthy Mexican Austrian father in Mexico City as emphasizing Mexican cosmopolitanism within a larger New World order. However, I read this moment as a consolidation of bourgeois *mexicanidad* racial order tied to racialized gender and sexuality. As stated above, Ruiz de Burton merges a Mexican national identity with her border Baja identity, and when she moved to the East Coast, she became even more invested in Mexican politics through her contact with the Mexican Legation in Washington, D.C.[43] This scene opens up the space to talk about how Ruiz de Burton views the French intervention as an "alternative to any assumption of geographic morality emanating from the concept of 'America.'"[44] She is taking hemispheric imaginings from Mexico, which she imagined as superior to the United States because of her position and landholdings in Baja California, and utilizing them in her narratives. At first Ruiz de Burton was completely against the French invasion in Mexico and was a liberal supporter of President Juárez, just like Don Felipe and Don Luis were when the invaders arrived at the port in Veracruz. However, with the execution of Maximilian in Querétaro in June 1867, her position changed. Feeling neglected by the central government in Mexico, but more importantly wanting stability for Mexico and for her own landholdings, Ruiz de Burton states, "Me dijeron claramente que 'mientras no haya un gobierno en México que nada espere para la Baja California.'" (They clearly told me that "as long as there is no government in Mexico then expect nothing for Baja California.")[45] The French intervention happened after President Juárez halted debt payments for foreign powers, which was catalyzed by near financial collapse. The French saw this neglect of debt as an opportunity to establish their world dominance while supporting the Confederacy and splitting the Union. Ruiz de Burton never writes about it in her letters, but this scene replicates anti-Black sentiment in Mexico (and the United States) coupled with resentment of Anglo-Saxon imperialism and her allegiance to *mexicanidad*.[46]

Rosaura Sánchez and Beatrice Pita state that "whether Ruiz de Burton herself favored liberal monarchy in Mexico is not clear nor really at issue" because she uses this scene to demonstrate that U.S., not European, empire was the greatest threat to Mexico.[47] Whereas Gretchen Murphy reads this scene in direct opposition to the Monroe Doctrine in order to establish a transatlantic culture where Mexico is esteemed, Jose Aranda reads it as Mexico "failing to secure North America for their white, educated, European elite."[48] In reading this scene as clearly anti–United States, however, this chapter falls in between this scholarship on Ruiz de Burton. Continuing with a discussion of the Bourbons and Habsburgs, who would have ultimately controlled Mexico under a French monarchy had Mexico never declared independence from Spain, this scene sets up a racial hierarchy of European bloodlines in relation to *mexicanidad* in the Americas, clearly elevating light-skinned Mexicans with ties to Europe as superior.

However, before we even get to this conversation about their newfound loyalties to Maximillian, we find out that when allied troops from France, England, and Spain landed in Veracruz in 1862, Don Felipe offered financial assistance to the government to fight off the invasion in Mexico, and Don Luis immediately joined the Mexican army. Their loyalties have always been to Mexico; however, Don Felipe and Don Luis enunciate them differently throughout the narrative, securing an anti–United States attitude throughout. This Mexican loyalty and the exact geopolitical place where the troops landed, in Veracruz, is telling. Veracruz has historically been the main port of entry for slaves, foreigners, and attacks, and Don Felipe and Don Luis were, at one point in the narrative, intent on protecting their nation and establishing themselves as superior in the New World. Veracruz is also home to the "La Mulata de Córdoba" legend that has more presence than any other legend in Mexican literature.[49] While Lola's storyline does not match the legend exactly (because there are many iterations of it), it mirrors it in ways that attempt to unveil excessive Black sexuality in Mexico in the nineteenth century.

However, scholars have long been tracking the similarities between Lola and other historical figures in the nineteenth-century United States. Andrea Tinnemeyer particularly has looked at the similarities between Lola's captivity narrative and the real-life Olive Oatman captivity narrative. Olive Oatman and her sister Mary Oatman were taken captive in 1851 by the Apaches and later sold to the Mohaves. They remained there until Olive was returned to her white family in 1856, while Mary died of starvation in captivity. The Mohave tribe gave the girls a chin tattoo that both male and female captives received and represented their belonging to the tribe. This would be the marker of recognition if the Mohave captives were to be stolen by another tribe. Tinnemeyer argues that Ruiz de Burton utilizes the Oatman captivity narrative as the basis for the captivity of Doña Theresa and Lola in her novel as a way to "redress grievances after the U.S.-Mexican War. Ruiz de Burton's revision of the captivity narrative operates under a different geographical and racial imaginary than the one commonly animating captivity narratives. It focuses attention on the Southwest Territory [and] on the broken promises of the Treaty of Guadalupe Hidalgo."[50]

While I agree that *The Captivity of the Oatman Girls among the Apache and Mohave Indians* bears directly on *Who Would Have Thought It?*, I am shifting the narrative from a U.S.-centric analysis, which is evident in that Ruiz de Burton writes the novel in English. However, as a strong proponent of Mexican stability, superiority, and economic freedom, I am shifting to a cross-national analysis of the text. There is an anti-Blackness that taints the novel that cannot be explained through the Oatman narrative. I am arguing that it is *mexicanidad* that lays the foundation for the sexual and gendered discourse that persists within the novel. Ruiz de Burton engaged in a Mexican literary discourse because of her contention with U.S. imperialism.

When we first meet Lola, the protagonist of the novel, she is not in Mexico but with the Natives in the Colorado River area who have taken her mother, Doña Theresa, into captivity and dyed Lola's skin black. Dr. Norval finds Lola and her mother in captivity in the Southwest borderlands and promises Doña Theresa that he will educate and raise Lola as Catholic in New England until he finds her father and grandfather in Mexico. Doña Theresa collects an array of gems, gold, and jewels and sends it all with Dr. Norval to take care of Lola in New England and eventually pass down to Lola when she is old enough. Lola's coming-of-age also mirrors her skin lightening, as her black dye wears off and she ends up in Mexico by the end of the novel, married to Julian Norval, Dr. Norval's son. Julian joins Lola in Mexico to live their life together following the Civil War. All this is happening to Lola while Mrs. Norval, the Yankee "abolitionist," exploits Lola's wealth and in the process "falls from Republican motherhood grace" when she has an affair with the Reverend Hackwell and falls ill by the end of the novel. While the Civil War is the background historical event for a portion of the novel, and scholars have linked Lola's Blackness with the discourse of Blackness in the United States through chattel slavery, this chapter reads Lola's Blackness and the cross-hemispheric relations between the United States and Mexico in relation to how Blackness flowed through Mexican discourse in the nineteenth century.

Black subjects were culturally irrelevant in the national imaginary of Mexico during the nineteenth century; however, they were instrumental to the proliferation of colonialism in Mexico through the discourse of *mexicanidad*. The most famous *mulata* figure in nineteenth-century Mexico, and one that Ruiz de Burton most certainly was familiar with, was the legend of La Mulata de Córdoba. The colonial legend of this *mulata* was that she was a woman of Spanish and African ancestry, dark-skinned, and a product of slaves imported into Veracruz—a woman born of violence and racism between colonizers and Black subjects. She was a figure who stood at the "intersection of colonialism and modern nationhood" and was not only denounced by the Inquisition because she would not marry the Inquisitor but also mediated the forbidden desires that construct the relations between white and Black and master and slave in nineteenth-century Mexico.[51] Why was she so popular in the imagination of this time? Ramos argues that "she became a singular medium for the development and dissemination of Mexico's national racial discourse, playing a critical role in the complex processes that came to define Mexican national identity as 'mestizo,' exclusive of blackness."[52] While Ruiz de Burton navigates U.S. Manifest Destiny discourse, she also navigates Mexico's position in the New World order. Just as La Malinche is a trope of sexual excess and a traitor in the borderlands, La Mulata de Córdoba was Mexico's licentious racialized female legend in the nineteenth century who was tied to Blackness and "dressed in tropical fanfare and woven into the national aural fabric through an acoustics of otherness."[53] La Mulata de Córdoba inherently possessed "unbridled sexuality."[54] Arce states that "as a person in-between two worlds, she enjoys a kind of tragic 'mobility' that at once exalts and condemns her sexuality."[55] This mirrors Lola's journey in uncanny but not exact ways. Lola is dyed black; however, she is still able to move around geopolitically, although tragically at first. If she were a mirror of the female chattel in the United States, she would not have the privilege of movement. Here begins Lola's fungibility as a Black female, but through *mexicanidad* and not through U.S.-centered discourse. Lola mirrors the legend of La Mulata de Córdoba, *except* for the "proliferating tropes that constituted black female sexuality as perverse, linking blackness to the devil."[56] Lola has a fungible Blackness that allows her to move in and out of Black sexuality, while she simultaneously is the focus of all the male attention in New England.

Doña Theresa tells Dr. Norval in her testimonio that she and Lola were dyed black, but "that black skin will certainly wear off."[57] In this moment, the novel is suggestive in its anti-Black sentiments; however, the gendered racialization that describes Lola is not totally apparent at the beginning of the novel. And while readers are well aware that Lola has a mother and family in Mexico, the novel makes a point of labeling Lola an orphan only while she is dyed black. Once her skin begins to lighten, the discourse of the orphan all but disappears. In fact, at the beginning of the novel, Dr. Norval tells the reverend that while his wife does not have sympathy, he feels pity for the "poor little orphan because her skin is dark."[58] In all iterations of the legend, La Mulata de Córdoba is also orphaned. No one knows who her parents are, and no one knows her past. While the Norvals know of Lola's parents and family, they still categorize her as an orphan while she is dark. When nine-year-old

Lola arrives at the Norval home dyed black, Mrs. Norval sees her "magnified into a very tall woman."[59] The novel goes on to call Lola a "little black girl"; however, Mrs. Norval's first impression is very telling of how Blackness is first read through a Mexican discourse. Arce states that La Mulata de Córdoba "immediately identities through the sexualization and racialization of her body." While the identification of Lola as Black is clear upon her arrival in New England, Arce goes on to state that "[her physical] descriptors are rife with latent sexual desire, and in the case of the Mulata, this can only translate into sin."[60] Lola is Black when she arrives and is treated as such in terms of her femininity, but she is never sexualized because of her Blackness in the novel. Hackwell takes great interest in Lola because she has wealth and she soon starts whitening. However, Ruiz de Burton is very clear to construct Lola as proper in terms of her sexuality and femininity. Hackwell is constructed as a villain character and "continually gazes at Mrs. Norval" but only becomes obsessed with Lola when he finds out how much she is worth. She does not fit into the Blackness of Mexico; rather, she fits into the esteemed category of whiteness in Mexico. This is where the legend of La Mulata de Córdoba does not map onto Lola's story, and I argue that Ruiz de Burton does so very purposefully. Lola could never embody the excessive racialized gender and sexuality of the time; not only is she able to move in and out of Mexican Blackness, but she is also on a journey to embody the perfect white Mexican femininity. When Lola arrives at the Norval residence and is revealed for the first time from under her red shawl, Mrs. Norval gasps, "Goodness! What a specimen! A nigger girl!"[61] In a poem published by Vicente Riva Palacio in 1884, the *mulata* is categorized as "strangely" foreign. This strangeness is mapped onto Lola's Black body as she arrives in New England. Just as La Mulata de Córdoba enjoyed "tragic mobility," Lola moves to New England as a tragic Black woman at the beginning of the text. But her mobility likens her more to Blackness in Mexico than it does to Blackness in the United States. Racialized gender for Ruiz de Burton signifies something much different from the *gender* Lola inhabits at the end of the novel—that of properness, pureness, and esteem. After the Norval women examine how Black and "tall" she is, they all notice how unlikely her features are for a Black girl. Mattie goes on to state "how pretty her little hand is, and all her features are certainly lovely! See how well cut her nose and lips are. And as for her eyes, I wish I had them; they are perfectly superb."[62] Ruiz de Burton engages a discourse of the Mexican Black female and allows for the mutability and fungibility of this Blackness. She establishes Lola in advance as having "white features," thereby setting up her impending departure for Mexico as a Spanish Austrian woman rather than a Black woman, married to a white New England male. Ruiz de Burton at once applies a Mexican discourse of the Black female while simultaneously constructing a superior femininity against it.

While the beginning of Lola's journey to New England marks her through Mexican Black gendered racialization, she moves in and out of Blackness and accumulates a position of reproduction through her wealth. In examining Lola's Blackness in the novel, it is clear that while Blackness is defined in terms of "social relationality rather than identity," Lola's "Blackness" is mutable, whereas in the nineteenth-century United States, blackness free or enslaved was an inescapable institution of violence. Saidiya Hartman states that the status of free Black people was shaped and compromised by the existence of slavery.[63] Alternatively, Blackness in Mexico in the nineteenth century attempted to unite colonial and modern Mexico into a new national space, as seen by the prominence of the legend of La Mulata in nineteenth-century Mexican literature. Mexico was more comfortable homogenizing Blackness through the figure of one *mulata* than through the historical presence that built much of the nation.

Lola is able to move back and forth between racist ideology and her whiteness. However, while in blackface, Lola falls out of the ontological violence of Blackness because she maintains her whiteness, whether ideally through her properness or physically though her lightening, throughout the novel. Mrs. Norval does not want her staying in the house because of the color of her skin, so she sends her to sleep with the Irish chambermaid and cook. Lola establishes her whiteness and states, "Hannah, the chambermaid, was not so repulsive to look upon." Still, the thought of sharing her bed was to Lola very terrible. Lola is disgusted with the Irish workers and cries the entire night while sleeping at the doorway of Dr. Norval's room, where he finds her. Blackness propels this narrative forward for two reasons. The first is that Lola embodies Blackness to unmask the hypocrisy of white New Englanders and American democracy. But second, and most important, is that Lola must start as Black to set herself against the racialized gender that would taint not only Lola's subject position but her wealth as well. During her presentation to the Norval family when she first arrives in New England, Ruth Norval states that Lola is a "baboon," since she is the daughter of "Indians or Negros, or both.... Anyone can see that much of her history."[64] Mrs. Norval sees her as "a true emanation of black art!"[65] Even with the pure repulsion at her Blackness, Mrs. Norval still categorizes Lola as art, just as La Mulata de Córdoba is described in the legend. What Lola does not embody are the negative aspects of racialized gender and sexuality we see in the legend. Setting up a standard of whiteness above white

New Englanders and against Mexican discourse on Blackness, Ruiz de Burton negotiated her own positionality within the Americas.

One stark contrast between the La Mulata de Córboda legend and Lola's Blackness is wealth. Wealth is at the center of Lola's move from the Southwest to the East in addition to her Blackness. Lola does not belong in New England at the beginning of the novel because of her Blackness. Mrs. Norval refuses to allow Lola in the house because she is nothing more than a "black" girl. She is foreign to everyone in the eastern space not only because of her pseudo-Blackness but also because once she does lighten, she is too proper for the deceitful space and leaves to live a life of honor in Mexico. Similarly, La Mulata de Córdoba is foreign in Córdoba, as Riva Palacio writes in his poem:

> Hace más de dos siglos que vivía
> En Córdoba, jardín veracruzano,
> Hermosa villa cuya sien adornan
> Del trópico los frutos sazonados,
> Una linda doncella que en sus ojos
> Del africano sol lleva los rayos . . .
>
> (It's been more than two centuries since she lived
> In Córdoba, garden of Veracruz
> Lovely adorned village
> Of tropical sumptuous fruit
> A beautiful maiden whose eyes
> Contain the rays of from the African sun) . . .[66]

Arce reminds us that locating La Mulata de Córdoba "del africano sol" "places the source of her unearthly power elsewhere, thus making her alien and not autochthonous."[67] Lola is "foreign" in New England, and in the United States for that matter, but she has a place in Mexico where she belongs. Lola's fungible Blackness can only work if she ultimately belongs somewhere. Simultaneously, Lola's foreignness is tied to her wealth as she is the only source of real wealth in the novel. La Mulata de Córdoba's foreignness is not only tied to her Blackness but also to her occupation that links her to witchery. This foreignness of Blackness in Mexico ontologically ties La Mulata de Córdoba to excessive sin, which extends to her sexuality. Her "otherness" is what attracts men in the first place, and her "witchcraft" is known in some iterations of the legend to seduce men through potions. When Mrs. Norval finds out that Lola comes with a great amount of gold and rare gems, she becomes overwhelmed with the desire to acquire Lola's wealth. Lola is desired in the capacity of her Blackness, but *not* because of her Blackness. Ruiz de Burton does not allow Lola to be sexually excessive and desirable, which was the case with Black female discourse in Mexico in the nineteenth century. When Dr. Norval finally reveals Lola's wealth contained in the boxes of gold and gems, Mrs. Norval "stood up, uttering a cry of delighted surprise, then clasping her hands, remained silent, with open mouth and staring eyes, transfixed by her amazement and joy."[68] Mrs. Norval states that "the despised black child she now would give worlds to keep. She would go on her knees to serve her, as her servant, her slave, rather than let her go."[69] Establishing slavery as the most degenerate position possible, she is willing to serve Lola to gain control of her wealth. And unlike the Black female figure in Mexican discourse, Lola's reproductive value lies in her wealth, not in her body. La Mulata de Córdoba is constructed through her hypersexuality as it defines her entire subjectivity; she is born to nameless parents through violent sexual miscegenation and desire that is mapped onto her body as Black. Riva Palacio writes of La Mulata de Córdoba's "ondulante seno y rojos labios" (bountiful breasts and red lips).[70] La Mulata de Córdoba is sexualized through her body and Blackness, while Lola is desired because of her wealth and despised because of her Blackness, which she overcomes.

Lola supports Mrs. Norval and her entire family not only through her reproductive bodily value, but also through her reproductive wealth value. Lola is able to mutate her Blackness. We immediately see a shift in their economic status when "all the Norvals wore new dresses to church, new cloaks, new furs, and new bonnets, again. There seems to be no end to their money."[71] The Norval girls are sent off to Europe in all of Lola's finest diamonds, and Mrs. Norval continues to lavish them with Lola's wealth. Later, Mrs. Norval cannot bear the thought of Lola possessing such wealth as she thinks, "And would that little nigger be so rich, and her girls so poor?"[72] Ultimately, Lola's Mexican white femininity is the most ideal. Whiteness functions not only as a cultural and racial formation for Lola, but ultimately also as a mark of gender and sexuality when she embodies white femininity through the Mexican female body politic. Lola's "whiteness" evokes innocence, naturalness, and wealth. Lola's whiteness is Spanish and Austrian, evoking moral, economic, social, and political authority.

While Lola is dyed black and gets older, her wealth and sexuality are combined as the novel progresses. The Reverend John Hackwell, the rogue who drinks whiskey behind closed doors and blackmails mostly women throughout the novel, lusts after Lola. While the novel comments on her beauty underneath the blackness, her wealth and "white" beauty become inextricable. At this point in the novel, as her blackness begins to wear off, she becomes "spotted" as if with some sort of "disease."[73] But by this time, Hackwell has already plotted a legal scheme to trap Lola in a common-law marriage and claim her wealth. Her sexuality is not tied to her hypersexualization, monstrosity, or grotesqueness, as the Black female of La Mulata de Córdoba is described. However, it is only when Lola turns white that Julian's love for her solidifies. Lola states, "No one but your father was kind to me. I could bear all this, but I could not bear to think that to you, too, I was an object of aversion because my skin was black. And yet I was too proud to tell you that the blackness of my skin would wear off, that it was only stained by the Indians to prevent our being rescued.... I hated to think that you *might* suppose I was Indian or black."[74] Lola is aware of the position her blackness puts her in, and she knows that she can escape that once it wears off. Finally, as she comes full circle into her whiteness, Lola's blackness fades and she marries Julian, the white New Englander and son of Dr. and Mrs. Norval who moves back to Mexico with Lola. As she embodies pure whiteness at the end of the novel, readers witness American white femininity's inability to compare with Lola's.

At the end of the novel, Lola suffers from a "malady [that] was nothing but a profound melancholy."[75] The scene mirrors her mother's own experience of sexual assault and violence, where Doña Theresa "did not wish to see her family now, after ten years of such life as had been forced upon her."[76] Lola's melancholy is reminiscent of her mother's own sexual assault and captivity—Doña Theresa's dehistoricized from Indigenous rebellion and Lola's at the hands of the Protestant reverend John Hackwell. However, both women establish and resignify the gender and sexual roles of the Mexicana body politic, which ultimately positions them as exemplar figures against Black and Indigenous subjects and above white U.S. femininity. Ruiz de Burton also utilizes blackface to articulate how racialized gender and sexuality are informed by the social relationship of abjection that marks Blackness in nineteenth-century hemispheric discourse. Through Lola's Black mutability and eventual "coming out" as white, Ruiz de Burton challenges the notion of "Mexicanness" as only dark and positions Lola's reproductive value squarely on her wealth and not her body. Lola's body remains pure and virginal throughout the novel, as opposed to the white female characters, who are not "moral." Lola unmasks the deceptions of white femininity, particularly through the character of Mrs. Norval, while Doña Theresa's gender, sexuality, and femininity are challenged through imperialist wars that ultimately construct her as a Mexican martyr.

Mexico Will Not Remain Captive: At the Crossroads of *La Cautiva*, the Mexicana, and *Los Indios*

On November 12, 1863, *La Estrella de Occidente* ran a story titled "Cuatro palabras al bello sexo.—Lo que pueden hacer las mexicanas en favor de nuestra independencia" (Four words to the beautiful sex—What the Mexicanas can do in favor of their independence). The story speaks to pure and proper Mexican women and directs them to protect Mexican independence after the French invasion in 1863. The author, Manuel Cabezut, begins the column by stating that he is writing "a esa hermosa mitad del género humano, que se llama muger" (to that beautiful half of the human race, who is called woman).[77] He rhetorically constructs proper Mexicana femininity in relation to protecting the Mexican nation while simultaneously using the image of the *la muger* (la mujer, woman) as a metaphor for the strength of the nation. The construction of the ideal Mexicana in Mexican print culture is in contradistinction to U.S. print culture. Anne Goldman makes clear in Anglo-American serials like *The Century* and *The Overland Monthly* that the overblown rhetoric in those writings "undermine[d] conventional representations of sexuality which maintained the purity of white womanhood by slandering everyone else."[78] Cabezut speaks to *la muger*, but he also speaks to Mexicans within the nation more generally, as he likens the nation to the feminine. He tells the Mexicana that she should aspire to be like the women of Spain because they had undying patriotism and were not barbarous. Cabezut tells *la muger* Mexicana that she needs "a salvar su honor y hermosura. El que asi no lo hiciere, será indigno de llevar el nombre mexicano" (to protect your honor and loveliness. Whoever does not do so, will be unworthy to bear the Mexican name).[79] This article interestingly mirrors but simultaneously juxtaposes Ruiz de Burton's stance on Mexico's place within the New World order. At first, the two genteel Mexican characters in the novel support Mexico's autonomy, but they later change their stance because of their affinity for the rightful French heir to the throne. While Cabezut constructs Mexico through a holy feminine presence and asks her people to support and defend her, he also uses anti-Native discourse when he states that the French took Mexico *cautiva*, likening it to the brute force of the "savage others" who wreaked havoc on the pure Mexico. Cabezut's construction of the pure and patriotic Mexicana and his simultaneous degenerating discourse of the poor *Mexico cautiva* advance an understanding of how Mexico saw itself in relation to the New World order. A destabilized country because of U.S. imperial forces and European invasion, the Mexican national imaginary blamed the weakened and informal diplomatic zones on the border and at the ports for the violence that ensued in the nineteenth century, just as Ruiz de Burton does. This blame results in an anti-Native sentiment and the construction of the proper Mexicana feminine subject seen in nineteenth-century Mexican print culture.

As early as 1860, *La Estrella de Occidente* newspaper runs stories of *los indio bárbaros* who come into the borderland region for "sus incursions en los pueblos de este distrito" (the incursions in the towns of this district)."[80] The newspaper records the actions of the Apaches in a column titled "Noticia de Apaches" (Apache News) and documents everything from the stealing of horses and cattle to the deaths and captivities that have taken place in the region.[81] In an 1867 editorial published in *Occidente*, the writer talks about the traitorous actions of some Mexicans mimicking what the *los indios bárbaros* were doing and states, "Hoy publicamos las relaciones de nuevas depredaciones y de nuevos asesinatos perpetrados por los apaches. A estos tristes sucesos tenemos que agregar la existencia de una nueva gavilla de latro traidores que segun estamos informados, andan cometiendo robos y salteos en este Disrite y en los inmediatos." (Today we publish the reports of new depredations and new murders perpetrated by the Apaches. To these sad events we have to add the existence of a new sheaf of traitors who, according to what we are informed, are committing robberies and running in this District and in the immediate vicinity.)[82] This Apache/Mexican explosion of captivities and robberies has everything to do with wealth hierarchies in Mexico and the encroachment of space from U.S. forces that pushed Native territories into Mexico. It also has everything to do with, as María Josefina Saldaña-Portillo states, the colonial invention of "the Indian" or "el indio."[83] Saldaña-Portillo makes us aware that there is not just one trope of "the Indian" or "el indio" that occupies a transhistorical phenomenon, but that there is a rich index of generic tropes that becomes an exploration of the *untranslatability* of these categories.[84] It was not that there were actual *indios bárbaros* running around lawlessly; it was that this concept needed to be framed as such because of the colonial acquisition of space by Spain, Mexico, and finally the encroaching United States. The newspaper makes sure to state that Sonorans were happiest and most content before the incursion of Apaches. However, this begs the question of who was happy?

The captivities and burglaries between the lower classes of Mexicans and the Apaches exemplify why Doña Theresa would be the target of not only the Apaches. The *Occidente* tells the narrative of how unhappy the Sonoran people were with all of the captivity, murder, and robbery going on and states that it was "por la falta absoluta de fondos en el erario, contenerlos en la obra de destrucion que con barbaro y cruel furor han iniciado" (due to the absolute lack of funds in the treasury, to contain them in their work of destruction that with barbaric and cruel fury they have started). The destruction of the "barbarous" Indigenous people and the lower-class Mexicans unveils the evident racial tensions in *Who Would Have Thought It?*, where Ruiz de Burton makes sure to position her Mexican characters with whiteness and wealth. According to the *Occident*, the situation in Sonora during the time that Ruiz de Burton was penning her novel was dire. Not only were the *indios bárbaros* and Mexican bandits attacking Sonora, "el triste cuadro que desde hace algunos anos viene presentando nuestra sociedad sonoresense a consecuencia de las prolongadas luchas, que el pueblo ha tenido que sostener contra las ambiciones y el partido del retroceso para hacer triunfar los principios democraticos y rechazar el imperio y la intervencion" (the sad picture is that our Sonoran society has been dealing with this for some years as a result of the prolonged struggles that the people have had to sustain against the party in order to make democratic principles triumph and reject empire and intervention).[85] The impending doom of U.S. intervention that was pushing the Indigenous populations in Mexico and in the borderlands was causing havoc for Sonora. The trope of the *indios bárbaros*, coupled with the fear of U.S. intervention and poor Mexican bandits, were reasons that the environment where Doña Theresa was taken captive was unsafe.

As Ruiz de Burton continues to construct her perfect Mexicana female subject against Black, Native, and U.S. white female ideologies and through white *mexicanidad, los indios* become excluded on both sides of the U.S.–Mexican border after the Treaty of Guadalupe Hidalgo (1848). Native Apaches and Comanches on the U.S. side refused to cede ground to U.S. expansion and fought back by taking Mexicana and Americans captives for collateral. The U.S. encroachment into Apache and Comanche lands caused them to expand their territories into Mexico, where border zones were weak and penetrable. On the Mexico side, "the indio bárbaro lost its colonial fluidity, ceased to be the potential economic and political ally, and instead became all that must be pushed out of the nation's borders."[86] Mexico no longer found *los indios* useful to their colonization project that needed them to protect the vulnerable frontier from Anglo-American settlers after Texas independence and the Mexican-American War. Contrary to early scholarship on Mexican immigration policies claiming Mexico wanted to "whiten" the nation, European settlement was actually encouraged to buffer an already hostile frontier space between Native peoples, Anglo settlers, and Mexican nationals (which, of course, shifted with different imperial powers).[87] Saldaña-Portillo puts it perfectly when she writes,

"If the emergent nations of the United States and Mexico colluded in their production of the indio bárbaro in the mid-nineteenth century, to solidify their own boundaries and establish peace between the two nations, the racial geographies of the two countries collided spectacularly in the annexed territories along the border in the late nineteenth and early twentieth centuries."[88] After Mexican Independence in 1821, Indigenous/Native subjects, who constituted 60 percent of the population at that time, were made citizens of Mexico.[89] Those behind the First Constitutional Congress in 1821 "believed that Mexico was in an era that will change the face of the earth ... putting commerce at the center of the nations among [them] in Anáhuac as the balancing point between Europe and Asia."[90] This is the same exact ideology seen in Ruiz de Burton's novel. Mexico becomes the focal point where transnational cosmopolitanism would suture the East and the West. Unlike Blackness in Mexico, Indigeneity was romantically included as an exotic history of the past until the rise of the ideology of *mestizaje*, which intended to "level" the national population makeup by erasing Indigeneity. Christina Arce reminds us, "[Indians] are relevant as small parts of a mestizo whole in which their infantilized 'noble passivity' constitutes the acceptable part of a 'cosmic race' that celebrates Indian history only in its glorious antiquity."[91]

Ruiz de Burton plays off this cross-border displacement of *los indios* by consolidating Spanish colonial displacement of *indio* subjects, Mexico's recognition of Natives as full citizens with land rights after 1821, and the U.S. expansion into what was formally Mexico, displacing landowners and making the new northern frontier vulnerable to Native attack by dispossessed Native people deprived of their land, labor, and resources. The first thing that Doña Theresa tells Dr. Norval in her testimonio is that her "name [is] Doña Theresa Medina [and] that she had been carried away from Sonora in Mexico, ten years ago, and she had never had an opportunity to escape until now."[92] Within Doña Theresa's testimonio is her captivity narrative, which mirrors Lola's captivity in New England with the Norval family. Ruiz de Burton dislodges the notion of *el indio bárbaro* as the only "savage" of the Americas. While she does not elevate *los indios* or the U.S. Native subject above U.S. New Englanders, she markedly levels them both as dangerous and utilizes this characterization to further her agenda of constructing an ideal Mexicana. After Dr. Norval agrees to take Lola, Doña Theresa dies in captivity, knowing that her daughter will be safe with New Englanders on the East Coast. Doña Theresa becomes a martyr. As a "sacrifice," Doña Theresa refuses to return to her family in Mexico or escape with Lola and Dr. Norval because she has had sexual relations with the tribe members and is tainted by the "savages." Doña

Theresa tells Dr. Norval to "take her child away from among savages and bring her up as a Christian, and educate her ... in case [he] should not be able to find her father."[93] Doña Theresa absorbs the trope of the sexually licentious Mexican woman and proves her courage and exceptionality in relation to white femininity. Ruiz de Burton utilizes the trope of *los indios* to exemplify how Mexicanas are co-constitutively constructed against other racial or marked bodies and proper *mexicanidad*.

Sonora, Mexico, was an overwhelmingly permeable border state where Apache natives were being dispossessed of their land through westward expansion and were simultaneously retaliating by taking wealthy Mexican women captive. Scholarship on captivity narratives in the United States spans the decades between the seventeenth century, with Mary Rowlandson's *A True History of the Captivity and Restoration of Mrs. Mary Rowlandson* published in 1682, to the late nineteenth century, with Emeline L. Fuller's *Left by the Indians: Story of My Life* in 1892. However, Ruiz de Burton merges discourse on Mexican *indios* and U.S. captivity narratives in constructing Doña Theresa's captivity and thus her ideal gender and sexuality as a Mexicana. In almost every issue of *La Estrella de Occidente* in 1862 and 1863 there is mention of the Apache *bárbaros* in Sonora, the same place where Doña Theresa is captured from her hacienda. In fact, the famous case of the Mexicana Inez Gonzalez, who was taken captive in Sonora by Apache natives, made it into the *New York Times* on September 30, 1851. In Mexican print culture, there was an entire column dedicated to the Apaches, which enunciated the political ideology toward *los indios (bárbaros)* and *las cautivas*. As early as 1860 in *La Estrella de Occidente* a large warning and headline reads, "La pacificaction de los Yaquis y Apahces requiere toda nuestra atencion" (The pacification of the Yaquis and Apaches requires all of our attention).[94] The column goes on to say, "El señor Don Pedro ... vió los cadaverse de us hombre, dos mugeres, y un niño que habian sido asesinados de una manera atroz y bárbara por los Apaches" (Mr. Pedro saw the cadavers of one man, two women, and one child that were assassinated through barbarous ways by the Apaches).[95] Most of the columns on the Apaches and *los indios* explained their supposed violence in great detail when talking about the Mexicans they took captive. But it is the intersection between discourses of *indios bárbaros* as captors and the consistent construction of ideal Mexicana femininity through support of the nation that explains the characterization of Lola and Doña Theresa in the novel.

Doña Theresa establishes her aristocracy apart from the *indios bárbaros* through the labor practices for which she employs the Native people. Dr. Norval tells his wife the story of the gems and gold that Doña Theresa gave him when he returns home and states, "She picked it up, and, as she had some knowledge of precious stones, she saw it was a large diamond, though only partly divested of its rough coating. Then, she looked about for similar pebbles, and found many more.... Afterwards the Indians bought her emeralds and rubies, seeing that she liked pretty pebbles. Thus she made a fine collection, for she took only that largest and those, which seemed to her the most perfect."[96] Doña Theresa establishes her femininity and aristocracy in relation to *los indios* by making them labor over the resources that were theirs in the first place. This concern demonstrates Theresa's refinement, nobility, and "self-sacrificing devotion," qualities that reflect her identity as an ideal Mexicana of "pure Spanish descent" and differentiate her from her captors.[97] The wealth Doña Theresa hoards as her daughter's "dowry" is entirely naturalized and masks the plunder of Indian lands and resources.[98] Sexuality, and particularly Lola's point of those desiring her, becomes tied to the wealth of the Native people. Doña Theresa, as *la cautiva* in Mexican discourse, has the choice to become a tainted woman or a woman of piety. Cabezut's 1863 article links invasion and captivity (of the French) to the *indio bárbaro*, while simultaneously painting a picture of the "perfect" Mexicana and states, "Al mismo tiempo que reside en el corzaon de la muger la inconstancia, la veleidad y el encono, se encuentra tambien lo mas grande, lo mas noble, lo mas bellom y lo mas poético que dares puede el amor." (At the same time that inconsistency lies in the heart of the woman, the fickleness, and the fury resides in the heart of the woman, there is also the greatest, the most noble, the most beautiful and most poetic thing that you can love.)[99] He asks the women of Mexico whom they want to be during the volatile times of capture. Doña Theresa faces the same decision. Does she want to go back to her life in Mexico as a tainted woman or die a martyr? She states that "she only wished to save her daughter from a similar fate, and then to lie down and die."[100] The threat of sexual violence appears throughout the novel, from the Native captors and the New Englanders, but is exemplified as more violent through *los indios* because it cannot be verbalized and figures in absentia. Being *la cautiva* means potentially being stuck as "hembras degradadas que componen la parte perdid del fanatismo y retroceso femenil, solo se ve entre ella algunas arpias" (the unpure females that make up the part of the loss of the pure fantasy and femininity, we can only see them as a regression of femininity).[101] Meanwhile, on the East Coast, Lola is shunned at the Norval household and "sent...to sleep with the cook and the chambermaid."[102] Mrs. Norval watches Lola's every move and makes plans to keep her away from her son Julian by sending her off to a convent. However, Lola rises above tainted white femininity in the end, and she functions in the narrative to suggest a new version of proper femininity superior to U.S. femininity and U.S. white, Black, and Native peoples.

White Circuits of Ministerial Sex Scandals and White Femininity

Reverend Hackwell and Mrs. Norval both exemplify all that is wrong with American democracy and white femininity. They are both greedy, deceitful, immoral, and manipulative. Mrs. Noval, a parody character from early sentimental American novels, is a racist, has consumerist proclivities, and is ill-equipped to deal with her sexual passions. When Mrs. Norval lets out her symbolic cry after Hackwell threatens to leave her, Ruiz de Burton is building off of a long tradition of ministerial sex scandals that were taking place in the United States during the 1860s and 1870s. This is one instance where Ruiz de Burton is evoking a long U.S. tradition of what could be considered the white feminine failure against puritanical democratic ideals. Between 1870 and 1914, at least 266 Protestant ministers left their religious posts, divorced their wives, and skipped town with other women to start new lives.[103] Between 1881 and 1914 a group of anti-religious authors documented over 3,500 cases of ministerial misconduct and catalogued them in a volume that led to ten expanded editions titled *The Crimes of Preachers in the United States and Canada*.[104] These ministerial sex scandals or "crimes of passion" were nothing new in the 1860s and 1870s, and according to Ann Douglas they began occurring because the minister moved in a world of women.[105] Whether that meant he mainly preached to women, women worked in the church offices, women did the charity work, or women ran all the social religious clubs, the minister was always around women. It was also women who helped the minister communicate his message to the rest of society because of the maternal power women had over their families.[106] The church and faith functioned off of a feminine preserve. This resulted in the clergymen forming close bonds with their female parishioners, many times crossing the line between platonic and intimate.

In 1877 Methodist minister Alfred Thompson was on trial for adultery, as newspaper headlines read, "The Pastor of Illinois Church Convicted as a Despicable Thief."[107] The *Chicago Daily Tribune* reported that he was unremorseful when he said, "We all do such things more or less," when he was testifying in court.[108] However, the ministerial sex scandal that got the most press in nineteenth-century America was the adultery trial of Henry Ward Beecher, an American Congregationalist clergyman at the Plymouth Church in Brooklyn, New York, who was an abolitionist and women's suffragist. He was charged with committing adultery in 1875 with his best friend's wife, Elizabeth Tilton. Beecher would drop in to visit Elizabeth "Libby" Tilton to read his novel-in-progress, *Norwood*.[109] However, Beecher having an affair with his best friend's wife was the least scandalous part of the ensuing drama. The adultery scandal was kept under wraps until Theodore Tilton, Libby's husband and Beecher's best friend, told Elizabeth Cady Stanton, Susan B. Anthony, and Laura Curtis Bullard, all leaders of the women's rights movement in the United States, and Stanton then told Victoria C. Woodhull, women's suffrage leader and the first woman to run for president in the 1872 election. Woodhull published the ministerial sex scandal in her paper *Woodhull and Claflin's Weekly* in 1872 and titled the piece "The Beecher-Tilton Scandal Case." Both Woodhull and Stanton were frustrated with Beecher's wavering support for the suffragist movement and decided to expose the adultery scandal. The "alienation of affections" trial began in 1875 and continued for six months, ending with a hung jury. Harriet Beecher Stow, author of *Uncle Tom's Cabin* and Henry Ward Beecher's sister, supported him until the end. The ministerial sex scandal overtook Reconstruction headlines and became the main focus of newspapers dedicating most headline space to the scandal. In the end, Beecher saw himself vindicated, but the stain remained in the American imagination.

Just like many people were involved in the Henry Ward Beecher ministerial sex scandal, the reverends in *Who Would Have Thought It?* are at the center of a scandal with many people involved in the deception for Lola's wealth. Hackwell makes a marriage proposition to Lola in a forceful manner, and when she declines and tells Hackwell she is going to tell Mrs. Norval about the whole thing, he consults with his sister Emma about a plot to marry Lola anyway and for Emma to marry Julian. He tells Emma, "Now as we cannot win Lola away from Julian, and we want money, we must try to get both Julian and money in some other way, and that way is the old woman—I beg her pardon—the madam."[110] Hackwell knows exactly how to get to Mrs. Norval's sensibilities, and he knows how to be manipulative through sexual advances. He begins his plan by softening Mrs. Norval up and calling her "Jenny" instead of the harsh-sounding Jemima.[111] She enjoys being with Hackwell and begins to dress more sophisticated while embarking upon cultural adventures she would have never considered. "This lady had changed more within the last five years than any of her metamorphosed family. She had grown younger and improved in appearance rapidly since her arrival in New York. She dressed now at the height of the fashion, as [Hackwell] admired finely dressed women, but she always dressed in dark, rich silks, and in a sort of dignified style which suited her very well."[112] Hackwell's love coupled with Lola's money is what brings Mrs. Norval to complete femininity. However, she falls disgracefully from the height of her white femininity because of her greed and unruly passions for the minister.

Whereas Lola remains beautiful regardless of how dark her skin is, Mrs. Norval only shines when she is having an affair and stealing Lola's wealth. The mocking tone of the narrator states that Mrs. Norval "had so far degenerated that she regarded her youth as misspent, her life a blank, until she loved Hackwell, until she was past forty."[113] Her original puritanical ideals had made her passionless and unattractive, and then as she was "coming-of-age," so to speak, she became more sexually liberated but just as vile and unattractive as before. There is no redemption in white femininity for Ruiz de Burton. Meanwhile, Hackwell is leveraging his white male patriarchy to convince Lola to marry him and expose the fate of her mother, Doña Theresa Medina, and Jemima's adultery—all in the name of gaining power over Lola. No one outside of those involved in the scandal can see just how chaotic the situation between Mrs. Norval, Reverend Hackwell, Reverend Hammerhead, Lola, Emma, and Julian really is becoming. Mrs. Norval begins to gain popularity in New York, and the narrator takes a jab at that false popularity by stating, "So the popular voice said and 'the people'—Mr. Beecher says—'can't make a mistake.'"[114] Referring to Henry Ward Beecher and the scandals that were surrounding him at the time, Ruiz de Burton evokes a long history of U.S. moral deterioration in relation to sex and white femininity.

In contradistinction to these sex scandals, Ruiz de Burton also evokes Mexico's *Laws of Reform* when Doña Theresa begs Dr. Norval to baptize and raise Lola as a Roman Catholic. At the time *Who Would Have Thought it?* was published, Mexico was consummating the final act that marked the end of a battle between the separation of church and state. This was the triumph of the Liberal Party in Mexico under President Júarez, and it was originally attained in 1861; however, the "tripartite intervention of France, England, and Spain, the Napoleonic-Maximilian régime, and the era of disorder which followed, had postponed the incorporation of the so-styled *Laws of Reform* as amendments to the federal Constitution."[115] As stated in the previous section, Ruiz de Burton shifted from Liberal to Conservative in her support for the French invasion, so it only makes sense that she would support the Conservative push for Mexico to remain Catholic. In her fierce advocacy for Catholicism in the novel, she has her empty and immoral characters poke fun at the Catholic religion. Reverend Hackwell muses on Dr. Norval's love for foreigners and Mrs. Norval's virtue in always setting him straight. Dr. When Dr. Norval sends Julian to be educated in Europe, Mrs. Norval sends for him right away because "Heaven knows what might have become of Julian if his heroic mother had not sent for him. He might have been a Roman Catholic for all we know."[116] This quick and humorous insult does not seem to hold much weight considering it is at the very beginning of the novel; however, this is a moment that foreshadows Hackwell's complete immorality and deception. Mrs. Norval is also a victim of this foreshadowing, as she states, "Finish her education! A Catholic Catechism!" when Dr. Norval tells her he is going to raise Lola as a Catholic, just as her mother asked. The outrage toward Catholicism in the most depraved characters allows Ruiz de Burton to carefully craft her pristine protagonist through the circuits of white, black, and red. Mrs. Norval's "fall of Republican Motherhood" is buttressed off of a "proper" Mexican white femininity, represented by Lola, but that is only a quarter of the story. Lola's ultimate white Mexicana femininity also comes from the circuits of *mexicanidad* that are nation-bound, delimited by national discourse, but simultaneously revealing hemispheric racial trajectories through anti-Indigeneity and anti-Blackness. And while this chapter has exemplified the discursive conversation of racialized gender, sex, and sexuality through *mexicanidad*, the next chapter reveals how *sexual capital* produces racialized gender and sex and then produces violence. Chapter 3 marks a turn to examine what happens when gender racial formations are only visible through violence and grapples with the overlay of racialized sexual difference, as witnessed in Rodríguez's already castrated body as the ultimate denouncement of her position in society. Racialized sexuality functions differently in this instance, in that it has less to do with the actual act of sex and more to do with the violence of the already racially sexed and gendered body.

CHAPTER THREE

Absent Presence
The Ghost of the "Only Woman Hanged" in Texas and the Abstract Labor of Gender Racial Formations

No soy culpable.
—Josefa Chipita Rodriguez

"I am not guilty." These were the final words of Josefa Chipita Rodríguez, sixty-three years old, before her execution by hanging in San Patricio County on November 13, 1863. Rodríguez was accused of murdering John Savage, a horse trader, when he stopped at Rodríguez's inn for the night after trading horses with Confederate forces. Rodríguez's inn was located on the Cotton Trail by Aldrete's crossing between Mexico and the United States on the Aransas River, a convenient stop for many travelers passing through to trade goods or cotton. Enslaved people of the Welder family found Savage's body in the Aransas River, and Sheriff Means immediately arrested Rodríguez and Juan Silvera. On Saturday, October 10, 1863, the Fourteenth District Court of Texas in San Patricio, under the judgeship of Benjamin F. Neal, tried them and found both guilty of murder. Judge Neal sentenced Rodríguez to execution by hanging, against the recommendation of the jury, and Silvera to just five years in jail. Rather than focus on the violent particularities of Rodríguez's execution, this chapter unveils her violent absent presence in history through a gendered racial formation of Mexicanas in the borderlands. The opening quotation is the only instance in the archive of Rodríguez actually speaking as a historical subject of violence in the borderlands. Her death was violently extraordinary, and while a plethora of cultural narratives attempt to provide her a voice, many of them reinscribe the same silencing violence that she experienced in life. In addition to her absent presence in the archive and cultural production, she is inherently gendered through her racialization, which ties the violence inflicted upon her to the economy of gender racialization in Texas.

Many scholars claim that the court transcripts documenting the events of her trial were burned, damaged by water, or just disappeared, and the only archival remnant of her trial consists of the criminal docket and transcript rulings from the week of her conviction, housed at the San Patricio County District Court Records office. But can we really know what happened to her archives? And most importantly, is her archival absence significant? Rodríguez's archival absence exemplifies the way racialized Mexicanas are constructed through a history of violence. Many have attempted to "reconstruct" Josefa Chipita Rodríguez and her life. After the 1984 execution of Karla Faye Tucker, the *second* woman in Texas to be executed, a rising interest in Rodríguez took hold. However, Rodríguez's and Tucker's cases were vastly different. This chapter uses the historical moment of Rodríguez's execution, coupled with her gendered racial formation, to compose a new narrative of Rodríguez and her life.

Vernon Smylie was the first to write about her in a book published in 1970 by the Texas News Syndicate Press titled *A Noose for Chipita*. Keith Guthrie, a Texas historian, followed suit in his book published in 1990 by Eakin Press titled *The Legend of Chipita: The One Woman Hanged in Texas*. These two historical texts are seen as the authoritative writings on Rodríguez, but they leave more gaps than they fill by ignoring the cultural production centering Rodríguez, particularly in constructing gendered racial formations in the borderlands. This chapter argues that Josefa Chipita Rodríguez is invisible through her labor and capital accumulation for the Confederacy, and only visible through violence, by combining references to Smylie's and Guthrie's texts with Rachel Bluntzer Herbet's 1942 epic poem, *Shadow on the Nueces: The Story of Chepita Rodriguez*; Lawrence Weiner, Leonardo Carillo, and John Wilson's opera *Chipita Rodríguez* performed on April 3, 1982, at the Corpus Christi Symphony in Corpus Christi, Texas; and Teresa Palomo Acosta's 1999 poem "Chipita." The history of Irish settlement in San Patricio, along with the burgeoning political unrest caused by Federal Union troops entering Texas to unsettle Confederate trading and market relations, were both issues that led to Rodríguez's execution. And while none of the previous historical accounts or cultural productions state this explicitly, racial tensions in South (Central) Texas coupled with these political realities hide the economy of gendered racialization that Rodríguez participated in and upheld.

This chapter is but one piece of the puzzle that constructs racialized gender and sexuality in the nineteenth century for Mexicanas in the borderlands. The previous two chapters provided the groundwork for racialized gender and sex in relation to elite landholding Californios who, whether they had real wealth or not, attempted to construct their bodies, gender, and sex against the racialized females in the borderlands.[1] This chapter marks a turn in the study to examine what happens when gender racial formations are only visible through violence. Instead of focusing on the discursive construction of racialized gender and sex, this chapter examines the material consequences of abstracted labor by racialized women on the borderlands and the gender economy of race. Rodríguez's body is fraught, invisible throughout her life, and only visible through violence after her death. The archival gap renders the numerous narratives surrounding her story fraught as well. This chapter grapples with the overlay of racialized sexual difference, as witnessed in Rodríguez's already castrated body, as the ultimate denouncement of her position in society. Racialized sexuality functions differently in this instance, in that it has less to do with the actual act of sex and more to do with the violence of the already racially sexed body. This transitional chapter purposely appears in the middle of the book because it connects the discursive construction of racialized gender and sexuality with the material consequences of those constructions on Mexicana lives.

Chipita Rodríguez spent her childhood and young adult years in Mexico with her family. "Chepita" was most likely a nickname for Josefa and was later either mispronounced or misspelled in public English records as "Chipita." During the Texas Revolution, when Santa Anna pledged to attack revolting Texans and settlers like the Rodríguezes, Chipita and her father Pedro fled Mexico for the McGloin-McMullen colony, which later became San Patricio de Hibernia. They settled by the Nueces River, several miles north of the Refugio County Courthouse. Pedro was killed in the Texas Revolution, leaving Rodríguez to survive on her own. Some claim Rodríguez had an illegitimate son by a white man who took their child away. During the 1850s, single and alone, she opened an "inn," which consisted of a cot on the front porch, and she served coffee and meals to her patrons. Irish empresarios owned the land that the inn was built on, and they allowed Rodríguez to run her business on the property. As the story goes, according to the *Texas Parade Magazine*, "John Savage [a horse trader] had sold some horses to the Confederate Army and on his way back to Corpus Christi had stopped for the night."[2] When he arrived at Rodríguez's inn, Savage had approximately $600 in gold, and he kept his gun strapped to his waist as he slept on her cot on the porch. By morning, the enslaved people of the Welder family had found his hacked body stuffed in a sack and Sheriff Means arrested Rodríguez and her supposed accomplice, Juan Silvera, and took them to Meansville before transporting them to the lean-to shed that served as a jail in the San Patricio Courthouse.

Who Was Chipita Rodríguez?:
Absent Archive, Violent Histories

The Latino nineteenth-century archive is at odds with forms of U.S. literary history because many of the narratives are written in Spanish and span the

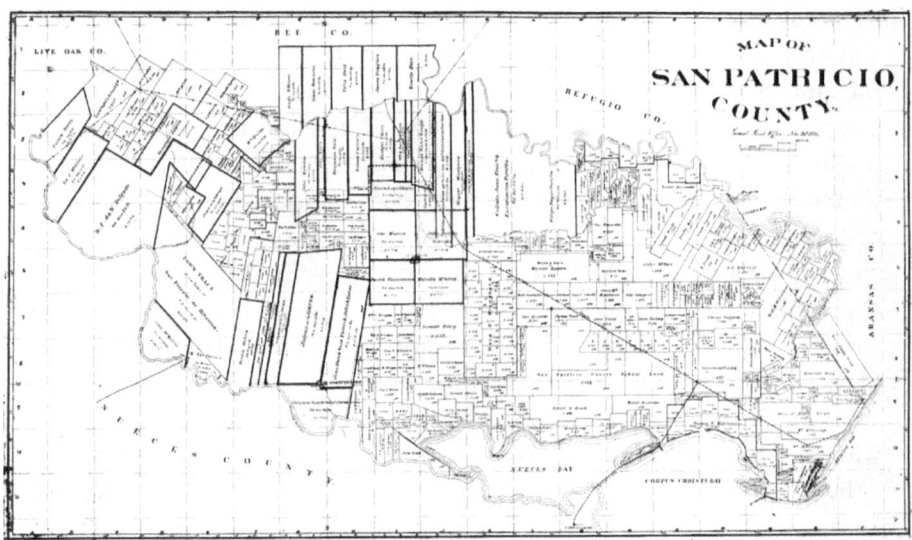

Map of San Patricio County, Abilene Photograph Collection at Hardin-Simmons University, Abilene, Texas, 1896.

writers' travels inside and outside of U.S. national boundaries; more importantly, the archive does not contain the narratives of poor racialized women in the borderlands. This book and this chapter in particular reckon with subjects in the archives who "reside in obscurity and are always at the edge of annihilation," what Rodrigo Lazo coined "migrant" archives.[3] Chipita Rodríguez's poor, brown female body is unseen in the history of capital in the Southwest borderlands, and her story is absent from the archive. So who exactly is Josefa Chipita Rodríguez? Very little is known of her life before her violent execution by hanging. What we do know comes from cultural artifacts that were produced long after her death. In reconstructing a partial life story for Rodríguez, we must cobble together what little remains in the archive and pieces of cultural production that focus mainly on the specter of her life and her violent end.

Part of that history comes from Rachel Bluntzer Hebert's epic poem "Shadow on the Nueces: The Story of Chepita Rodriguez." Published in 1942, this five-part narrative poem written in traditional form centers on the life and death of Chipita Rodríguez (spelled "Chepita" by Bluntzer Hebert). This work is the first and only epic retelling of a life no one will ever really know. Bluntzer Hebert attempts to construct Rodríguez as a figure larger than life, a figure of mythical proportions. Yet at times, the narrative pushes Rodríguez back into the periphery as a historical figure. The poem begins with a foreword written by J. E. Conner, head of the history department at Texas College of Arts and Industries (now Texas A&M University–Kingsville). In conventional Whitman cataloging form, Conner identifies Bluntzer Hebert's epic poem as a unique vein of lore that touches on all the themes of the rugged frontier, from "the stoic Indian with his tribal philosophy; the clash of war with its unnatural race alignments; the cowman with his innate honesty; the frontier judge, the conscientious sheriff..." to "the man of one race, the one of the other shown as narrators or tales; the call native wild life, the winds on the prairie, the changing of seasons, and finally a belief in signs and ghosts."[4] In this opening move utilizing a "discovery" lens, Rodríguez exists alongside many romantic frontier notions, particularly notions of white men and outsiders. In the catalog of the frontier, Rodríguez is but one of the people Conner lists; to recreate Rodríguez's life, he argues, is to better understand civilization. In the introduction, Bluntzer Hebert reveals that her great-aunt Josephine Sullivan first told her the story of Rodríguez. Sullivan was personally connected to the story because Rodríguez allegedly confessed all to Sullivan's descendant, Kate McCumber, the night before her execution.[5] To this day, no one knows the real story. In an attempt to humanize Rodríguez, Bluntzer Hebert draws a genealogical line connecting them. The prologue situates readers in the present time and explains, "Years had passed since Kate had listened / To a woman's full confession."[6] In this moment of the poem, Kate McCumber remembers the story of Rodríguez and

> drew it straight from its hiding where,
> Pigeon-holed in her possession,
> It had lain like a faded letter.[7]

Rodriguez is no longer hiding in the memories of the past. She is called forth as a specter to tell her story, and with this summoning, a wail is heard. Kate then tells her daughter, to whom she is relaying Rodríguez's story, that she will reveal what Rodríguez divulged to her the night before she was executed. She will finally expose the truth about the night of John Savage's murder. This establishes authoritative voice in the historical placement of Rodríguez's subjectivity. It is this white woman who will set the record straight for Rodríguez. But instead of focusing on the life and death of Rodríguez, the epic poem becomes just another iteration of her death. There is very little narrative establishing Rodríguez as a living subject in the borderlands.

The first part of the epic poem is titled "Flight and the Prairie," and it tells the story of Rodríguez and her father, Pedro Rodríguez, fleeing Mexico to escape Antonio López de Santa Anna. Bluntzer Hebert writes,

> Back in the early eighteen hundreds
> Pedro Rodríguez reached the border. . . . Then as Santa Anna threatened,
>   Pedro again decided to flee him.
> He and Chepita began to swim
> Side by side from the river brim."[8]

These opening lines relegate Rodríguez and her father to a certain type of positionality. They are unbound to safe space, they move insecurely from place to place, and most importantly, there is no feminine presence to take care of young Chipita Rodríguez. Her father, Pedro, knows the secrets of the Aztecs, secrets Antonio López de Santa Anna wants to know, and he tells Rodríguez these stories over and over as she sits on his lap and looks at him adoringly. Rodríguez's story hinges on the great epic presence of her father, Pedro, and his mythological tales of the Aztecs. Pedro sets the strong foundation for the poem as he takes up arms against Santa Anna, "with a hate that burned in his bosom,"[9] after his wife (and Rodríguez's mother) dies while crossing the river into the United States. Once her father dies, Rodríguez is left alone and moves to the prairie, where she opens an inn on the Aransas River. Bluntzer Hebert describes Rodríguez, stating, "She would sweep the earthen floor," and then again, through the performative language of absence or invisibility, stating,

> Empty-armed, she moved to the prairie
> Near a river arched by branches.
> There on the live oaks, moss, and vines
> Looped and hung to weave designs.
> Like a brother, the bordering ranches
> Opened their doors for the prairie to welcome her.[10]

Bluntzer Hebert constructs Rodríguez's narrative against the strong and welcoming nature of the prairie, which accepts her when she has no one else. This linguistic construction of the absent presence of Rodríguez ultimately mirrors her abstract labor value in South Texas society, which I explore in the next section. Through this construction of loss and Rodriguez's secondary characterization in relation to her father, Bluntzer Hebert delves deeper into her negative construction of Rodríguez and reveals that a "thief" gave Rodríguez a son and snatched him away. This folktale is one of many stories that constructs Rodríguez in the imaginary of Texas. According to legend, Rodríguez's unnamed son came to visit her after his white father took him away from her, and it was her son who killed Savage; by disposing of the body with Silvera, she acted to protect her son.[11] Again, Rodríguez is situated in relation to what she no longer has, people who are no longer in her life, and her absence from the historical record and archive.

The epic poem is told through omniscient narration and the voice of Kate McCumber, the only woman said to know the *real* story of what happened the night Sullivan was killed. We only hear from Rodríguez through the telling of her story by the narrator. The first of two occasions when Rodríguez speaks in the poem occurs when her son apparently kills Savage and "she had whispered, 'I am his mother!'"[12] Rodríguez's white male partner took her son away from her while he was an infant, so her narrative goes against the construction of proper Mexican motherhood. One of the few times we hear her speak, Rodríguez is relegated to her failure as a mother. The poem goes on to say,

> When [Juan Silvera] asked her, "Where is his saddle?"
> But her lips like the silent water
> Held a secret of midnight slaughter.[13]

Here Rodríguez redeems herself as a mother by protecting her son, who apparently killed Savage in this particular narrative. The poem looks over the trial and narrates,

> Like a key lay her tongue lay hidden,
> But it still could liberate her.
> What if doors were locked and bolted
> If the key within revolted?[14]

Reminiscent of La Malinche and her translating for the Spanish, Rodríguez fears that her wild tongue will revolt against her will to protect her son. She screams in the courtroom, "I am not guilty," and in a narrative turn of events, Kate McCumber becomes the narrator. McCumber goes on to tell her version of the execution; later, when the sheriff asks McCumber to borrow her cart, she tells him, "Never would I be accused of giving / Cart of mine as a hearse for the living."[15] Bluntzer Hebert ends her poem with Rodríguez's looming execution, but the actual execution is not present in the poem. While Rodríguez prepares for her execution, readers hear

> Miserere mei Deus.
> Prayed the padre interceding.
> There were the dying prayers he was reading.[16]

Throughout the poem, a religious tone attempts to denounce the execution as wrong, not because the evidence was circumstantial, but because Rodríguez was denied her proper last rites. The last stanza of the poem reads,

> It was then she joined the procession
> Formed by a world-old line of mothers—
> Some who died while giving breath,
> Some who had known a living death,
> For she not only died like the others—
> Kate was hushed by her daughter's whisper,
> "Listen—a phantom footstep falls;
> Chepita treads historic halls!"[17]

In an odd ending, Rodríguez transforms into the "dying mother," joining all the other mothers who died during childbirth or during their lifetime, unheard and unseen. However, there is no mention of her botched trial, of the racial tensions that obviously led to her execution, or of the unseen racialized gender economy that Rodríguez participated in, which left her open to surveillance and violence. In an attempt to make Rodríguez seen, she is almost completely erased and nonspeaking. Bluntzer Hebert attempts to elevate Rodríguez out of her degraded racialized gendered positionality by placing her in a universal category of proper motherhood to evoke sympathy and pathos. However, in thinking about *how* Rodríguez died, we cannot sidestep her positionality as a Mexican woman who *did not* raise her son, ran an inn to sustain herself, and potentially killed a Confederate horse trader and then disposed of his body in the Aransas River.

Beyond Bluntzer Hebert's epic poem, the archive fills in rudimentarily, and the folktales become inconsistent and conflicting. In August 1863, Rodríguez was accused of killing John Savage. When the enslaved people from the Welder family's plantation found Savage's body in the Aransas River, John Welder rode fifteen miles to Meansville to get Sheriff William B. Means. No one knows if Sheriff Means ever even talked to Rodríguez before arresting her, but according to the court minutes that remain, he arrested Rodríguez on circumstantial evidence, namely bloodstains on her porch, which she claimed came from killing a chicken.[18] Authorities recovered Savage's $600 worth of gold downstream on the Aransas River, and there is no mention of robbery or gold in the surviving court minutes. Sheriff Means also arrested and charged Juan Silvera as an accomplice.

Once the trial started, Sheriff Means presented evidence against Rodríguez and also sat on the grand jury that eventually indicted her. At the time of the trial, the Confederacy was shipping cotton through San Patricio into Mexico, and the Union planned to invade the border's coastal cities to sever this trade route. Many of the men in Texas were enlisted in the war or were aiding the impending Yankee invasion, so there were very few men who could be considered Rodríguez's peers to sit on the jury. Illegal actions and cronyism ran rampant within Judge Benjamin F. Neal's Fourteenth District Court of Texas.[19] According to the handwritten minutes of the Fourteenth District Court in San Patricio, Texas, from the fall 1863 session, Attorney of the Court Thos H. O'Callaghan was charged in two separate cases, but Judge Neal dropped these cases so O'Callaghan could prosecute Rodríguez's case.[20] Five of the fourteen grand jury members were indicted for murder and also had their cases dismissed. In the courtroom, William C. Carroll and Pat O'Docharty represented Rodríguez. There is no information as to who testified in the trial or what type of evidence was presented to the jury.[21] The court minutes read, "Evidence is presented to the jury.... The arguments of counsel are heard."[22] The handwritten notes do not indicate that Rodríguez spoke at all throughout the trial. Even Bluntzer Hebert makes this fact clear when her poem states,

> She recalled the words of her father
> When she knew that danger was prowling.
> Juan had not questioned any more—
> She was never so silent before.
> The coyotes commenced their howling;
> Theirs was a wait which ended with yelping.
> Once she thrilled to this voice of the prairie.
> Now it only made her wary.[23]

Here she reiterates Rodríguez's silence, but she also evokes the epic figure of Rodríguez's father, who remains center stage in the poem. When the jury came back to read the verdict, it stated, "We the jury, find the defendant Chipita Rodríguez, guilty of murder in the first degree, but on account of her old age and the circumstantial evidence against her, do not recommend her to the mercy of the court."[24] Court was adjourned until the next day, October 6, 1863, when Judge Neal pronounced his sentence for Rodríguez: execution "according to law by hanging by the neck until she is dead" on Friday, November 13, 1863, between the hours of 11 A.M. and sunset.[25] Rodríguez was the first person convicted of murder to be executed by hanging in San Patricio County. Rodríguez's attorneys withdrew a motion for appeal. On November 13, 1863, Josefa Chipita Rodríguez was hung, against the recommendation of the jury for clemency because of her age. Before her hanging, she was confined for several weeks before her trial for her own safety. Ironically, the indictment for murder lists Juan Silvera before Rodríguez; however, he received less time and punishment than she did. Her "accomplice," Juan Silvera, received a five-year sentence for the murder of Savage.[26] Silvera may have told officials that Rodríguez killed Savage to get a lighter sentence for himself. Silvera is not mentioned in the court documents that remain, except for the verdict and his sentencing.

The Hidden Economy of Gendered Racial Formations in the Borderlands

Rodríguez's body is simultaneously a spectacle and a representation of gendered racial formations. Race is an important component for both women and gendered structures of power.[27] To suggest that racial formation is fundamental to gender and sexual processes is to suggest that Rodríguez's body signifies an onslaught of racial imaginaries that conjure up masculine and feminine characteristics in contrast to conventional feminized bodies.[28] Through this racial imaginary of poor, dark Mexicanas in South Texas, gender works to signify and constitute racial categories. To begin, like most racialized women in the borderlands, Rodríguez fell outside of conventional femininity. Her mother died, leaving her without a female role model; she had a child out of wedlock with a white Anglo-American settler, who then took her child away because she was not "fit" as a mother; and she ran an inn for settlers, traders, and others passing along the west bank of the Aransas River at Aldrete Crossing. Bluntzer Hebert writes,

> Hoping the Rio Grande would free him,
> Pedro again renewed his courage.
> There his wife had died with fever.
> Pedro wept, but he had to leave her.[29]

For all intents and purposes, she was an entrepreneur before the Irish settlements knew how they wanted to run business in their new colony. She failed at proper femininity because she was outside of the domestic space; in fact, her domestic space and public workspace collided and were not separate at all.

While the first part of Bluntzer Hebert's epic poem briefly examines Rodríguez's life before the murder and trial through the lens of the epic figure of her father Pedro, Part II, titled "Strange Visitor," follows Rodríguez's nontraditional economic endeavors running her inn for people on the Cotton Trail. The McMullen-McGloin colony, established in 1831 in Mexican Texas before the Texas Revolution (1835–36), was a "land of possibilities" for new Irish settlers. Ultimately, Irish pioneers settled in two communities, San Patricio and Refugio in South Texas. The Mexican government–sponsored empresario land grants aimed to populate the most vulnerable of Mexico's northern states, which led to the Irish settlement of San Patricio County (the jurisdiction where Josefa Chipita Rodríguez was executed in 1863). Stretching from the Nueces River to the Medina River, near San Antonio de Béxar, San Patricio was a large land grant, which called for the settlement of two hundred Apostolic Roman Catholic families on the left bank of the Nueces River above the coastal reserve within six years of 1828.[30] Two Irish empresarios, John McMullen, born in east Donegal County in 1785, and James McGloin, born in Castleregal, County Sligo, in 1801, founded the McMullen-McGloin colony, which was renamed San Patricio de Hibernia in 1831.[31] Two other successful Irish empresarios, James Power and James Hewetson, were granted land between the Guadalupe and Lavaca Rivers, which was later extended west to the Nueces to abut the McMullen-McGloin colony.[32] The United Sates annexed the Republic of Texas in 1846, but the Treaty of Guadalupe Hidalgo brought an end to disputes over the Rio Grande border at the end of the Mexican-American War (1846–48). The American Civil War began in 1861, when Texas declared its seccession from the Union. By October 5, 1863, when Chipita Rodríguez's trial began, San Patricio was feeling the surge of the Civil War as well as other racial tensions between Mexican Texans/Tejanos, Irish, and Anglo-Americans.

Aside from the way Rodríguez is gendered racially, a racially gendered economic system also emerges from her "abject" position as a woman on the border. Rodríguez was not a landowner, unlike the Irish empresarios or Mexican ranchers with land grants surrounding her. Wealthy Mexican ranchers held land on both sides of the Aransas River, most likely granted to them by the Irish empresarios as part of their agreement when applying for settlement. Chipita Rodríguez established her "inn" at the crossing on the "Aransas River about one mile above R. Aldrete's."[33] Deed records from Refugio and San Patricio Counties show no records of land in Rodríguez's name. The particular plot that Rodríguez's inn sat on was part of empresario James Power's land, and it was later purchased by John Welder; today the Welder Wildlife Refuge owns it.[34] While records state that Chipita had an inn at the crossing, it can more accurately be described as a shack consisting of a small room with some chairs and the cot outside on the porch. Nonetheless, she utilized her space to keep herself afloat economically. Even so, her self-sustaining business venture is absent from all archival accounts and records.

The economy of gendered racial formation that Rodríguez participated in centers on the unseen labor that led to her racialization, or what Marx would call *abstract labor*. However, Marx fails to understand how racialization leads to the law of value. Marx states, "The basis, the starting point for the physiology of the bourgeois system, ... is the determination of value by labour time."[35] Labor time is the law of value in society, particularly a capitalist society. The commodity is the "cell form" of modern society. Many early Southwest studies scholars have pushed back against the idea that capitalism was in fact flourishing before the arrival of the railroad and more industrial interdependent markets. But Texas was in a precarious position between the Union and the Confederacy geopolitically, and the commodities garnered from slavery flowed through South Texas, making it a flourishing space in full possession of exchange economy and exchange value. Marx ties concrete labor to the exchange values of commodities, which is the most important aspect of value in modern society. He further claims that the useful qualities of commodities are excluded from consideration and that we ignore the useful character of concrete labor, which is reduced to human labor in the abstract.[36] Contemporary scholars of ethnic studies and economic studies alike have recognized that Marx asks readers "to ignore both the *heterogeneity* of commodities and that of labour."[37] The economy of gender racial formation in the borderlands can be understood through what Iyko Day terms concrete and abstract capital, but through a lens of racialized exploitation as opposed to congealed labor. Instead of thinking about concrete and abstract capital as two sides of the same coin functioning in opposition to one another, abstract labor relates to concrete labor in the way capital "abstracts highly differentiated gendered and racialized labor *in order to create value.*"[38] Rather than view all laborers as homogenous, this part of the chapter grapples with the work of the economy of gendered racial formation in South Texas and what happens when that congealed labor becomes abstract. More importantly, I examine how certain bodies fall outside of the ideology of "proper" labor because they contribute economically through exploitation and become racialized *through* capital.

Rodríguez's labor is vastly different from what we would commonly think of as "conventional labor" because she was racialized during her migration to South Texas. She was not actually a wage laborer producing commodities; however, she occupied a "sphere of non-labour or extra necessary labour which envelopes the process of transforming labour, that is commodities purchased with the wage, into the living labour capacity found on the market."[39] This means that terms like "reproductive labor" are insufficient for identifying use-value and the concrete character of reproductive labor. What we come to think of as reproductive labor is cut off from social production because it is nonwage and nonlabor, which is naturalized.[40] What Rodríguez was doing at her inn was value producing, regardless of how we conventionally think that value is produced. The man doesn't always produce commodities while the woman reproduces him in the domestic space. This construction not only denies that gendered labor is commodified and monetized, but it also denies that there is an intersection of racialization that goes into veiling this production.

Rodríguez was not an Irish empresario, did not have accumulated land or wealth, and did not attempt to ascend to whiteness like other colonists did during her time. She did not function within the proper terms of femininity in her domestic sphere. She built her own shelter on the very trail the Confederacy used as the back door to move its cotton south.[41] In fact, less than two weeks before her hanging, the federal expeditionary force landed at Brazos Santiago, the pass south of Padre Island and twenty miles from Brownsville, to burn Confederate stores and cotton on their way to the Cotton Trail. As a stop along the Cotton Trail, Rodríguez's inn, and the labor she performed through it, enabled cotton to move through South Texas into European markets.[42] Besides performing domestic tasks that supported travelers, such as feeding and housing them, legend states that she also assisted in making and fixing their wagons so they could continue to travel in the sparsely populated area. Federal forces made their presence known on the Texas coast and attempted to block the Confederate trade into Mexico and then on to European ships, where "the precious bales could be safely transported across the Atlantic on ships flying neutral flags."[43] The destination for cotton on the Cotton Trail was Bagdad, Texas, near the Gulf of Mexico.[44] While the cotton passed through many different points of the U.S.-Mexico border, all routes went through San Patricio. Rodríguez was not a primary part of the cotton trade, but even so, her labor went unseen, a labor that ultimately helped foster the capitalist market and the beginnings of wage labor before such ideas even hit South Texas with the arrival of the railroad in the 1880s. On November 7, 1863, federal troops occupied Brownsville, and exactly six days after this occupation, Rodríguez was executed. Her hanging is indicative of capital and war because she served as a port of entry into the European market. But again, her significance in this role is ignored. Her absence is present.

The Civil War, the Cotton Trail, and Rodríguez's inn are all interrelated in the story of gendered racial formations in South Texas. As Bluntzer Hebert continues with her epic poem, her language constructs Rodríguez's life as one that hinges on the capital that passes through her inn instead of on her own subjectivity. She states,

Years had passed and Chepita's living
Came from the pittance of each stranger.
Death or Time could not erase
Pedro's dark and stoic face . . . [45]

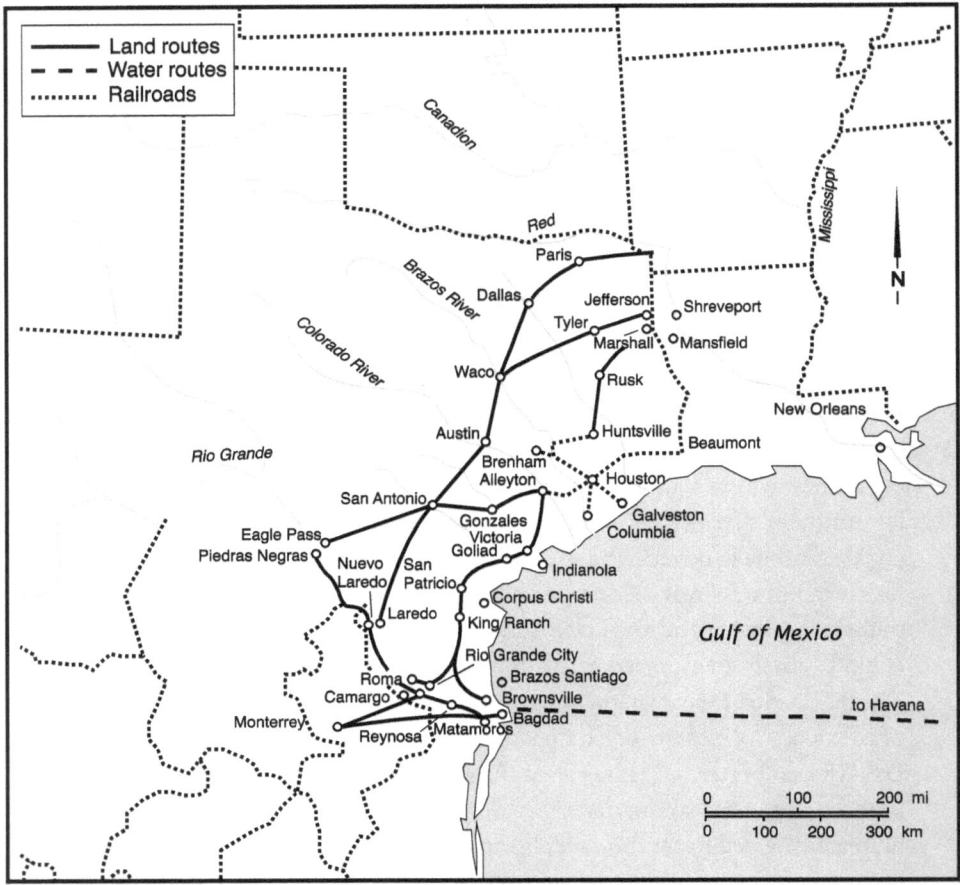

The Cotton Trail to the Rio Grande. Created by Martin Wannam, 2021.

Bluntzer Hebert centers Pedro's personal ethics and his dark complexion in place of a detailed description of Rodríguez's appearance. The poem again sidesteps Rodríguez, but she is an absent presence throughout. Rodríguez recalls her father telling her that if she ever finds herself in danger, she should "'be as quiet as the water.'"[46] This statement goes on to shape Rodríguez as a historical figure; she never actually speaks in any of the archives or any of the cultural production that ensues. This hypermasculine notion of enduring torture instead of speaking out cements Rodríguez as a caricature of the "silent" Mexican woman. She is never able to tell her story. Instead, she becomes "trapped with the evidence of murder" and the memories of her long-lost son.[47]

"Her Face Bore the Marks of Many Hard Years in South Texas": Absence of Body and Phallus of the Racialized Woman Hanging

Just as Rodríguez's labor and voice remain an absent presence in history, her actual body remains absent as well. No one knows the actual location of her grave. Although much cultural production has focused on her in recent years, she remains visible only through the violence she endured. And that violence is tied to the economy of gendered racial formations in Texas. Bodies within this geopolitical space are assigned a social and political position that presumes a different regulatory impulse and contradictory investments for racialized Texas Mexican women.[48] Rodríguez became the face of racialized female violence in South Texas, but she was not the only one. Her story persists because of her brutally violent death and the way she becomes visible only through this violence.

Deputy John Gilpin and the two-wheeled cart pulled by oxen transported Rodríguez's coffin along with her the day of the hanging. Spectators followed the cart from the courthouse down a trail that led west toward the Nueces River.[49] The execution site, a mesquite tree with a grave dug at its feet, was about a mile from the courthouse. The deputy stopped the cart under the tree and gave Rodríguez a handkerchief to cover her face. She declined. Gilpin placed the noose around Rodríguez's neck and drew the other end over the tree. He then got into the cart and cracked the whip on the oxen, causing them to lurch forward. Rodríguez was of thin frame, and her neck did not break at first, so her body tightened and flailed about under its own pressure. Some legends say that her face mirrored the horror of strangulation.[50] As soon as Rodríguez was pronounced dead, after a slow and agonizing death, Gilpin cut her down, dumped her body with the noose around her neck into the handmade coffin, and buried her.

This is the way her death is narrated in many historical documents, websites, biographies, and cultural productions.[51] I hesitate to detail her hanging at all, but the narration of her excessive and violent death is important because it is the only time that we are privy to Rodríguez's subjectivity. Racialized gender opens the brown female body up to all types of violence, rather than just masculine or feminine violence. Racialized gender does the gender work to "signify and constitute racial categories."[52] Gender operates as a racial project, and Rodríguez's execution functioned in the same way. She was disposable, but more importantly, she signified the enunciation of racial terror that was rampant in South Texas in the late nineteenth century.

According to legend, spectators followed the cart from the jail to the mesquite tree, and others met them directly at the place of hanging. Laws were broken to make Rodríguez's execution possible, so how can we differentiate it from a lynching? According to William D. Carrigan and Clive Webb, "From the California Gold Rush to the last recorded instance of a Mexican lynched in public in 1928, vigilantes hanged, burned, and shot thousands of persons of Mexican descent in the United States."[53] In Texas, from 1848 to 1928, there were 597 documented victims of mob violence.[54] Monica Muñoz Martinez reminds us that mob violence did not occur only in regions where there was no law enforcement. On the contrary, mob violence went hand in hand where the criminal justice system was very well established.[55] Mob violence against Mexicans peaked during the 1850s and then again in the 1870s, bookending the time of Rodríguez's execution.[56] Just as in the South young Black men were seen as a "threat," most targets of mob violence in Texas were young Mexican men. However, Rodríguez's experience of this type of violence speaks volumes about how she was discursively constructed as a Mexican woman in the first place. Racialized Mexican women in the nineteenth century were vulnerable to any type of gendered violence, even if the violence was supposedly reserved for men. And the fact that Rodríguez only becomes visible through horrific gendered violence speaks to the complicated history of lynching in America.

While Rodríguez awaited her execution in the San Patricio jail, an Irish mob of about fifteen men stormed the jail, demanding access to Rodríguez to lynch her themselves. Henry Alonzo Maltby, the editor of the *Ranchero* out of Corpus Christi, stated, "Fourteen or fifteen men demanded [Chipita] from custody, in order to deal summarily with [her]."[57] This, coupled with her capital punishment conviction (against the recommendations of the jury) based on questionable circumstantial evidence, exemplifies the racial tensions and hierarchy in San Patricio. Racial tensions were high among the Irish and Mexican Texans in San Patricio, and mob violence and lynching were becoming common practices in the larger region. The sheriff's deputies at the jail did eventually stop the vigilante group before they got to Rodríguez, but where do we draw the line between lynching and hanging by execution, given the questionable trial and sentencing and the large groups of spectators who came to witness her death?

The conventional definitions for legal execution by hanging versus lynching are distinct. However, how do we define what happened to Chipita Rodríguez when she had a "trial," but all the steps that ensure a fair trial were negated and the judge went against the recommendation of the jury to spare her execution by hanging? While Rodríguez's hanging was not extralegal, Muñoz Martinez reminds us that "violence [often] superseded judicial procedures regularly [and] articulated popular distrust of the justice system or local frustrations with the bureaucracy of criminal prosecutions."[58] Lynching is above the law; it is vigilante, if you will. Capital punishment by hanging entails a process where a person is proven guilty beyond reasonable doubt before a jury of their peers in a courtroom. However, as evidenced by the lynch mob and the unfair trial in Rodríguez's case, state-sanctioned violence must be interrogated through the discourse of lynching if we are to see a full picture of violence against Mexican women. Robin Weigman defines lynching as "the towering patrolman who re-narrates the body and sadistically claims it as a sign of his own power, and the symbolic as law, the site of normativity and sanctioned desire, prohibition, and taboo."[59] Lynching highlights a topos of bodies that delineates chaos while parading as social and political "order." Weigman notes that as lynching "operates according to a logic of borders—racial, sexual, national, psychological, biological, as well as gendered—lynching figures its victims as the culturally abject, monstrosities of excess whose limp and hanging bodies function as the specular assurances that the threat has not simply been averted, but thoroughly negated, dehumanized, and rendered incapable of return."[60] Rodríguez's absent body crosses many borders—the border between the United States and Mexico, the border of sexual difference between conventional male and female punishments, and lastly, the border between proper and improper femininity.

Throughout U.S. history, lynching was coupled with the castration of Black and brown males to symbolically sever their masculinity, "interrupting the privilege of the phallus, and thereby reclaiming, through the perversity of dismemberment, his (masculine) potential for citizenship."[61] Freud states that the sight of female difference traumatizes man by bringing up notions of castration. Man then creates a fetish through a surrogate penis, a representative of power.[62] However, David Eng complicates Freud's castration anxiety by claiming that it is marked not by singular difference but by multiple differences.[63] Castration of the Black or brown male before a lynching signifies the merging of race with sexual difference and inferiority. Lynching takes the hypermasculine male (who is often accused of rape) and feminizes him through castration. For white male supremacists, this is the most degraded position the Black or brown male can occupy, for a "woman provides the nexus against which masculine *disembodiment* can be achieved."[64] The white male feels threatened by the masculine sameness. However, what happens when the lynching victim is a racialized woman, without a phallus to begin with? The gendered violence that Rodríguez experienced as a racialized woman is completely indicative of her sexual and racial difference.

Even without a phallus, Rodríguez was still racially gendered through notions of masculinity. Every written iteration of Rodríguez's trial and hanging describes her as a "little, old Mexican woman," yet every drawing of her (and there are many) portrays her as masculine.[65] Guthrie states, "Chipita's face bore the marks of many hard years in the South Texas sun but was devoid of any expression. Her calloused hands were limply clasped in utter resignation in [her] lap."[66] In one breath, Rodríguez is described both as a small Mexican woman and as tough with a hard face. Keith Guthrie's book, *The Legend of Chipita: The Only Woman Hanged in Texas*, includes a drawing of Rodríguez that places her hairline particularly low, indicative of a larger head. The shadow of a beard also appears on her neck. What might be considered a slip of the hand actually portrays an invisible Rodríguez as a visibly masculine Mexican woman. Rodríguez's hair is thin, and whether we can attribute that to the pencil drawing or a deeper articulation of what Mexican women look like, there is a certain lack of femininity that goes along with portrayals of Rodríguez. Following this logic, Rodríguez never needed a phallus, because her racialized gender constructed her through a sexual difference that made her body available to any type of violence, male or female.

Rodríguez is a perfect example of how racial capitalism functions. Cedric Robinson's theorization of racial capitalism states that racism and capitalism formed from an older world order "to produce a modern world system of 'racial capitalism' dependent upon slavery, violence, imperialism, and genocide."[67] The intersection of race, gender, and capital unveils a violent system that renders the Mexicana flesh outside the boundaries of gender normativity and produces visible violence on the flesh, which constitutes the gender racial formation as a conduit for capitalism and accumulation of wealth through abstract labor.

This representation of the laboring body, whether we think of Rodríguez as laboring or not, comes to be reassembled by Iris Guthrie through her imagining of what Rodríguez looked like. Marx tells us that the body is an "expenditure of human brains, muscles, nerves, [and] hands" that shapes the "body of the commodity" and is a *membra disjecta* that comes together to make a whole.[68] The process of production takes pieces of body and makes them work in unison. Through the artistic process of "constructing" a whole Rodríguez, Guthrie produces a fictional body that does not exist and at once abstracts the labor and value of the historical figure of Chipita Rodríguez. In the process, Guthrie constructs Rodríguez through a masculine lens that

"Chipita," by Iris Guthrie. This drawing is in Keith Guthrie, *The Legend of Chipita: The Only Woman Hanged in Texas*, illustrated by Iris Guthrie (Austin, TX: Eakin Press, 1990).

begs us to evaluate the tropes and stereotypes assigned to Mexican women. The abstract representation of Rodríguez takes parts of what poor Mexican women "look" like in the national imaginary and puts them together to construct a whole. It is the abstract body that is cut into parts that is not seen on the borderlands as someone who produces value. Rodríguez is not represented as herself in this drawing. She represents all other poor Mexicanas on the borderlands, which renders them masculine and interchangeable.

Absent Archive, Abstract Language: Conceiving of Rodríguez through Violence

Just as Rodríguez's racialized gender labor during her life is invisible and her body is absent after her death, her archive is also glaringly silent. The language that makes Rodríguez whole always rests outside of herself, and her person is always abstract. To return to the concept of concrete and abstract labor for a moment, Marx states, "Along with the useful qualities of the products themselves, we put out of sight both the useful character of the various kinds of labour embodied in them, and the concrete forms of that labour; there is nothing left but what is common to them all; all are reduced to one and the same sort of labour, human labour in the abstract."[69] As this chapter has established, abstract labor is not just the specific character of labor that becomes homogeneously the "expenditure of human labor power," which Marx states is the actual concrete labor; abstract labor also racializes certain bodies *through* capital. If Rodríguez's racialized gendered labor remains hidden and she is only made visible through violence in the borderlands, we must trace the abstract ways in which her body appears in language. Diana Taylor ruminates on performance and how it can embody a "hauntology." Taking cues from the intersection of performance studies and literary studies, I examine performance as "skeptical of what remains" and language as the continuum in which bodies are transmitted to the archive.[70] I utilize the term "abstract language" in the same sense as the economic term "abstract labor," which takes into consideration how abstraction further racializes Rodríguez's body. Rodríguez's body is completely erased from the archive; only by appearing in cultural artifacts is her execution connected to abstract capital, at best, and to language as nonhuman, racialized, and degraded without phallus, at worst. Rodríguez's narrative is not solely about what her body *tells* us, which is that brown female bodies in the borderlands were killed and then erased from the archive, but more importantly about what her body *does not* tell us, which is embodied through her re-creation in contemporary cultural production.

The absent presence of Rodríguez through the abstracted language economy further racializes her. *Chipita Rodríguez* is an opera in two acts composed by Lawrence Weiner, with the libretto by Leonardo Carillo and John Wilson. The first performance was on April 3, 1982, at the Corpus Christi Symphony in Texas. It was also performed in the fall of 1992 at the University of Texas, Austin. Weiner's opus comprises more than 160 compositions for a wide range of musical solos and ensembles, some 50 of which are published. These include 40 compositions for symphonic band, 15 pieces for orchestra, numerous choral and chamber works, works for solo instrument, voice, and percussion ensembles, and an opera/ballet of *Chipita Rodriguez*. While the opera was performed before an audience and was recorded and archived at the Briscoe Center at the University of Texas, Austin, a written script from

1982, with no identifiable publisher, is more accessible. The actual performance was recorded, but the affect of the performance in that moment could never be recorded, saved, or documented. Therefore, I choose to focus on what is replicable, and that is the language economy that this cultural artifact deploys. The opera opens with a corrido about the death of Rodríguez. The ballad reads,

> Ay que tragesia tan grande
> La que les voy a contar
> La historía de una señora
> No se les vaya olvidar.
>
> (What a great tragedy
> That I am now going to tell you.
> It is the history of a woman;
> may you never forget it.)[71]

This scene accompanied by the corrido shows the sheriff and his men arresting Rodríguez as she is convicted of murder. Directly after this short scene to ground the historical incident, Psalm 130 is read in Latin; it translates to "If Thou shalt observe iniquities, O Lord, Lord, who shall endure it?" The *de profundis* call within the psalm is a call to prayer for the dead. The spirit of Rodríguez is called upon here, and the audience is invoked in the praying and calling for her dead soul. The language of the play hinges on the dead body of Rodríguez.

A bilingual opera, the narrative does not focus on Rodriguez's life before or during the trial and hanging, but instead focuses on her unverified granddaughter Rosita's journey "to clear [Rodríguez's] soul" through the patriarchal Catholic Church.[72] When Rosita asks the Catholic priest, "Where are the records [that speak to my grandmother's execution]?," the father replies, "The few that are left are in the care of the county clerk."[73] Here again we witness the clear and present absence of Rodríguez. When Rosita goes to visit Father Murphy to see if he can do anything to acquit her grandmother, the play reads, "The old priest did not permit a Christian burial, and some say the ghost of Chipita still weeps as she walks the banks of the river."[74] This reference to La Llorona makes it clear that Rodríguez is being constructed through a Mexican maternal trope. La Llorona is a folktale that has many iterations. However, in the most common tale of La Llorona (who is mostly named María in legends), she marries a rich man, and he cheats on her constantly, so she drowns the two children that she has with him. She continues to roam the riverbanks where she drowns her own children and weeps until her death.

After death, she is heard and seen on the riverbanks as a ghost. This evocation of La Llorona in the story of Rodríguez exemplifies the fungibilty of Mexican women and their bodies in society. Rodríguez does not kill her son but instead takes the blame for his murder of Savage. The correlation is off; however, we can see that the Mexican woman always takes the brunt of the blame in different situations. Father Murphy tells Rosita there is nothing he can do to clear the name of Chipita Rodríguez through the church, but when Rosita is about to leave, the church maid Agapita tells Rosita that she is familiar with her grandmother's story and urges her to see Lupe Garza so she can help her.

On her journey to redeem her grandmother, Rosita realizes that neither the state of Texas nor the Catholic Church can redeem her, so she turns to a *curandera* named Lupe who has contact with the dead. Weiner connects Lupe to Mexican iconography through La Virgen de Guadalupe, who is the mother of Mexico, as she finds an alternative way to contact the lost soul of Rodríguez. Here we see Weiner breaking the traditions of the Catholic Church but simultaneously evoking it through the sacrilegious ceremony of the *curandera*. However, Lupe is still invested in the Catholic religion. While Lupe attempts to contact Rodríguez in the afterlife, she states, "I believe in God and all that is holy. . . . Holy and immortal God, Holy and immortal God, have mercy on us."[75] Lupe then goes into a trance while contacting Rodríguez, and the apparition of Rodríguez's son, Rosendo, appears. He asks, "What do you want of me?"[76] The opera pins the murder on Rosendo and makes clear that Rodríguez only took the blame to protect him. Here, Rodríguez takes on the role of the martyr, which Mexican women embody through the construct of the La Virgen de Guadalupe (virgin) and La Malinche (whore) dichotomy.

According to Octavio Paz, La Malinche was an Aztec interpreter, mistress of the Spanish conquistador Hernán Cortés, and "the Mexican Eve."[77] The historical triangulation of Spanish, Indigenous Aztec, and mestizo maps onto Rodríguez's narrative. She, a Mexican woman, has sex with a Euro-American man, bearing a mixed-race baby with him. In Rodríguez's narrative, the Euro-American father takes the child away from her, and when her son murders Savage, she sacrifices herself for him. Like Malinche, whose son was largely raised by Cortés, Rodríguez's son is raised by the Euro-American father who takes him away from her. Rodríguez is a "traitor" because she has a son with a white man but simultaneously sacrifices herself by taking the blame for his crime. The opera has a high anxiety about Rodríguez's racialized gender and attempts to transform her into a martyr through sacrifice. While Rodríguez was not an active mother in her son's life, according to the historical record, many of the cultural narratives reconstructing her life do not actually construct her as a person but rather as a ghost, mother, and martyr. This language construction of Rodríguez through a gender racial formation abstracts her actual person. At this point in the opera, the apparition of Rodríguez appears, but she speaks through Lupe to say, "Let my son rest. What is a mother if not a woman who loves and protects her child. A mother's love for her child never fades, even in death ... never fades ... never fades ... no, judge ... no ... no ... I am not guilty!"[78] After this scene, Rodríguez and her son Rosendo appear as apparitions and dance until the lights fade, ending the first act.

After the intermission, Lupe announces to the audience, "We have seen the very spirit of Chipita; the unjustly accused. Her soul is without hope."[79] Lupe tells the Catholic father that Chipita harbors a mother's love for her son. The Catholic canon lawyer then tells the audience, "You would think that she is a martyr."[80] Again, constructing Rodríguez as a mother taking the blame for her son elevates her through sacrifice. Women, thus, are only meant to sacrifice for their families and are expected to be nothing else. Ultimately, the Catholic Church does not rectify Rodríguez's soul and moves on to other matters. As the opera closes, Rodríguez appears as a ghost and dances as her granddaughter, Rosita, sinks to her knees in despair; the lights fade on Rosita as we see Rodríguez move away, revealing the "horror of her eternal fate."[81] In the absence of an archive, the opera acts as an ephemeral form of knowledge. However, the opera reinscribes Rodríguez's body with the same gender racial formation it tries to undo. Centering her racialized motherly ambitions, mapping the Malinche and the Llorona narrative onto her already invisible body, and having her speak through someone as a ghost only furthers the violence against and trauma of Chipita Rodríguez. The opera functions as fate and design, and there is nothing it can do to resolve the history of Rodríguez herself, so it reinscribes her as she always was, an absent presence.

In the last part of the opera, Father Murphy tells Rosita and Lupe that even though they all saw and heard the apparition of Rodríguez, he does not think the canon lawyers will exonerate her in the eyes of the Catholic Church. Three canon lawyers appear left of stage and they carry papers and large books. They deliberate among themselves and begin reciting a Gregorian chant, which is a form of monophonic, unaccompanied sacred song in Latin. At the end of the chant, they say, "Let the matter stay as it is."[82] With Rodríguez not exonerated in the eyes of the church, "Chipita slowly [moves] away and [reveals] the horror of her eternal fate."[83] The opera ends and Rodríguez remains in the neutral space of purgatory, where her soul cannot rest.

Teresa Paloma Acosta, a poet from McGregor, Texas, attempts to navigate the appropriation of Rodríguez's story and her voice through cultural artifacts. Her poem is titled "Chipita," and she opens with an italicized note stating that "Chipita's life is clouded in mystery."[84] She goes on to write, "First a preface to prove to myself that you are dead, I sift through someone else's footnotes. They weigh like lead. I find I cannot carry them or you—alone."[85] She evokes here a language of imposition that she has to carry the "truth" about Rodríguez when it weighs so heavy on her.

> So, ok,
> Only *now* someone asks
> about you
> Wants to know the truth
> And insists on loving you—
> Myth, legend, lie. All.[86]

Acosta attempts to lean into the abstracted language economy by telling readers that Rodríguez is a myth, a legend, and a lie. There is no authentic construction of Rodríguez, and even though she is a legend, she remains a mystery. Acosta goes as far as to say many of the legends about Rodríguez are lies. When Acosta tells readers that

> All the truth
> Is buried deeper still
> —Within your dust,

she is telling readers that the truth about Rodríguez has not been told and is waiting where Rodríguez lays, "But we cannot hear the language you speak / Anymore."[87]

Acosta writes first-person to Rodríguez, where she tells her, "Chipita— / The last time I thought of you, I was alone and tired."[88] She conjures Rodríguez back to life in her own imagination. The poet tells us that Rodríguez was dressed in sea blue and had a face that was softened with a smile. This is the only reference to Rodríguez being soft or feminine in any of the stories or legends about her. Acosta then says that after she thought about Rodríguez, she quickly wrote her name down. On Acosta's own terms, she writes Rodríguez back into existence. And in a turn of the poem, Acosta gives Rodríguez a voice. Rodríguez says,

> I ate pears, manzanas.
> I often enjoyed coffee.
> I loved my son.[89]

Here we see that Acosta stops capitalizing on the absent presence of Rodríguez and imagines her speaking, while simultaneously evoking her motherhood. Acosta ends the poem with Rodríguez stating,

"When they take you away,
Insist you pay for me.
Forever."[90]

Acosta attempts to keep the spirit of Rodríguez alive by imagining her speaking. The last word, forever, is symbolic of where Rodríguez lies in our memory.

Conclusion: (Not) A Resolution to the Racialized Gendered Violence of Chipita Rodríguez

Some claim that the ghost of Chipita Rodríguez walks the banks of the Nueces River near San Patricio at night with a tattered noose around her neck. In one legend, she moves silently in the dress she wore when she was executed, and in another iteration, she somberly cries, surrounded by a light mist radiating a mystical glow. There are many legends in San Patricio that revolve around the Irish population that settled there. Many legends paint pictures of gender violence against women of all races and nationalities, but Chipita Rodríguez's is particularly reminiscent of the Southwest legend of La Llorona. Rodríguez's execution narrative was specifically regional to South Texas, but it was not until the 1984 execution of Karla Faye Tucker, the *second* woman in Texas to be executed, that Rodríguez's narrative gained renewed national attention. In 1985, Texas state senator Carlos F. Truan of Corpus Christi proposed Senate Resolution 14 to pardon Rodríguez for the murder charges. The resolution states that Rodríguez "may have been wrongfully convicted of the crime for which she was executed,"[91] making clear that the surviving court records "cast great doubt on the propriety of her indictment and trial and hence the validity of her trial."[92] The resolution makes note of the violation of procedure in the selection of the grand jury and the trial jury and reiterates that all evidence presented in the murder trial was circumstantial. It also highlights the fact that Rodríguez's arraignment, trial, and conviction occurred within a single day, a highly unusual practice. In addition, there were no continuances granted or appeals made for the outrageous conviction. The resolution emphasizes the "volatile nature of the community, involving, on the one side, vigilantes who attempted to lynch the two defendants, and on the other side, townspeople who sympathized with them and jeered the verdict."[93] But ultimately, pardons are prohibited in the case of the dead, making the resolution only a "symbolic redress"—a mere sentiment of expression by the Texas legislature.[94] Years after her execution, Rodríguez still does not speak.

To this day, no one knows the location of Rodríguez's grave. Her body is never present in history or cultural production, and when she does become visible, it is only through violence. The abstraction of her labor, her body, and her voice further complicates her racialized positionality and relationship to gender and sexuality in the borderlands. Even before industrialization and wage labor came into existence, Texas functioned within capitalism because of its role in the transnational market through the products of slavery and the Cotton Trail. However, even though Rodríguez's inn was situated squarely within this capitalist system, her labor has never been considered concrete because it did not produce a direct commodity for the market. It is only through the notion of abstract labor that I argue Rodríguez creates value, even if it is not "counted." Her racialized abstract labor is tied directly to the racialized gender violence that she experiences. The next chapter builds off the conversation of labor, sex, and the materiality of the body, but in relation to racialized sexual production and reproduction within the sexual economy of debt peonage in New Mexico.

CHAPTER FOUR

Productive Racialized Sex
The Sexual Economy of the Southwest Borderlands, the Nuevomexicana Body Politic, and Memory Archives

In 1867, the U.S. federal government prohibited debt peonage in the Union. This decision came after two essential rulings by the New Mexico Territorial Supreme Court that set the foundation and the boundaries of debt peonage in the United States. An important social and economic system in the Southwest borderlands and México, debt peonage was invested in labor control and the evolution of the Americas through racial capital. New Mexico was the focal point of the U.S. national debt peonage debate because the system did not have a clear definition when the United States annexed Northern Mexico in 1848. Debt peonage was not slavery and it was not free labor; it sat at the interstices of these two economic and labor systems. And while debt peonage was not slavery in that the *patrón* (bosses) did not own the peon's body, he did own his or her labor, and the economic system carried the same hereditary condition as slavery. However, unlike chattel slavery in the U.S. South, which followed the status of the enslaved mother, debt peonage followed the status of whomever was indebted, most times the father. And while scholars agree that males and females both labored in debt peonage, there was a clear masculine component to the economic system that not only specifically indebted sons after a father or mother passed or ran away, but also created working conditions that were male-centered.

But this chapter is not concerned with the males of debt peonage or the masculine component of this borderland economic system; instead, it shines a light on the violent gendered and sexual components of debt peonage, and the poor Nuevomexicana women who were at the center of it.[1] This chapter is concerned with the sexual capital that comes out of debt peonage. The elite landholders or *ricos* of New Mexico harnessed their cultural capital and their relations with transnational trade to exploit poor Nuevomexicana women and utilized their bodies and sex violently in ways that do not appear in historical records and are not visible within the nineteenth-century economic modes of production that built racialized sexuality. Whereas some elite women throughout the Southwest borderlands in the early nineteenth century were central brokers of cultural, social, and economic capital through sex, as indicated in chapter 1 on Californianas before the U.S. invasion, *patrones* in New Mexico used poor Nuevomexicana women's sex as one facet to enhance mercantile/monopoly capitalist relations and transnational trade in the late nineteenth-century borderlands. *Patrones* utilized the racialized sexuality of poor Nuevomexicana women for sexual capital. With the convergence of American imperialism with old economic systems of Spanish colonialism and Mexican nationalism in the Southwest borderlands, the *ricos* in New Mexico used the women's bodies to keep up with American trade and emerging monopoly capitalism in the Southwest, but the *ricos* had fleeting economic power during westward expansion and white settlement. This chapter looks at the institution of debt peonage during the transitional years when New Mexico became a part of the newly annexed U.S. territory and examines it as a moment in history when racialized sexuality was mobilized. I argue that while U.S. empire did not want to accept New Mexico into the union because of anti-Mexican ethnocentrism and anti-Catholic nativism, and also because of the "primitive" institution of debt peonage, the *ricos* utilized the racialized sexuality of poor Nuevomexicana women to attempt to maintain their power in the region. While this system of sexual capital did not work for the elite landholders and *ricos* of the region, because they were ultimately ousted by white settlers, it solidified the portrayal of racialized women's bodies in the histor[i]al record as sexually excessive. Nonetheless, by 1835, New Mexicans were "the majority of those traveling into the Mexican territory, owned a substantial portion of all the goods freighted south, and specialized in hauling *efectos del pais* [local merchandise]."[2] Whether through mercantile trading, the sheep or bison economy, or the beginnings of transnational trade with Mexico, America, and Europe, the *ricos* utilized the racialized Nuevomexicana female body not only for her labor, but also to reproduce the labor force, which was then able to lead caravans, maintain the land, and be indebted for a lifetime through the condition of debt peonage.[3] This is to say that the bodies of these poor Nuevomexicana women had a dual capacity in the productive and reproductive system of debt peonage. As Rosaura Sánchez states, "There is no essential gender discourse, only gender discourses in articulation with other discourses, like those of nation, race/caste, religion, family, class, and sexuality, all of which articulate with one another and generate a variety of social identities."[4] Sex, gender, colorism/caste, and class could not be disentangled from one another, and this chapter reckons with the larger argument of the book, which unveils the complex role racialized sexuality played in the construction of racialized subjectivity and how sexual capital is not necessarily a commodity itself that is sold and traded, but rather is unseen labor that produces commodities for the *ricos* and elite landholding Hispanos.

Given this history, I examine the materiality of sex for women of color on the border and how that materiality affects sexual politics and life value in a certain historical moment. This chapter serves as a partner to chapter 5, as I think about the "productive" uses of sex and the body and then shift in chapter 5 to the "unproductive" discourse of the racialized female body on the borderlands in relation to sex. As I stated in the introduction to this book, the materiality of sex is the physical act of sex, and the material results from sex that are historically utilized to control populations in the Southwest borderlands. The body of the poor, racialized Nuevomexicana woman exemplifies the theoretical and practical discomforts of pleasure and power. As race emerged as a heritable category that defined social reality, the biological capacities linked to the Nuevomexicana woman were also linked to her status and place in New Mexico. Her reproductive life was always signified by her public location in the space of the accumulation of wealth in the borderlands, rather than in the private space of the domestic. She became a site for the resignification of gender and sexuality because she could *never* attain proper femininity, but her body was required to propel commerce forward. In contrast, the elite landholding Hispanas and their families in New Mexico conceptualized and positioned themselves in relation to the growing nation through gender and sexual norms, against the poor Nuevomexicanas who built and maintained the elites' homes and wealth. The body of the poor, racialized Nuevomexicana resignifies the limits of reproductive labor, which has no value in society, though her sexual reproductive capacities are *productive* and forced violently by *patrones*. This history explains the political economy of the borderlands. I identify the economic system of debt peonage as a sexual economy and an extension of sexual capital that reveals the nuanced ways gender and sexuality are utilized as a technology of power and, in this particular history, how the Nuevomexicana body was engaged in a cycle of wealth and racialized sexuality.

I examine six texts: two recovered New Mexico Territorial Supreme Court cases on debt peonage; two short stories about debt peonage written during the Work Projects Administration (WPA); one WPA testimonio by peon José Librado Gurulé; and Fabiola Cabeza de Baca's memoir *We Fed Them Cactus* (1954). The multi-genre sources in this chapter locate an economic abstraction not only in the texts, but in the materiality of the body as well. I begin this chapter by laying out the economic system of debt peonage as a paternal system in the nineteenth century. Next, I examine two New Mexico Territorial Supreme Court cases, first to outline the condition of debt peonage in the legal system through the 1857 case *Mariana Jaremillo v. José de la*

Cruz Romero, and second to map out the sexual and gendered conditions that were central to the economic system of debt peonage through the *Marcellina Bustamento v. Juana Analla* case, also from 1857. I interweave the findings of these court cases in my reading of the narratives from the WPA and Cabeza de Baca to reveal how debt peonage was a sexual economy and how the racialized Nuevomexicana's body was a vehicle for wealth. Exploring how narrative authority is asserted, controlled, denied, and manipulated in these texts, I argue that the WPA narratives are examples of dependent production, where the narrative falls between autonomy and subjection; they address the court rulings, but they do so through an interlocutor, which threatens authorial intent. In contrast to the WPA pieces, Cabeza de Baca negotiates narrative authority by ventriloquizing *El Cuate* to reinforce gender and sexual roles that uphold family wealth. Taken together, these accounts expose how debt peonage built racialized civility. There is a strict line drawn within the system of debt peonage and U.S. empire, where idealized femininity is mapped onto the elite landholding Hispana, who is tied to land and inheritance, and sexual utility is assigned to the Nuevomexicana, who is tied to a complicated system of productive and reproductive labor. This chapter follows the arc of the book, beginning with the brokering of the daughters of wealthy and elite Californios to maintain cultural capital in the building of empire, and moving on to the sexual economic system of debt peonage, which illustrates how the interplay of racialized sexuality/sex and capital are productive. The WPA narratives have symbolic and metonymic meaning that conveys how racialized women in the Southwest borderlands were part of a sexual economy that produced wealth for the *ricos* in New Mexico. In contradistinction to the WPA narratives, *Cactus* speaks from a position of privilege that maintains "proper" gendered and sexual codes and customs, which are starkly the opposite of what poor Nuevomexicanas were experiencing in the same regional location.

The signification of the poor Nuevomexicana body remains hidden in Cabeza de Baca's memoir and the WPA narratives themselves. Neither text centers the poor Nuevomexicana body, but this chapter reads the absences of the archive through memory. In other words, I read the peripheral female characters in the three WPA short stories and the "proper" feminine narrative voice in Cabeza de Baca through the New Mexico Territorial Court cases. Products of a sort of nostalgia project, none of the texts in this chapter disclose the nuanced history of the borderlands in relation to racialized sexuality. However, upon closer examination, the narratives unveil the unwritten ways in which bodies were violently put to sexual work. The notions of productive and reproductive labor help us unravel how the poor, racialized Nuevomexicana body had a dual capacity that Karl Marx and even Marxist feminists have failed to take into account. Marx notes that productive labor is any form of labor that produces surplus value, which can constitute a tangible commodity or merely a service.[5] For Marx, labor power has value. Labor power is also a commodity, and labor power makes commodities themselves. For Marx, reproductive labor has use-value but no exchange value; therefore, only labor power produces value. Thus, reproductive labor power falls outside of the category of value and becomes naturalized as social labor, not as a productive process of capital. Marxist feminists rewrite Marx and state that reproductive labor is very much mystified labor and has value. Marxist feminists like Leopoldina Fortunati remind us that the basic unit of capitalism is the family.[6] As Fortunati argues, reproductive labor has value through reproducing the worker in order for him to produce commodities and value. She states that the "process of reproduction is a process of value formation ... the direct transformation of the work of producing commodities into capital is a necessary condition of its productive existence, so too is reproduction work's indirect transformation into capital a necessary condition of its productive existence."[7] For Fortunanti, reproductive work *is* directed toward production (versus toward consumption) and therefore surplus value. Fortunati theorizes the dual character of reproductive labor as labor that is abstract and social. First, she states, "Reproduction work is abstract human labor, but unlike the work that produces commodities, it omits the exchange value of the product—labor-power—and not the use-value."[8] As abstracted as productive work is within capitalism, reproductive work is further abstracted within the system. Second, she states, "Reproduction work is social because it is social work, not because it is socially determined."[9] Regardless of who does the reproductive labor, it becomes labor-power that must be standardized. While I agree with many of the points that Marxist feminists make in relation to reproductive labor, they utilize a universal notion of "female" and center the heteronormative family as the nucleus of capitalist production. In doing so, they cannot think about capital and race simultaneously and make a grave error in theorizing the reproductive labor as centered in the home. The poor, racialized Nuevomexicana exemplifies the limits of how reproductive labor has been theorized through Marxist feminism because she, too, has a dual characteristic in producing wealth for the *ricos* and *patrones*, who attempt to use this wealth to maintain power on encroaching U.S. westward expansion.

This chapter examines this dual capacity of production and reproduction as a result of racialized sexuality. The Nuevomexicana not only reproduces the labor force but also produces for her family and the *patrón/hacienda* system, while her husband's wages continue to be given to the *patrones* for clothing, shelter, food, and medicine. We must rethink how she reproduces the worker (through her indebted children) and produces for the worker (through her reproductive labor of survival in debt peonage) as a dual capacity of her racialized body. The materiality of her sexuality is tied to the multiple ways she is able to produce and reproduce for the *patrón* and foregrounds heteronormative sexuality. Her sexual labor in reproducing the labor force in debt peonage is *congealed*, for if we follow Marx when he states that labor power produces value, then labor "becomes value only in its congealed state, when embodied in the form of some object."[10] While Marx and Marxist feminists would never think of the reproduction of children for the labor force as a commodity, this act of reproductive labor unveils the congealed labor performed by the poor Nuevomexicana to reproduce the indebted peons through sexual capital and the sexual economy of debt peonage.

I define sexual economies as colonial/modern structures, enacted through sexual and economic systems (in certain historical moments determined by rape, racial miscegenation, and violence), that build racialized civility and racialized capital.[11] I link systems of violence and economy to the production of settler subjectivity in New Mexico, where idealized femininity and the fraught social figure of the elite landholding "Hispana" woman are sites through which empire and nation-state are "properly" reproduced in contention with subjugated Indigenous and poor Nuevomexicana bodies. Expanding upon Black feminists' definition of the sexual economy of slavery, I deploy the term to think about the system of debt peonage and the lasting effects it had on racialized gender and sexuality in the Southwest. And I add to the foundational work to consider the paternal lineage of debt peonage in relation to the production of the *patrones*' wealth. The tasks that peons performed under bondage depended on their gender, age, and strength. Males made up most of the peons in the Southwest, but if they were peons, their family was indebted indefinitely because of them. When the male could no longer work or needed more hours than he could provide individually, the *patrones* used his family, mostly sons, to continue payment to his account, which could never be rectified. While the majority of the stories regarding debt peonage in the Southwest center on the male peon, when interrogating the gaps and silences, it becomes clear that debt peonage also very much affected the wife of the male and shaped her excessive racialized sexuality.

This chapter is situated in relation to the discursive work on racialized sexuality that produces sexual capital discussed at the beginning of the book, but it is the second chapter examining the material consequences of sexual capital and racialized sexuality. As I theorize in the introduction, racialized sexuality is the point where the deployment of sex and sexuality intersects with the deployment of race. The historical economic system of debt peonage is linked to the process of sexualization, which situates the utility of poor Nuevomexicanas to their racialized bodies. They labor *through* their sexual bodies, which are always tied to heteronormative notions of family and reproduction, but are utilized by the *ricos* and elite landholding Hispanos for the ways in which they can contribute offspring to the institution that produces wealth for a small number of people. In addition to *how* racialized sexuality materially contributes to sexual capital, this chapter also builds off the first two chapters by bringing to the forefront how racialized pathology for women in the borderlands is held against "proper" sex and gender of wealthy racial subjects on the border. By buttressing superior Mexican (American) gender and sexuality through the hemispheric logic of Ruiz de Burton and marriage arrangements of wealthy Californios, this chapter unveils the subsidizing process of racialized sexuality that allows wealthy Hispanos to engage in other enterprises.

Court Ruling: The Sexual Condition of Debt Peonage in Territorial New Mexico

While conversations surrounding westward expansion were happening in relation to slavery in the newly annexed territories of Northern Mexico after 1848, many did not know how to categorize or think about debt peonage or involuntary labor in the Southwest. Debt peonage had become a mainstay in the Southwest by the 1800s. Some scholars of debt peonage maintain that is was a regionally specific system in Mexico and Latin America that was not limited to race. Historians have questioned the institution of debt peonage in the present-day Southwest, and some say it was not fully established under Spanish and Mexican governance. However, it is recalled in oral testimonies like the WPA narratives, memoirs, and the *guia* (guide) records in the Mexican Archives of New Mexico (addressed hereafter as MANM).[12]

Different from debt peonage, the *encomienda* (the labor system of the Spanish colony) and *repartimiento* (which stems from the definition "an American Indian hired to work" but means distribution) systems were established under Spanish colonialism and spanned from British Carolina to French Louisiana, Spanish New Mexico, and Alta California.[13] The Spanish crown targeted Indigenous populations for cheap labor. The commercial agrarian system of debt peonage "matured after independence from Spain," and it evolved differently in different parts of the newly annexed U.S. territory, Mexico, and Latin America.[14] In Yucatán, Mexico, where haciendas were concentrated, the economic system "involved a small class of predominantly European-descent landowners (hacendados) who attempted to exert social and economic domination over the indigenous Maya majority through the institution of debt peonage."[15] Alternatively, in the territory of New Mexico, the descendants of Spanish-Mexican colonists exerted control over the *mestiza/o* (*casta* terminology) and Indigenous populations through this same institution but on their land grants and communal land grants.

Particular to the Southwest was Native or Indigenous slavery, which resulted in the *genízaro* (Indigenous slaves in the American Southwest in the 1880s) population that settled mostly in Abiquiu, New Mexico. Elite landholding families kept these Native or Indigenous slaves, who were different from peons, well into the 1880s, as the *encomienda* and *repartimiento* systems became extinct due to disease and the transfer of private enclosures, haciendas, and ranchos. Rebolledo notes that from the sixteenth to the late nineteenth century, "the use of these Indian servants was rationalized, unlike the African slave experience, by the fact that they were 'adopted into the family' and their souls saved by Christianizing. These 'slaves' were kept within the family, were not sold from person to person, and were sometimes able to barter for their freedom. Many of those released became detribalized Indians, called *genízaros*, who later formed townships."[16] Much recent astute scholarship has focused on Indigenous slavery. As James Brooks has noted, the Apaches, Comanches, Navajos, and Utes were the tribes most taken into Indigenous slavery.[17] New Mexico carried out Indigenous slavery throughout the 1820s and 1830s, and when American occupation began in 1848, the raiding of Indigenous communities by Hispano civilians in search of slaves was at an all-time high. Kiser reminds us that even with American occupation, "so common were Indian slaves in New Mexico in the mid-1800s that even the army officers charged with suppressing captive raiding benefited from the services of such abductees while at their posts."[18] By 1860, more than two hundred years of forced Indigenous slavery had resulted in the displacement of Indigenous people from their tribes and families.[19]

The Spanish crown renounced the *encomienda* and *repartimiento* systems in the 1600s (not Native or Indigenous slavery specifically), but *patrones* on haciendas, ranchos, and communal land property still needed cheap human labor, and debt peonage emerged as one of the fastest-growing labor sources. In the Southwest, peonage was characterized by work in agrarian and pastoral areas, and in its earliest Latin American manifestations it targeted lower-class, racialized citizens. Before New Mexico became a state, political conversations around admitting the minority-majority territory—both prior to and following the Civil War—carried racist undertones. Some scholars have cited debt peonage as one reason why New Mexico was not granted statehood. However, the so-called repulsion for the "savage" coercive labor practices of New Mexicans disguised a racist attempt to withhold equal social and political rights from the "mongrel" Mexican. While Congress was split on the slavery debate in New Mexico, many members of Congress wanted New Mexico to be admitted as a slave state. Menchaca reminds us that congressional representatives warned New Mexico officials that unless they supported slavery, proslavery legislators would vote against New Mexican statehood.[20] New Mexico did not become a slave state, but it also did not abolish Native slavery or debt peonage.[21] Debt peonage did not end with the signing of the Thirteenth Amendment in 1865, which supposedly liberated all persons subjected to slavery and involuntary servitude; it was not until 1867 that the U.S. federal government prohibited it. Even then, convict leasing and debt peonage remained in practice well into the twentieth century in the South.

Even though New Mexico felt pressure from proslavery legislators to become a slave state, it was the only jurisdiction in American history to institute a slave code as a state that did not have slavery. Territorial and statehood factions fought over whether or not New Mexico should vie for statehood. Mexico technically abolished slavery when it won independence from Spain in 1821, but when the United States entered Northern Mexico in 1846 for conquest, "slavery was *de jure* illegal, although involuntary servitude continued *de facto* in the form of both American Indian and Hispanic peonage."[22] The Compromise of 1850 designated New Mexico as a territory, but New Mexico simultaneously attempted to compete for statehood with a state constitution. In that state constitution, New Mexico rejected slavery; however, when statehood was no longer on the table and New Mexico was admitted as a territory, the territorial legislature adopted "black codes" in 1857 to discourage African Americans from moving there and in 1859 to protect the right to hold property in the form of slaves.[23] The curious slave codes enacted by the New Mexico territorial legislature seem out of context, given that New Mexico was not a slave state. But New Mexico became closely aligned with slave states in the South when Southern Democrats were placed in Southwest Territorial offices. More importantly for this chapter, New Mexico needed a way to keep debt peonage and Indian/Indigenous slavery alive in the territory in order to keep economic pace with settlers coming West. New Mexican politicos and *ricos* sought an alliance with the South because of the dominant Democratic government in Washington around 1853 that would guarantee the placement of the transcontinental railroad in the territory of New Mexico, thus guaranteeing commercial opportunities for elite landholding Hispanos in power. Besides this, Southern sympathizing from elite landholding Hispanos in New Mexico was all but guaranteed because they did not want to see their economic system of debt peonage and Indian/Indigenous slavery banned, just as Southerners did not want to see slavery abolished. Just as racialized sexuality was mobilized in the territories through debt peonage, New Mexico was simultaneously enacting slave codes allowing slaves to be held as property in order to align with Southern interests.

Shelley Streeby traces the history of debt peonage as linguistically appearing in "English in the mid-nineteenth century as a way of describing an array of labor arrangements."[24] Alan Knight states that from the late colonial period to the early nineteenth century there were two forms of peonage: coercive and non-coercive, or traditional.[25] However, William Kiser notes that peons performed tasks, and the *patrones* "paid all their laborers' tributes, advanced them money, clothed them, gave them medical attention ... and thus kept permanent debt accumulating."[26] Debt peonage in the Southwest was coercive and functioned as a form of bondage, and while David Weber maintains that a peon could "end his obligation by paying off his debt and his condition was not hereditary," it was not voluntary servitude, and family members, particularly sons, were indebted once a father or mother died with a debt.[27]

Many elite families in the Southwest attempted to mask peonage as a "system of apprenticeship or voluntary servitude," as territorial representative of New Mexico Miguel A. Otero wrote in his letters.[28] In an attempt to sustain its autonomy, New Mexico held tight to its debt peonage system while simultaneously attempting to integrate into the larger emerging and transactional capitalist system the United States was pushing west. Lieutenant Philip St. George Cooke, accompanying General Stephen W. Kearney's expedition of conquest in August 1846, noted that "the great boon of American citizenship [is] thus thrust ... upon eighty thousand mongrels who cannot read—who are almost heathens—the great mass reared in real slavery, called peonism."[29] This feudal system set the foundation for other modes of production to come. The capital invested in peons was minimal and thus provided more leverage for the debt system based on the use of the master's store for health care and clothing; the landowner also gave them small tributes, which the peons could never pay off, adding to the debt incurred throughout their lives. Unlike slaveholders, *patrones* did not own the peon's physical body, only their labor; thus peons were valuable for their productive work and were not a commodity themselves. Kiser reminds us, "Unlike most Southern slaves, peons did sometimes receive monetary compensation for their work, but their meager earning went toward satisfying the debt owned, and compounding interest ensured permanent bondage. Average adult male peons earned between $2 and $5 per month.... Such stipends never came in the form of hard currency but were instead applied directly toward the cost of food and clothing at the master's store."[30] The *patrones* inflated the prices in their stores and, in this way, increased a peon's debt rapidly, which held them in bondage for a longer period. Peons in the Southwest could also be transferred, but usually in an open forum trading meeting, as was the case with slavery.

In 1857, the New Mexico Territorial Supreme Court finally defined the ambiguous labor system of debt peonage as a class of "servants, menials, or domestics, 'bound' to some kind of 'service' for the payment of their debts due to their masters."[31] This ruling came after Mariana Jaremillo left her service to José de la Cruz Romero, resident of the County of Bernalillo in New Mexico. De la Cruz Romero filed suit against Jaremillo because she owed him $51.75 for leaving. At the time, the New Mexico Territorial Supreme Court was attempting to outline peonage in stricter terms. Slavery established a system of economic growth in North America, but debt peonage was not so clear in its form and function. This economic system was not slavery, because the masters or *patrones* paid the peons, regardless of how much they were indebted to their *patró*; however, it was similar in that it followed a bloodline for indenture. Said differently, debt peonage was not slavery because the peons were not "owned," and it was not free labor because the peons were not allowed to leave the *patrón* since they were always indebted to them for different reasons. Debt peonage came out of vassalage from Spanish rule; then the conditions of the peon in Mexico originated in the workings of the *repartimientos*. However, when José de la Cruz Romero sued Mariana Jaremillo for abandoning her work and service to him, owing the sum of $51.75 advanced to her, the New Mexico Territorial Supreme Court was unable to find any law creating and defining the duties and rights or the civil and domestic relations under the specific denomination of "peon." The invariable rule was that the peon could discharge himself from service by paying his debt to his master, and the master could not refuse to receive payment from his peon and still hold him in service. Interestingly, the language in this court case states that peons were "not any particular color, race, or caste of inhabitants," but later the ruling reveals that they "generally had none or small amounts of property."[32] The lower class of individuals the court case classified as "peons" were linked to a racialized population in the Southwest who were mostly made up of American Indians/Indigenous people, *mulatas*, and mestizos.[33] While New Mexico does not represent the entire Southwest, it becomes the focal point that sets the foundational boundaries, definition, and legislation of debt peonage in the Southwest. This 1857 case distinctly maps out the terms of debt peonage in the United States and states that all free men and women, when no legal impediment exists, may enjoy this type of contract. The only way a peon can leave his or her master during the time of service is mutual consent; motive, such as the injury of the peon (through work or at the hands of the *patrón*); or if the master keeps the peon's account unclear so they do not understand it. As almost a side note, the court ruling states that parents cannot contract away the services of their children, except if agreed upon beforehand. This is the vaguest part of the court ruling, and it seems for good reason. If a peon died, often from excessive punishment or malnutrition, the oldest boy would usually be contracted to take the position of the deceased parent. This was not "legal" and was only reserved for special contracts and circumstances, but it was normal for many peon families.

After the 1857 court case outlining debt peonage for the U.S. federal government, peonage became a mainstay in the United States until it was abolished in 1867, two years after the signing of the Thirteenth Amendment. However, many wealthy landowners in New Mexico did not follow the law that required them to emancipate their peons who were being held because of their debt to the *patrones* or masters. And while this economic system was about labor control, there remains a gendered and sexualized component that has yet to be discussed. The peripheral sexual and gendered condition of debt peonage consolidates race, sex, and capital in nineteenth-century New Mexico. While the 1857 *Mariana Jaremillo v. José de la Cruz Romero* case in New Mexico outlined the condition of debt peonage, it was the *Marcellina Bustamento v. Juana Analla* case in the same year that mapped out the way sexual capital was central to the economic system of debt peonage. *Bustamento v. Analla* paved the way to interrogate the sexual economy of debt peonage, kinship ties within the institution, and the legality of bondage of a minor. The case states that Catalina Bustamento was a child born out of wedlock between a *patrón*, Carpio Bustamento, and his peon, Juana Analla. In the case, the judge stressed that Catalina was the illegitimate child of Carpio, but the power dynamics within the case that reveal the violence of pleasure and power were never questioned or examined. Carpio's wife, Marcellina Bustamento, took Analla to court because she claimed the child belonged to her and wanted to keep her in her care, most likely to utilize her labor. When the judge asked Marcellina Bustamento if the child was an indebted servant, she refused to respond, though she did state that Catalina Bustamento was not detained illegally and was there of her own free will, as a child. Bustamento repeatedly stated in the court case that Analla was an unfit mother because of her social and racial status. Interestingly, the judge more likely ruled for Catalina Bustamento to be returned to Analla not because of kinship and blood ties, but because Marcellina Bustamento did not respond to the allegations that she was holding the child in peonage and servitude. Bustamento made it clear in her response that Analla was a woman of "immoral habits and conduct, and unfit to have the care and custody of the said Catalina."[34] The judge, James J. Davenport, ruled that Catalina Bustamento was illegally detained as a peon. According to historian William S. Kiser, Davenport "adjudicated that the biological mother, despite her marginalized social status as a peon, retained legal guardianship over her child and that neither the father nor the surrogate mother could claim the girl as a servant.... Thus, Davenport granted protection to the bond between mother and child and in so doing rendered a stunning legal blow to a tradition of servitude and fictive kinship that had proliferated in the Southwest for over two centuries."[35]

The 1857 *Mariana Jaremillo v. José de la Cruz Romero* court case outlined the condition of debt peonage for the first time. There was not a precedent before the 1857 case laying out the legal terms and conditions of debt peonage, which allowed *patrones* to mistreat peons, even after the judge set out the legal terms. However, this case did not outline the sexual condition of debt peonage. It was the *Marcellina Bustamento v. Juana Analla* case that established kinship ties and how sex functioned, mostly violently, in debt peonage. While Analla had her daughter under debt peonage by her *patrón* and the judge ruled it unconstitutional to keep the child or any child of a peon indebted, the *patrones* did not follow the law. The case exemplifies how kinship and sexual capital worked within debt peonage and how it was the poor Nuevomexicana's body that was exploited for her racialized sexuality. The case also exemplifies the dual capacity of the poor Nuevomexicana body, which I will explain in the next section. While this decision in 1857 began to shed light on the sexual and gendered condition of debt peonage in the Southwest, the implementation of the law was slow-moving. These foundational cases in the U.S. Southwest were legitimized in New Mexico and the Southwest borderlands, and reveal how the mediating forces of economies, social formations, and cultural practices shape the Nuevomexicana body and the borderlands.

The WPA Narratives: The "Dual Capacity" of the Nuevomexicana Body in Debt Peonage

How can we view cultural practices and production in New Mexico through these historical cases? What type of narrative authority do these texts claim in relation to the way they were produced? The resignification of the Nuevomexicana body and the issue of kinship in relation to sex, sexuality, and place is exemplified in the WPA stories. Memory is (re)constructed through the New Mexico WPA narratives, or as they are now published, *Women's Tales from the New Mexico WPA: La Diabla a Pie*; these were stories collected from the community of New Mexico, designed to help destitute writers during the Depression. An oral history project in the late 1930s and early 1940s attempting to recover New Mexico's Spanish past for the modern U.S. state, this New Deal–era federal initiative employed eligible writers to collect, transcribe, and submit stories about New Mexico's folktales. The WPA, or Work Projects Administration, formerly the Works Progress Administration, was known locally as *la diabla a pie* (the devil on foot).[36] There were similar projects that took place in rural states across the United States, particularly in the Deep South, where the tradition of collecting slave folk narratives goes back to the time of Reconstruction. Just as slave narratives are living traditions, so are the complex New Mexico WPA stories. However, unlike slave narratives in the nineteenth century, the New Mexico WPA stories were published by Tey Diana Rebolledo and Teresa Márquez in 2000 through the Recovering the U.S. Hispanic Literary Heritage Project, where more than sixty story collections by Annette Hesch Thorp and Lou Sage Batchen are accessible. The WPA narratives and the complicated position of Thorp and Batchen in collecting the stories reveal how race, gender, class, and sexuality shape New Mexico and U.S. empire. The stories also reveal the most intimate spaces, which uncover the political position of the Nuevomexicana woman.[37]

As Tey Diana Rebolledo explains, "In the later 1930s and early 1940s, the administration of Franklin D. Roosevelt sponsored the Federal Writers' Project, designed to help destitute writers during the Depression."[38] This was a "back-to-work" project where writers collected materials for a series of state guides. The main component of the project was interviews with elder residents, who gave information "document[ing] the culture and history as a 'human interest' section of the guides."[39] The first collection and writing of data began in 1933 under the Civil Works of Arts Project. While the interviewers and writers tapped the vein of folklore and culture, many of them did not speak the language of the people of New Mexico—Spanish—and even with the little Spanish they did know, could not recognize, as Rebolledo states, the "jocularity and linguistic playfulness of the phonetic and mimetic representation."[40] Along with this misinterpretation of the information, the interviews tended to romanticize New Mexican culture and the land. However, even with these problems, the representation of periphery populations within New Mexico weaves a rich narrative of the negotiation of memory.

I examine three WPA narratives in this section: "The Panic of 1862," "Mateo y Raquel," and "José Librado Gurulé's Recollections, 1867." "The Panic of 1862" is about the Perea family in Las Placitas, New Mexico. The Perea family flees their home because of the threat of Texan raiders, but they leave the peons behind to look over the *rancho*, during which time one sack of gold is stolen from their property. "Mateo y Raquel" looks at debt peonage from the vantage point of the peon's wife, who is indebted to the same *patrón* as in "The Panic of 1862," one of the richest men in the territory of New Mexico, José Leandro (or Leander) Perea.

"The Panic of 1862" was narrated on March 16, 1941, by José Librado Gurulé, who was born in 1850 lived in Las Placitas, New Mexico. He was a direct descendant of the twenty-one families of the San Antonio de Las Huertas land grant, and he was able to give Batchen information about Las Placitas because he held a list of *mayordomos* (people who looked after community water rights) and appears as a source for many of the WPA stories collection by Batchen.[41] Gurulé centers the male peon workers but incidentally exemplifies the glaring connections between the male peons, the female peons' dual capacity to produce and reproduce labor, and the accumulation of wealth for the *ricos*. The narrative illustrates how the *patrones* stretched the boundaries of the *Marcellina Bustamento v. Juana Analla* court case by indebting the young peons to watch over the *rancho* as they fled the Texans who wanted New Mexico to join them in their seccession from Mexico. When New Mexicans refused to join the secession, Texans raided their properties. The "panic" in the title would seem to refer to the fear and panic New Mexicans had when they heard of the Texans coming to raid Bernalillo, but that is not a correct reading. The "panic" actually refers to the *patrón* Don José Leander Perea flogging and punishing every man in the vicinity of his hacienda for what he accused the peons of—stealing his gold. The narrative begins, "A small army of natives at and around the town of Bernalillo were practically in bondage to Don José Leander Perea, head of the family."[42] The household had Native slaves and also peon workers in bondage. The large room was "a store, which supplied the needs of the Perea household, and at which every peon roundabout had a charge account. The peons lived in little adobe houses of their own, on land outside the Perea estates or in the Native villages in the vicinity. What they earned was applied on their accounts at the Perea store. Eight dollars a month was standard wage for the men."[43] As the story lays out the conditions of the peons, we get a glimpse into how the family of a male peon was utilized.

After the small town hears of the Texans raiding New Mexico, the Pereas all flee to Colorado and leave the peons to protect their *ranchos*. The peons helped pack the Pereas' bags and carriages. They also helped barricade the house and were given orders as to what to do when the Texans arrived. "The youths of the peons were left to guard the house and the adjoining property. They were to stick to their duties, no matter what."[44] Although it was illegal to utilize the family of the indebted peon, this did not stop most elite landholding Hispanos who held peons. While the condition of debt peonage was not supposed to be hereditary, this story exemplifies the contrary. The children guard the Perea house, and while the mother is not present in the story, it is her reproductive capacity that supplies the labor force of those in bondage, therefore utilizing her sex in this economy. However, she is removed from history, narration, and the national imaginary. When the Perea family returns to New Mexico, José Leandro Perea comes to find out that someone has stolen a fortune he and his son buried in the middle of the *rancho*. They automatically blame the children for taking the treasure. The narrative reads, "Without warning the youths left to guard the house were dragged into the fearsome presence of the Don José and his son Pedro. They were scared half to death."[45] After many men were accused, flogged, and tortured, with no one admitting guilt, Don Perea built a pillory, and all the men in the surrounding areas knew they were open and available to Perea's violence. This "panic" spread far and wide. It was José Librado Gurulé's father, Nicolás Gurulé, who confronted Don Perea when he accused two innocent men in his village of the theft. He "invoked the law" when he told Don Perea that the law needed to be involved in these floggings and that he could not accuse all the men while going on a vigilante tirade.[46] No one was ever found guilty, the extralegal flogging by Perea stopped, and Perea never found his gold.

The narrative authority in the "The Panic of 1862" is complex. The story is told by José Librado Gurulé, whose father was one of two men who intervened in the extralegal flogging of peons. Gurulé's father is twice removed from the actual narrative, as his son tells Batchen, who then records the story for publication. The WPA narratives mark but one instance of textual practices that take the main protagonist, the person telling the narrative, out of written authorial intent. Just as the Treaty of Guadalupe in 1848 was not written *by* the conquered but about them, so are the WPA narratives, even though they are being dictated. These are narratives and literary contestations of New Mexico historiography that attempt to create a memory of territorial community.⁴⁷ Stuck in between a *testimonio*, a mediated narrative about life and experiences told in first person to an interlocutor, and an *interview*, where an interlocutor asks pointed questions that tap into a vein of folklore culture, the WPA stories are narratives of "dependent production," where Rosaura Sánchez firmly roots *testimonios*.⁴⁸ The dependent production goes through multiple interlocutors where the collaborative effort produces the literary text. What becomes interesting is *how* these stories are then utilized. The final product for New Mexico, which included mostly anonymous narratives and interviews, was titled *New Mexico: A Guide to the Colorful State*. Rebolledo states outright that it was not only late in being published, but it was ugly, and many of the gathered narratives were never even published.⁴⁹ "The Panic of 1862" is written as free, indirect discourse that never centers the narrator or any other character. It thus falls in between autonomy and subjection, which exemplifies the lack of production time and care that went into crafting these narratives. It also exemplifies the time period of the Depression, with lack of aesthetics and lack of literary technique. While the dual capacity of the peon's wife—the production and reproduction of the economy—is evident in the periphery of the narrative, the production and reproduction of the actual literary text is sparse, uncontrolled in form and distribution, and not a commodity that had much value during its first publication run. In contradistinction to the Nuevomexicana sexual body, "The Panic of 1862," as a narrative to get people back to work, did little for the people who were actually dictating the story.

The 1857 *Marcellina Bustamento v. Juana Analla* case underscores the economic relations of the state that were tied to sex and labor. This case resignified the Nuevomexicana body politic by shifting how we understand the materiality and management of gender and sexuality, or sexual capital, in relation to sexual violence, production/reproduction, and proper femininity. "Mateo y Raquel" is a story about a man named José María who was held in bondage by Don José Leander Perea as well. José Librado Gurulé also gave Batchen this narrative, because his father was a contemporary of Mateo. Again, in this narrative, the authorial intent becomes blurred and is hard to track. Gurulé first tells the story of José María as a peon. This was a debt that José María's father left to him, which kept him in bondage and would then be carried by his son, Mateo. We witness firsthand the reproductive capacity of the peon's wife, even if she is not in bondage with her husband. The story states that José María received five dollars a month—an average of about seventeen cents a day—and had no days off because he was a sheepherder; the other *rancho* hands, however, had Sundays off if there was no urgent work. Food was provided to them but was minimal and just enough to keep them going. The "debt" to the *patrón*'s store was what kept the institution of debt peonage going, because by law the peons had to purchase whatever they needed from the *patrón*. The story goes, "It was the privalege [sic] and the custom of the rich dons to see to it that such [debt] grew rather than diminished. The law was on the side of the rich dons, in fact, they were the law unto themselves. They must have the labor of the poorer class (los peons) and they laid down all the rules of the game."[50] The condition of hereditary debt peonage was illegal in the Southwest, but as the passage above states, the rich *patrones* enforced, or ignored, the laws.

It was not until the 1857 *Marcellina Bustamento v. Juana Analla* case that the hereditary condition of debt peonage went to the New Mexico Territorial Supreme Court. The "Mateo y Raquel" story was set in the nineteenth century, pre-1848, but as the court case reveals, the conditions of debt peonage had hardly changed by the 1850s. As the story progresses, José María arrives late to work and receives a flogging and beating by the *patrón*. He cannot take the conditions of his bondage any longer and escapes. He "knew all about his debt to his patrón and how his patrón held money far above the life of any peon."[51] When he is captured and sentenced to hanging, his son, seventeen-year-old Mateo, takes his place in 1836. By the time the American invasion occurred in 1848, the institution of debt peonage was so embedded in the Southwest that the peons would not see their freedom for another twenty-one years.

While Mateo is at work acquiring more debt, his wife, Raquel, becomes the center of the story, as she raises their family, clothes them, teaches them, and raises goats for sustenance. Mateo can do nothing but work for the *patrón* and use his labor to build the landowner's *rancho* and care for the goods and animals the *patrón* traded and sold, but Raquel is the one producing and reproducing not only her own family, but for the family of Mateo's *patrón*, even though she is not an indebted peon. While Mateo cannot take care of his family because he is overworked and the *patrón* takes his weekly paycheck, the story reads, "But Raquel knew her needs and if Mateo could not meet them, she would meet them herself. . . . So Raquel set to work to acquire a goat."[52] Interestingly enough, the goats that Raquel raises, which symbolize production and survival, keep the family alive. They also represent Raquel's dual capacity and reproductive labor as emblems of fertility, vitality, and ceaseless energy. The generative power of the representation of the goats speaks to the abundance and duality of Raquel's positionality within New Mexico and the utilization of her racialized gender and sexuality. In fact, the metonymic meaning of the goat is emblematic of Raquel as the overworked body or "working like an animal." Raquel becomes associated with animalistic qualities and the excess that comes with the nonhuman. The narrative compels us to acknowledge that Raquel soon "had a few goats of her own."[53] Coupled with this reading, Raquel symbolically reproduces the peons and is likened to the goat as reproduction. Linguist Ronald Langacker conceives of metonymy as a reference-point phenomenon in which one conceptual entity, the reference point, affords mental access to another conceptual entity, the desired target.[54] If we think of metonymy as more than a figure of speech that consists of using the name of one thing for that of something else it is associated with, and instead as a discourse that interrelates them to form a new, complex meaning, the metonymy of the literary archive enunciates the historical trajectory of racialized sexuality.

She also becomes associated with the excess of the primal figure of the nineteenth-century westward expansion. The goat represents Raquel and the Mexican women of the border as open for sexual exploitation, utilizing the offspring of their fertile bodies for trade. Through travel narratives and other discourses in the nineteenth century, readers are confronted with discursive constructions of Mexican women as whores, excessive, and licentious, to name a few. In her archival research, Deena Gonzalez has consulted over 250 travelogues, diaries, and printed collections in New Mexico, only to find that Mexican women were referred to as treacherous, flirtatious, and seductive. They were "swarthy thieves and liars," and their dress was a "study in negligence."[55] As the poor, racialized Nuevomexicana takes on meaning, it is the metonym that makes a new meaning, which is carried on in the present day. As we move from agrarian and mercantile capital to global capital, her sexual role shifts, but the signification of her body remains the same. As Rodrigo Lazo clarifies in his seminal essay on the archive, the history of the modern archives is inextricable from the establishment of nation-states; therefore we must read for *how* memory is constructed up and against the national discursive ideology that permeates not only the archive but also the subjugation that keeps certain violences out of the archive in the first place.[56] Narrative authority falls to the wayside because of the dependent production of creating the text, so reading for metonymy is not only reading against the grain for absences; it is also reading for what is present and putting the cognitive pieces together to see how they frame nation-state discourse. This means that we see a shift from the poor, racialized female on the border to a productive body in relation to the needs of Hispanos who were desperately attempting to maintain power in their new territory.

As the narrative progresses, we witness just how important Raquel's body is to her family and the economic system of debt peonage. While Mateo's five dollars a month was applied to his store credit, Raquel kept her family alive with clothing and bedding from the goatskin, and sustenance from the milk and meat. Her productive labor produces a livable situation for her family. Raquel utilizes not only her labor to sustain her children and husband, but also her reproductive capacity to reproduce the labor force of peons. The productive capacity of racialized sexuality becomes a tool for exploitation. Like Marxist feminist Leopoldina Fortunati, who unpacks reproductive labor in the transition from pre-capitalism to capitalism, I explore an older economic form, debt peonage, and the reproductive labor capacity inherent to it.[57] This chapter also considers the sexual economy of the institution of debt peonage, the *rancho*, and the hacienda system of land grants as constitutive of the emergence of capital accumulation.

Fortunati argues that through previous modes of production, the aim within specific communities was the reproduction of individuals and the *production of use-value*.[58] In these modes of production, the aim is the *production of exchange value*—that is, the creation of value for value. Fortunati states that production is "the creation of value [while] reproduction appears as the creation of non-value ... posited as natural production."[59] In an attempt to expand upon Marx and rethink female reproduction, Fortunati thinks through how the reproduction of individuals implies the reproduction of labor power; this is because bodies only have exchange value and cannot create value for themselves. Thus, bodies can only "present themselves in relation to their capacity to produce" and are offered as a "commodity by [the person in] exchange for [the body's] exchange-value."[60] Debt peonage, while a residual mode of the economy, simultaneously reproduces the conditions for capitalism and exists within it.[61] For contemporary Marxist thinkers, reproduction has a double meaning. The first refers to the reproduction of labor power and the worker. This is where Marxist feminists make a huge intervention in the definition of "value." The second, according to Jasper Bernes, is called "social reproduction," which refers to the entire process by which the capital/labor relationship is reproduced.[62] This means that the industries involved in the circulation of commodities, the industries designed to manage the reproduction of capital, and the administration of the flow of goods and bodies are all part of social reproduction.[63] And while Raquel's labor is all unwaged labor, we must take into consideration how her body is utilized to produce capital. I entertain Raquel's body and sex as being a part of the social reproduction of the economy of debt peonage because her sexual labor is congealed as part of the way the economy functions.

In my own rethinking of reproductive labor, we can remap Fortunati's critique of Marx by reconceptualizing how Nuevomexicanas within debt peonage (whether a peon or a wife to a peon) have dual characteristics through racialized sex (their children constantly replenish the economic system) and their own function to produce commodities for the *patrón*. The peon is not a commodity but occupies a unique position where he earns a low wage but never sees it. His meager wage goes directly toward his bill at the store of the *patrón*, who moderately clothes and feeds him. Raquel's reproductive capacity, as the wife of a peon, yields economic profit for the *patrón* by producing children who will become peons. Even though it is illegal to force the children into bondage after their parents are dead or cannot work, reality tells a different story, as we see in the narrative. As the story comes to a close, "Mateo became very ill. He could not work. His pay was cut off and he was told to 'get out.' And as all the curanderas yerba failed to cure him he was ordered to send his son Juan to take his place and assume the just debt to the patron, and likewise add to the account at the store."[64]

Patrones and *ricos* like Perea utilized their peons to their maximum capacity, even though the peons were "part of their family." As exhibited above, it was not uncommon for peons to exhaust themselves under debt peonage and either die or run away with their debt unpaid. As part of the same WPA project, José Librado Gurulé tells a third narrative about himself, a young sixteen-year-old indebted boy who had gone to Missouri and back on the Santa Fe Trail as a herder, guide, and retainer for Perea. The captain of the freighting outfit was Esquipulo Romero, El Capitán.[65] Gurulé remembers "some ten wagons ... loaded with wool, each of them drawn by five spans of oxen; for the road they were heavy with mud, especially on the *plana* (level ground)."[66] The wives and mothers would continue to work their own household, plus the household of the Pereas at times. Many of the young boys signed on with Perea, seeking sustenance to help their families survive, but more of them were indebted to him through their fathers. The *ricos/patrones* benefited tremendously from this indebted help, which was made available to them by the Nuevomexicanas who occupied a dual capacity. Perea benefited from mercantile trade and the beginnings of transnational trade through the sexual capital of debt peonage while growing his fortune through shipments and trading of American and European products. In the Mexican Archive of New Mexico, the trade logs show that Perea remitted over $40,000 worth of merchandise to Chihuahua, Zacatecas, and Aguas Caliente.[67] In all these trips down the Santa Fe Trail and into Mexico, Perea's peons drove the caravan and made the trades. By 1867, Perea was one of the wealthiest men in New Mexico. Susan Boyle states that "periodic financial summaries between 1851 and 1875 show that American business firms considered him to be one of the most prominent men in the territory."[68] By 1875, Perea's wealth had grown to $800,000, with $100,000 in real estate and $75,000 in sheep. The recorded WPA debt peonage stories show how Perea utilized the Nuevomexicana body that is not legible to borderland history and how *ricos* like Perea upheld capitalist relations through the sexual capital and economy of debt peonage.[69]

Upholding the Normative Nation: Gender Norms and Space in Cabeza de Baca

Fabiola Cabeza de Baca was not nearly as wealthy as Perea, but she came from an elite family residing in the village of La Liendre, eighteen miles southeast of Las Vegas. Her narrative tells the stories of her peons and ranch hands in the nineteenth century and how that lifestyle was violently taken away from her at the hands of white settlers and homesteaders. In relation to the WPA stories, Cabeza de Baca tells her own nostalgic story for a New Mexico of the past. Cabeza de Baca upholds "proper" gender and sexual norms throughout her memoir that keep the hierarchical system of debt peonage firmly in place and cement the juxtaposition of the "excessive" racialized female in relation to the "proper" female through memory and language. In doing so, she maintains the spatial structure that privatizes land for the benefit of one person, keeping intact inheritance language that is invested in heteronormative genealogies of the nation. In complete contradistinction to the New Mexico WPA stories, which reveal the gendered and sexual condition of the economic systems of the Southwest borderlands, Cabeza de Baca's memoir reinforces and legitimizes the nation's gender and sexual codes to establish herself and her family as gatekeepers of a progressing nation, with a notion that is challenged when her position as an elite landholder is called into question. While the Supreme Court of the Territory of New Mexico cases tell the actual history of the region and how the poor and racialized female body was utilized in relation to capital and wealth, Cabeza de Baca utilizes a third-person narrative strategy through a masculine gender to reinforce the sexual economies of the Southwest borderlands and establish the inability of Nuevomexicana female bodies to ever satisfy gender and sexual norms because of their racialized sexuality. This reinforcement helps establish properness and participation in U.S. imperialism and empire, while simultaneously faulting it for dispossessing elite landholding families in New Mexico. The Cabeza de Baca family was an acting agent in Indigenous and poor New Mexicans' inferior positionality.

Similar to the WPA stories that romantically remember the past to comment on the present, Cabeza de Baca's memoir nostalgically looks back on a better time and place in New Mexico. However, her text is not mediated by an interlocutor; rather, she employs a male narrator to tell her stories in her memoir. She focuses heavily on space to maintain hierarchal familial and worker relations within privatized land, which solidifies the inheritance of property and enforces heteronormative sexuality. In other words, the memoir reinforces normative gender and sexual roles and examines inherited land and the employees that work the land. Published in 1954, *We Fed Them Cactus* tells the story of the shifting space and evolution of El Llano, New Mexico. Landscape and people are woven tightly together in this narrative of a heterogeneous past. Cabeza de Baca writes her memoir as she witnesses the shifting of her own social space as a result of the nuclear landscape in New Mexico, ongoing racial stratification, and economic decline in 1945. Her writings reflect this tension between the past and the present. In the face of a nuclear wasteland, Cabeza de Baca retreats back into a New Mexico of the past. The first nuclear bomb was developed under the Manhattan Project in 1942 and located in Los Alamos, about twenty-one miles from the Cabeza de Baca hacienda. The "A-bomb" was eventually tested on the White Sands Proving Ground near Alamogordo, New Mexico. Cabeza de Baca narrates the social landscape of El Llano and states, "In the pre-Hispanic era, the Llano Indians walked—with Spaniards came horses and the life of the Indians changed. Then came *Ciboleros* using *carretas* pulled by oxen to go into the Llano for their meat supply, and later wagons with horses began to wind their way over the Llano's rough roads."[70] She packs this multi-genre autobiographical memoir with residual, dominant, and emergent modes of production for different groups and employees on El Llano, but one thing always remains constant: her investment in the hierarchy of the employees, or peons, on her grandfather's land, which intersect seamlessly with her unyielding investment in the gender and sexual norms that construct stability for her. She states, "I can remember my paternal grandfather's sheep camps and the men who worked for him."[71] She also briefly acknowledges the many histories of colonization and loss. And while she does not go into a historical account of the discreet erasure of "Indians" (as she terms them) in the text, she speaks to how social and labor relations between groups literally configured the spaces on El Llano. Genaro Padilla states of *Cactus*, "Traces of Mexican American lives do indeed reside in autobiographical narratives that transform life into history into textual permanence: memoirs so long out of print they are nearly forgotten; social and cultural histories in which the 'I' encloses itself in a language of topographic identity, cultural practice, and political intrigue; diaries, family histories, personal poetry, and collections of self-disclosing correspondence."[72] As exemplified in the quote above, Cabeza de Baca utilizes the "I" to unveil a forgotten history when she states that she remembers her grandfather's sheep camps and the workers who labored for her grandfather. But whose history is she unveiling and remembering? This construction of autobiography, or in this case memoir, assumes a subject position above, against, and within social, cultural, and political spaces and relations in the United States, as Padilla describes above. However, in an antagonistic relationship to the community, the "I" in *Cactus* predates the historical displacement of Hispanos with the coming of Anglo settlers after 1848 and speaks from a position of privilege that maintains gendered and sexual codes and customs that are in stark opposition to the experiences of poor Nuevomexicanas in the same regional location.

Chicana/o scholarship first criticized *We Fed Them Cactus* for being an elitist and imperialist text while simultaneously negating the many histories of settler colonialism and dispossession. Cabeza de Baca identifies with her Euro-Spanish genealogy and positions herself as a privileged subject who lost everything to Anglo colonization.[73] Current Chicana/o scholarship, however, examines the text through a different lens—that of settler colonialism and critical gender and sexuality studies, among others. Utilizing a discourse of resistance in the context of U.S. empire and dispossession, Padilla argues that *We Fed Them Cactus* is complicit on the surface and resistant in the subtext. Padilla states that *Cactus* resists Anglo colonization through "the dense texture of language and reified memory."[74] Pointing out small "whispers" of resistance throughout the novel, Padilla argues, "In such whispers we discover those gaps in the narrative where the Native cultural 'I' voices itself against the imperial 'Other' to speak through the bars of the ideological prison in which it is confined."[75] From a Chicana feminist perspective, Rebolledo suggests that Cabeza de Baca's nostalgic and romantic view of New Mexico, which some Chicano scholars claim to be an internalization of class, sexual, and racial attitudes because of her socialization process, should be reevaluated and pushed even further than Padilla's critical limits. Rebolledo maintains there are "narrative strategies of resistance" that are visible in the text through Cabeza de Baca's recognition of her colonized identity, her sense of a communal sentimental past, and her blurring of various literary forms and genres.[76] While these perspectives are valuable and have merit, the running narrative of resistance in early Hispano, Mexican American, and contemporary Chicana/o literary discourse must be troubled by the multiple forms of power that are not all equivalent, particularly when thinking about economic systems, sexual violence, and the peons on Cabeza de Baca's land.

Fabiola Cabeza de Baca was born near Las Vegas, New Mexico, on May 16, 1894, into a distinguished, landowning, ranching family. At the age of four, after her mother passed away, Cabeza de Baca's paternal grandmother raised her on her grandfather's hacienda across the Gallinas River from the village of La Liendre, eighteen miles southeast of Las Vegas. As someone who was intellectually curious and had a family with the means to support her interests, Cabeza de Baca received her teaching certificate in 1913 and later received her bachelor's degree from New Mexico Normal in 1921. In 1927 she joined the Agriculture Extension Service, where she served as an extension agent. A copious writer, Cabeza de Baca published articles for local newspapers, published two cookbooks, *Historic Cookery* in 1939 and *The Good Life: New Mexican Food* in 1949, and *We Fed Them Cactus* in 1954. As an agent of the state's project of modernization, similar to the WPA collection stories, Cabeza de Baca was rooted in the preservation of traditional Hispano culture while simultaneously undertaking, as Maureen Reed states, "work that required her to inform clients about the benefits of making modern changes in the way they managed their homes."[77] Rebolledo states that Fabiola Cabeza de Baca came from an "old, landed, upper-class New Mexican family. [She] extols the Spanish (and not the mestiza or Indian) heritage and sees the past as a utopia in the pastoral tradition where humans were integrated with nature and tied to the land."[78] As with any conflicted colonial subject, Cabeza de Baca's desire to position herself within a Spanish colonial past speaks to multiple histories of loss, violence, and domination. It is a method to map her way through her elite landholding class status, a racist class structure, and the ever-changing land relations in the geographic Southwest. While she centers the male voice through her memories, folk stories, and even narrator (El Cuate), Cabeza de Baca utilizes gender and sexual norms to reveal how the private space of the "home" reinforces the production of nationalism through the bodies of poor and racialized bodies.

This reinforcement of gender and sexual norms, which attempts to prove "proper" femaleness, is exemplified through the narrator, El Cuate. El Cuate is the ranch cook for the Cabeza de Baca hacienda and also the main storytelling voice in the memoir. There is a collision of El Cuate's voice mediated through Cabeza de Baca's vis-à-vis the stories she remembers him telling her when she was young. She tells the reader, "We were always glad when El Cuate spat out his tobacco. We knew he was in the mood for storytelling. What stories he could tell! There were stories of buffalo hunts, Indian attacks, about Comanche trade, of rodeos and fiestas."[79] From this point on, we receive the narration through El Cuate, but from the perspective of Cabeza de Baca. This is very telling of her gender politics. She upholds the stability of traditional gender roles in her decision to have El Cuate narrate more than half of the memoir with his stories about how things "used to be" on El Llano. Karen Roybal states that Cabeza de Baca's ventriloquizing through El Cuate is an "androgynous rhetorical style" that provides a "middle voice" to inhabit both the masculine and feminine literary voice, which gives Cabeza de Baca the same amount of power as men, the typical storytellers of the time.[80] While I agree with Roybal that masculine storytellers were typical of the time period, I expand on her claim that Cabeza de Baca politicizes the appropriation of the masculine voice to reclaim her agency through a gender-modern lens.[81] The rhetorical strategy of occupying a male narrator might very well allow Cabeza de Baca to transcend her position as a female subject in the borderlands; however, she continuously reinforces the heteronormative relations of males and females by cementing the male figures as authoritative and the female figures as centers of the domestic space. Cabeza de Baca was a modern woman, as exemplified by her position as an agent of the Agriculture Extension Service, but she was not a modernist writer or one that broke with romanticization of place and conventional gender roles. Roybal reminds us that her position was complex and inherently against modernist formal innovation. However, her celebratory and romantic writing style goes against her fragmented identity of her present, which could have opened up doors for her to experiment with genre and characterization.[82] Yet this was not the case in utilizing El Cuate. El Cuate does not tell only stories of "male perspectives" that Cabeza de Baca was not allowed to witness, forcing her to utilize his voice. He also relates stories that Cabeza de Baca could very well have told herself, such as the story of the "Fiestas at San Hilario," where "every man, woman, and child in village, as well as families from the surrounding plaza, had gathered."[83] Ultimately, she depends on the same heteropatriarchal norms that give her power through her privilege.

Later, when she takes the text back into her own voice (the first time her "autobiographical" voice returns), she discusses the traditions of the "home" and domestic life, stating, "The women on the Llano and Ceja played a great part in the history of the land. It was a difficult life for a woman, but she had made her choice when in the marriage ceremony she had promised to obey and to follow her husband."[84] The heteronormative family structure remains front and center in her analysis of El Llano and the domestic space, which is very much tied to maintaining a Hispano/Nuevomexicano national identity. In this discourse, the figure of the woman acts as a "primary marker of an essential, inviolable communal identity of tradition."[85] The conversation surrounding a Hispano nationalist voice leads us to interrogate, as Anne McClintock states in her examination of nationalist discourse, how gender reveals the construction of the nation in terms of familial and domestic metaphors, "where 'the woman' is enshrined as both the symbolic center and boundary marker of the nation as 'home' and 'family.'"[86] Furthermore, the discourse that surrounds the domestic space and the nation utilizes the vocabulary of motherland, something that one is "naturally" tied to. This association of women within the private space reinforces the merging of nation/community, as the woman occupies the role of selfless mother and caretaker in the household. Cabeza de Baca does not question this role; rather, she utilizes this very nationalist rhetoric, not only in her discussion of the home space on El Llano, but also in her remembering of hierarchical social relations, where the employees on her grandfather's ranch were all "family." This privileged positionality allows us to understand how the distinct economic systems in the Southwest and South are connected—though not conflated—in terms of establishing alternative kinships. Cabeza de Baca's staunch stance on creating a New Mexico "Hispano" voice exemplifies the collision of colonialism, racism, empire, and sexism.

Continuing to uphold a gendered language that situates her as "proper," Cabeza de Baca constructs the space of El Llano as masculine and passed down through generations. El Llano is "vast" and "strong" and curves along the Llano's high northern and western rim.[87] Cabeza de Baca describes the space along El Llano as an "eyebrow, above the plain."[88] This phallic construction of the land is paired with a discussion of the "inheritance" of traditions from family and the "unsung heroes of an industry which was [her] livelihood for generations."[89] *We Fed Them Cactus* delineates distinct geographical places that are permeated with meaning as a result of social interactions and cannot deny the significant gendered relations occurring as Cabeza de Baca maps the past onto the present. Space becomes a place when it is infused with history and meaning.[90] Place incarnates the experiences and aspirations of a people. Cabeza de Baca moves us from the utopian "wide open spaces" of El Llano, where her connection to land is immense and almost religious, to places of interrelatedness as well as spaces of complete foreclosure that impede any type of utopia from forming. Instructive in the way she sees spaces, Cabeza de Baca *tells* the reader that the hierarchy of who owned space was likely a given in the vast land and doesn't interrogate the ways in which the use of space is heteronormative and nationalist. She writes, "Then, of course, herding was one of the few kinds of employment available in New Mexico. If a man became indebted to a *rico*, he was in bond slavery to repay. Those in debt had a deep feeling of honesty, and they did not bother to question whether the system was right or wrong."[91] And she does not question this system of bondage either. Later she tells us that her paternal grandfather was one of the *patrones* who held the indebted people accountable on El Llano.

Fabiola Cabeza de Baca's great grandfather, Luis María Cabeza de Baca, *el patrón*, lay claim to a swath of land on the plains of northeastern New Mexico in 1821. Luis María was a prominent sheep man and conducted business along the Santa Fe Trail and into Mexico, where he took a significant trip that made him a lot of money in 1837. According to Thomas Sheridan, Cabeza de Baca and his seventeen sons and son-in-law "received title to the grant of Las Vegas Grandes, which stretched for more than half a million acres east of the Pecos River."[92] The Cabeza de Baca family herded their sheep on this vast grassland for no more than a decade after Mexican Independence in 1821, when the Comanches forced them to retreat to their Peña Blanca hacienda on the Rio Grande, where Fabiola Cabeza de Baca was raised by her grandmother. Luis María Cabeza de Baca did very little to develop the land and gained most of his cultural capital through genealogy (Spanish) and the dominant mode of economy at that time, which was the sheep trade and mercantile capitalism. In fact, in the summer of 1837, Luis María Cabeza de Baca took a caravan to Chihuahua and Sonora loaded with three hundred blankets, two hundred varas (units) of rough cloth, and eleven sarapes.[93] While "nearly 400,000 sheep valued at 200,000 pesos were driven south, accounting for 47 percent of the total measurable exports for the period," it was the smaller cargoes like Cabeza de Baca's that stood to garner real profits.[94] Even with the dominance of the trade and mercantile market being controlled by the Chávez, Otero, Sandoval, Perea, and Yrrissarris families, the way different merchandise had different value signifies inferior and superior positions that are the precursor to what we know as our global capital moment.[95] And while Cabeza de Baca did not have as much trade capital as the other more influential *ricos* in New Mexico, Brooks reminds us that these smaller traders straddled the spaces between bison economy, the Navajo trade, and the Mexican exports sector while integrating the domestic production of weavers and knitters from their own households.[96] The domestic production mostly came from indebted peons in the household. With the cultural capital that came with being *ricos* in New Mexico and the profits from not only trade caravans, which peons led, but also the domestic production from their own households, the Cabeza de Bacas were part of the contingency of New Mexicans who profited off the sexual capital of debt peonage, just as the Pereas did. New Mexican *ricos* were attempting to expand their wealth before settlers seized their territory and resources, and the poor Nuevomexicana body was at the center of that expansion.

Fabiola and the Cabeza de Baca family saw many forms of racist ideologies and dispossession at the turn of the century. However, the Cabeza de Baca family held cultural capital during the nineteenth century that ruptured when New Mexico began to modernize. Cabeza de Baca was a modern woman who expressed a spatial relationship to the land that was changing with modernization, which interrupted a normative attachment to *her* land. This means that while Cabeza de Baca had a dependency on the land and resources, this dependency relied on upholding hierarchy, gender norms, and inheritance on *her* land. El Llano becomes a type of Foucauldian heterotopia, where "mixed [and] joint experience[s]" are juxtaposed with each other in one single space/place.[97] From the dependency on the wet and ripe landscape, about which she states, "I began to understand that without rain our subsistence would be endangered," to the communal use of land for food when "caravans met on the way" to hunt for buffalo, "it became a small world, this big land of New Mexico."[98] The geography of *Cactus* fetishizes these past sites that are infused with meaning. Through her construction of "properness," space in this memoir can never be imagined as anything else but owned property. The moments of geographic nostalgia exemplify the impossibility of alternative kinship spaces. Cabeza de Baca reminds us, "The women on the Llano and Ceja played a great part in the history of the land. It was a difficult life for a woman, but she has made her choice when in the marriage ceremony she has promised to obey and follow her husband."[99] She goes on to say that the wives of *patrones* kept the domestic space running and were trained to handle plants to cure their household of sickness. In contrast, the racialized women in the WPA narrative had no choice but to function through sexual capital for survival. The *ricos*, like the Cabeza de Baca family, chose to pass on inheritance through "proper" forms of sex. We can thus identify nostalgia in the context of *Cactus* as reimagining and reconstituting her particular fraught relation to multiple sites of power and as rethinking the very notions of "home" and nostalgia. Negotiating multiple geographic sites that have been permanently ruptured by U.S. empire, Cabeza de Baca narrates the transformation of space and place, or as Brady states, "the turn from the lived, embodied space to the abstract space of capitalism."[100] El Llano shifts from an imagined "abundant" space where "different communities ... banded together for protection against the building of fences on their grazing land and to help each other with crops and farming," to a place of homesteaders that saw New Mexico as the "land of promise."[101] When we prioritize the space of the feudal mode of production over time, we begin to rethink the limits of spatial heteronormative inheritance tied to a capitalist political economy committed to "progress."

Kerwin Lee Klein states, "Where we once spoke of 'folk history' or 'popular history' or 'oral history' or 'public history' or even 'myth,' we now employ memory as a meta historical category that subsumes all these various terms."[102] Memory went from an archaic mode of being to a remaking of historical imagination. Memory, and more specifically a critical memory, that intervenes in a conventional historical narrative maintains close ties with other forms of folk, myth, oral, and popular histories and establishes an inextricable link between a past, present, and future while (re)mapping history. Because American history is fraught with one-sided and limited viewpoints, a critical memory that establishes links to the past is crucial. Geographically speaking, New Mexico is a location where multiple histories collide as a result of colonization and settlement. Klein states that memory is oftentimes paired as an antithesis or antonym to history. This contrast suggests that memory is positioned to counter history at any moment. On the complete opposite spectrum, memory can serve as a synonym for history, oftentimes "softening" the term "history" while giving it a relatable connotation. While memory can certainly add depth and context to traditional historical accounts, Klein suggests, "We need to reconsider the relationship between historical imagination and the new memorial consciousness, and we may begin by mapping the contours of the new structures of memory. Memories appeal to us partly because they project an immediacy we feel has been lost from history."[103] From a Chicana feminist perspective, the uncovering of the gender and sexual condition of the Nuevomexicana within debt peonage is a retrofitted memory.[104] This is a new gendered political identity produced through history that creates new contestated identities and political practices. Thus, memory complicates structural systems of oppression but does not necessarily function completely outside of these ideological systems. History is not a linear model of isolated events that collapses into the present. With New Mexico occupying such a conflicted historical space in the Southwest, it seems necessary to turn toward a politics of critical memory to interrogate the (mis)constructed histories of violent colonization, racial, gender, and class conflict, and dispossession. Remembering the residual economic system of debt peonage in New Mexico unveils the distinct social relations and gendered and sexual conditions of racialized sexuality through the dual capacity of the Nuevomexicana body; it also uncovers its political position through geography, place, and personhood.

While Cabeza de Baca provides us with moments where she positions land, space, and place as a priority over time, her shifts to discourses of land-ownership and inheritance are much more abundant and confirm her status as a descendant of the landowning class. She states, "My grandfather inherited Baca Location Number One, known as El Valle Grande, near Los Alamos of atomic renown."[105] She also inherited certain gender norms, including a paternal language of sexual norms that limits the possibility of space and place for women. Her positioning within the context of an elite subjectivity while simultaneously working within a conflicted context of colonialism and modernity is evident throughout the memoir. There are three main frames that contextualize this memoir: the colonial time, the changing time during the rise of the U.S. empire, and her present, modern time. We can also refer to them in relation to residual, dominant, and emergent modes of production. Cabeza de Baca's present, modern time is examined from the perspective of U.S. empire. But she also offers a perspective of the past during the emergence of U.S. empire, through the memories of El Cuate, who recalls the pre-1848 colonial times. The ideology of private property, tied to U.S. ideologies and white supremacy, serves to introduce the new emerging modernity of the Southwest. These multiple time frames allow us to see colonialism and modernity running parallel to each other. Through gendered and temporal discourses, Cabeza de Baca seeks to make known her entitled position, and for this reason, given New Mexico dispossession, she reinforces bloodlines. At the same time, and as if in contradiction, she attempts to establish a romanticized, ruptured time of communal land not tied to inheritance on El Llano by stating, "There have been many class distinctions in the larger towns, but the families on the Llano had none; the *empleados* and their families were as much part of the family as the *patrón* and his own children. It was a very democratic way of life."[106] The power politics involved in this nostalgic representation ignore the very real power structures under the guise of alternative kinships within the domestic space. As stated before, while the *patrón/peones* system was structured around dependent interpersonal relationships, the land clearly belonged to the *patrón*, and there was a definite, if not transparent, hierarchy with divisions of labor based on racial constructions that go back to Spanish colonial times. In Cabeza de Baca's memoir, identity is a flattening notion that does not take into account the discourses of private and public space or the division of gender and sexuality tied to social location. Identity becomes problematic because "the home" space, where her family and the *empleados* live, has different meanings for the two groups. "Home space" for Cabeza de Baca means the domestic center where private space is primary. For the *empleados*, "home space" means the home they labor and live in.

While Cabeza de Baca's notion of a Hispano identity is tied to a particular elite space of home, where the *patrón's* wife upholds the space of the hacienda, the identity of the *empleados* is tied to the space of the workers' quarters, the space of production and reproduction. As critical sites of political, ideological, and discursive struggle through which hegemonic ideologies are questioned, the memoir should aim to work out processes of racialization, gendering, and class positionality. However, Cabeza de Baca does not attempt to do this. Even though the *casta* system was abolished long before the United States took control of the lands that were Northern Mexico, the racial sentiments of those who owned the land and place were still dominant. The Cabeza de Bacas' claim to Hispano-ness is tightly linked to Euro-Spanish subjectivity. And while the Cabeza de Bacas were rightfully displaced from their land, first by the Comanches and later by homesteaders during U.S. imperialism, they held peons and desired a softer version of Manifest Destiny that would include rich racialized bodies.

Like the rest of the *ricos*, Cabeza de Baca utilizes a discourse of heteropatriarchy and paternalism that is very much invested in biological affiliations and inheritance, a positioning that forecloses a space of alternative kinships that dismantles uneven power relations and subsumes a "proper" type of sexuality and femininity. While she forecloses this space, she simultaneously constructs a domestic space where the family structure remains centered. It is out of the family home and the traditional family structure that the stories emerge and are paternalistically told within the familiar/familial place. The concept of the nation also remains centered, which is nostalgically tied to the home, communal identities, and inheritance. The woman maintained the family and "held a very important place in the villages and ranches on the Llano," as discussed previously.[107] Gender plays an important role in precluding spaces of communal possibility and alternative kinships by keeping places intact and maintaining a specific order for the nation. This type of discourse from Cabeza de Baca's memoir also concretely fixes normative gender roles as pure forms of an archaic past, a sexual purity. "Deviant" or sexual bodies of production (poor Nuevomexicanas) that fall outside of this construction of a Hispano identity are not included in the literary form of this memoir, but more importantly, the queering of Cabeza de Baca's voice as she takes on the persona of El Cuate engenders a form of "resistance" that falls into the nationalist logic: a woman speaking on behalf of the men of El Llano, disguised as a male ranch hand. In her fraught and complacent positionality within race, class, *and* gender, Cabeza de Baca chooses to nostalgically remember the places of the past that are informed with discourses of racism, colonialism, and sexism in complex and contradictory ways. Ruptured in a myriad of ways, nostalgia enables Cabeza de Baca to (attempt) to confront these confluences of violent structures in an idealized past while occupying violent spaces in the modern present/future.

Conclusion

The tension in these three narratives and two foundational court cases reveals and then attempts to hide the inherent contradictions in Nuevomexicana female subjectivity and the economic systems that revolve around the historical conditions of racialized gender and sexuality. The two New Mexico Territorial Supreme Court cases define the boundaries of debt peonage in the Southwest borderlands, while also setting the terms for how debt peonage was a sexual economic system. In relation to the WPA narratives, I have elucidated how the peripheral bodies of poor, brown women in the narratives are the actual main component of keeping debt peonage running and also the main component in accumulating wealth. Her body serves as the catalyst for production and reproduction in the sexual economy of debt peonage. This historical moment exemplifies how one-way racialized sexuality had a material effect through violent heteronormative conditions. And even though the *Marcellina Bustamento v. Juana Analla* case ruled that it was unconstitutional to indebt children of peons, *patrones* continued to do it well after it was ruled illegal. On the other side of the spectrum, elite landholding women in New Mexico, like Fabiola Cabeza de Baca, upheld normative gender and sex norms through inheritance language and land. The bodies of the poor, racialized Nuevomexicana women were sites of violent productive and reproductive labor that produced wealth. The elite, landholding Hispanas juxtaposed with the *mestiza* peons exemplify a rich history of social, economic, and political entanglements that were constructed by Spanish colonialism and maintained by regional wealth. The collision of the romanticized past of New Mexico comments not only on the changing place, dispossession, and displacement of Nuevomexicanas in New Mexico, but also on how racialized sexuality juxtaposed "proper" femininity in the growing Southwest borderlands. The materiality of sex for women of color on the border effects sexual politics and life value. But where does history go from here? There is a shift in how poor, racialized female bodies are consumed at the turn of the century. We see a shift from productive sexual bodies in the Southwest borderlands to unproductive sexual bodies.

In conjunction with the intervention of the brown female serving as a dual-capacity economic marker, this chapter also interrogates how narrative authority gets asserted, controlled, denied, and manipulated. The WPA narratives all serve as examples of dependent production, where the narrative falls in an in-between space where the production of the text is embedded in "custom" more than literary technique or authority. Meanwhile, Cabeza de Baca's memoir negotiates narrative authority through the ventriloquizing of El Cuate to reinforce gender and sexual roles and therefore cements inheritance through monogamous sex in her construction of New Mexico. As the United States pushed westward and life transformed at the end of the nineteenth century on the backs of women of color, the move from agriculture, cattle ranching, and mercantile capital to industrialism and global capital shifted the material utilization of racialized sex and sexuality. Merchant capitalism opened up new markets and modes of economy that would change the landscape of the frontier. While Mexican Americans were navigating the large-scale trade market, a new economic system was taking hold: monopoly capitalism and industrialism. And at the turn of the century, poor brown female bodies went from being a productive force in the borderlands, as exemplified by the racialized sexual economy of debt peonage, to the unproductive racialized sexuality of prostitution.

CHAPTER FIVE

Technology of "Unproductive" Brown Bodies
The Political Economy of Prostitution and Racialized Sexual Pathology in Arizona at the Turn of the Century

In 1898, George H. Smalley, the editor of the *Tucson Daily Citizen*, supposedly ran a story about a madam of a bawdy house in Tucson, Arizona's, Gay Alley who was "fair, fat, and forty."[1] Decades later, in 1954, Smalley described the encounter with the Tucson madam in the reminiscences section of the newspaper titled "Arizona Album: Pioneer Anecdotes—Fair, Fat, and Forty," in which he tells readers of the *Daily* that she was a businesswoman and influential in local politics. The story goes that one evening she appeared at a meeting of the local Common Council in Adobe Hall and confronted the mayor and other council members with a "menacing gesture," shouting, "Gentlemen, I came to warn you that if you do not have the girls kicked out of the saloons and gambling houses, I will move my girls from Gay Alley to a house I own up near the Methodist church. Those dames are interfering with my business, and every one of you fellers know it as well as I do."[2] As Smalley notes, her threat was not to be taken lightly; she controlled many votes, and the gamblers and saloon men who bought the women in her house were even more powerful.[3] The mayor smiled and told her that he would appoint members of his council to investigate the matter.

According to Smalley, after his story about the council meeting came out, he was sitting at his desk at the *Tucson Daily Citizen* when he felt something hard against his back. He heard the click of her six-shooter as the madam cocked it and denounced him with raw language. Though this woman "had a bad reputation," he later recalls, she still had an enormous amount of local political power. She told him if he ever put her name in the paper again she would shoot a hole so big in him a rat would be able to jump through it. After threatening Smalley's life, she turned to leave, but not without first clarifying, "I may be fair, and I may be fat, but I am not forty."[4]

As colorful as the story is, it is nowhere to be found in the *Daily Tucson* newspaper archive for 1898. Whether it was fabricated by the imaginative spirit that Smalley possessed in his long career as a journalist or for the advancement of a certain political agenda, the local political power of prostitutes in Tucson and Arizona was waning.[5] During the Progressive Era (from

1890 to the 1920s), local policing, moral-reform politics, and immigration law took down red-light districts everywhere. And while prostitution in Tucson, Arizona, aided in building the city through local ordinances that charged the women for existing through volitional prostitution, things shifted for Mexican prostitutes on the border when their occupation became de jure nonconsensual and racist in the early 1900s. Tied to whiteness through moral reform and federal immigration laws that were instituted locally, Arizona prostitutes that were Mexican were pathologized because of their racialized sexuality and foreignness in the country. Projecting blame for prostitution onto faceless procurers, usually foreign, was a convenient way to avoid more sweeping social change focusing on why women went into prostitution in the nineteenth century and early twentieth century in the first place. The racialization of sex in the borderlands became tied to a discourse of unproductiveness instead of the thriving political economy it had been attached to for decades before in Arizona. The border was porous for Mexican women to cross back and forth for work in prostitution in both locales until local officials in Arizona and national immigration officers began to slowly imagine a space simultaneously free of sexual excess and foreigners. While Mexicans crossing the border were not the national target of immigration control in the nineteenth and early twentieth century, Mexican women in Arizona became targeted for prostitution in the first decade of the twentieth century through conversations that were taking place at the national level regarding statehood tied to moral reform laws, anti-Chinese immigration law and sentiment projected onto Mexican prostitutes, and the targeting of males for deportation that made Mexican women vulnerable to deportation because of sexual excess. The present scholarship on the origin of violent militarization of the border against the entry of Mexicans came with the passage of the Immigration Act of 1917.[6] However, this chapter pinpoints the dangerously pathologizing process of targeting Mexican prostitution for racialized sexual excess in 1909.

This chapter has multiple moving parts and archives that tell the history of prostitution in Arizona at the turn of the century. It also tells the story of how the local political and economic power of prostitutes in Tucson and throughout Arizona dwindled and became racially pathologized and dangerous within the first decade of the twentieth century. The reason for the decline in power was twofold. First, Arizona was involved in heated discussions regarding statehood in 1902, which resulted in nonadmission to the Union because of the confluence of racialized bodies and sexually excessive economies in the territory. Better said, Arizona did not receive statehood at the turn of the century because it was too Mexican, too Indigenous, and too sexually excessive for the moral purity reforms and nativist agendas that were sweeping the nation. Secondly, Mexican prostitutes in Arizona became racially sexualized through immigration laws, which made prostitution dangerous for them because of deportation in the borderlands as they were being equated with foreignness. I begin with a brief discussion of the economic shifts on the border in relation to prostitution at the turn of the century. I historicize the borderlands by looking at both sides of the border economically and through prostitution laws nationally to exemplify just how porous and common it was for Mexican women to border cross in order to survive impending monopoly capitalism and the modernization of Mexico. Next, I move into the archive to elucidate the history of racialized sex and sexuality of prostitution in Tucson and Arizona. I examine the shift from the growing political economy of prostitution to when prostitution became dangerous and sexually pathologizing in Arizona, particularly for Mexican women who were frequent border crossers. First, this chapter dives into the Arizona historical archive by examining territorial newspapers from the end of the nineteenth century to around 1915. The newspapers tell an interesting narrative of the powerfully productive political economy that prostitution fostered in the community through local ordinances in the Tucson municipality. I look at these archival newspapers that uncover the thriving sexual economy of prostitution in relation to discussions of statehood that pathologize prostitution through moral reform laws introduced by the biggest advocate against prostitution at a national level, Josephine Hughes, who was based in Tucson. Next, the archive takes me to moments in history when prostitution became dangerous for Mexican prostitutes in Arizona. I examine the unlikely yet material relationship between Mexican prostitute deportation through the discourse of the Page Law in 1875 and the Chinese Exclusion Act in 1882. I examine recovered newspapers that name immigration officer Brown McDonald as the main agent in Tucson who deported Mexican women for prostitution.[7] The archive shows that Brown McDonald clearly tracked prostitutes for xenophobic reasons and not necessarily to "save" these women, which further racially sexualized them in problematic ways. This section also looks at immigration reports filed for Arizona that focused on male procurers but incidentally deported only the Mexican prostitutes instead of the males. While these situations exemplify when prostitution became dangerous and sexually pathologizing for Mexican women in Arizona, the archive also visually exemplifies this narrative. In closing this chapter, I connect the history of prostitution in the Arizona archive that begins with economic power to racialized sexual excess to the prostitution photography of the Gustav Schneider archive (1912). This last section examines how racialized sex and sexuality was used as a technology of power that targeted Mexican prostitutes on the border. I interrogate the Schneider photographs through the notion of "technologies" of power in relation to racialized sexuality, deportation practices, and the technology of the photograph on the borderlands. The Gustav Schneider archive of photography in Gay Alley visually represents the history of racialized Mexican prostitutes at the turn of the century.

This chapter closes the book not only because it is the logical historical chronology to close it, but because it exemplifies a shift from the productivity of the brown female, through upholding certain economic systems like debt peonage, to the unproductivity of the racialized prostitute. The impetus for this chapter, and book for that matter, is not to fill historical silences or "recover" history in any form, but to interrogate the active silencing that happens in the archive in relation to racialized sex, gender, and sexuality. We hear whispers from women sprinkled throughout the archive, yet there is a distinct push to erase and eradicate certain bodies from the history of the borderlands. As the last chapter of the book, the examination of prostitution on the borderlands, particularly in Arizona, exemplifies how certain Mexicanas at the turn of the century were connected through capital. That is to say, this chapter examines how sexual capital (produced through racialized sex) is a productive force of capital, while it is simultaneously labeled excessive and improper. I began this book with the discursive construction of racialized sex in relation to elite and wealthy Californios. I moved on to how racial gender formations are always only visible through violence, as exemplified through the execution of Josefa Chipita Rodríguez. Lastly, I focused on the productive and unproductive nature of racialized sex on the nineteenth-century borderlands and at the turn of the century. I end this book with how the exploitation of *the body* on the borderlands reflects the positionality of the racialized brown female.

The transition from agriculture and mercantilism to capitalism in relation to racialized sex led to a shift from productive racialized sex of women in debt peonage, who were tied to a dying economy of *patrón* and hacienda culture, to the racialized sexual excess of nonproductive prostitution. While landholding Hispanos were not able to retain their cultural power and wealth with encroaching white settlement and monopoly capitalism, they were able to use the racialized sex of poor Nuevomexicanas to open up large transnational routes and maintain their status for some time. However, at the turn of the century, a shift was occurring in the borderlands that not only saw a shift in power but also saw a shift in economic models. This shift saw the beginnings of industrialism in the Southwest borderlands. These economic shifts further bound many Mexican and poor brown women to a condition of sexual excess and offered them a semblance of economic stability. But more importantly, poor brown women on the border already occupied a sexually excessive space because of their position in colonialism, imperialism, and previous economic systems. Essentially, this transition from bondage to a non–living wage was called "modernization." This chapter unravels the fleeting political and economic power of prostitution in Tucson and Arizona while interrogating the moment Mexican women in Arizona became targeted for prostitution. It does this work to exemplify how racialized sex was mobilized at the turn of the century as something excessive, immoral, and therefore worthy of pathologizing; but more importantly, it uncovers the lives of Mexican women who would be invisible in history while they contributed the economy of a city in the borderlands. Regardless of the economic system in place in the Southwest borderlands, prostitution has always flourished. However, what this chapter tracks is the regional power of prostitution before industrial capitalism to the diminishing power it began to possess as industrial capitalism and immigration policy started to interlock. Arizona is a distinct place within the Southwest borderlands, because while there were few Anglo settlers before and after 1848 and non-Anglo people outnumbered Anglo settlers, the narrative that gets solidified in history is that Arizona was a *terra nullius* with boundless economic opportunity waiting to be tapped by Anglo settlers.[8] Unlike New Mexico, which loudly uplifted its Spanish-speaking populations while rejecting U.S. settlers, and Texas and California, which served as economic development models in the United States because they had large Tejano and Californio populations, Arizona has a whitewashed history that opened its space up differently for white supremacist terrorization.

The fleeting local power of Tucson prostitutes was firmly connected to Arizona gaining statehood in 1912. While madams had local political power in Tucson, the excessive anti-foreigner sentiment of Progressive Era politics pervaded Tucson moral reform activism from powerful political wives like Josephine Hughes As Arizona was entering the United States as a legitimate state after years of being rejected on the basis of its minority population, national efforts focused on how to curtail immigration and prostitution simultaneously, mapping sexual excess onto brown female bodies that crossed the border. There was a certain type of volition behind prostitution work on the borderlands at the turn of the century (while still dependent on class status) that aids us in understanding how prostitution was productive work, as understood through the bodies of women on the border. Prostitutes in Tucson paid modest fees to work in prostitution, and as indicated by George Smalley's sensational story above, they had power to negotiate with political authorities in the city. However, we witness a shift in Arizona, particularly in Tucson, where "foreignness" became tied to sexual excess, and sex for Mexican women became unproductive and quite frankly dangerous. It was around the early 1900s that prostitution became dangerous for Mexican women under the conditions of foreignness being tied to sexual excess and contamination. This shift was clear not only to Arizona journalist George Smalley, but also to Arizona cultural historian Gustav Schneider, whose photographic archive of Gay Alley prostitutes shows us how racialized sexuality functioned at the turn on the century on the borderlands.

This chapter reckons with how sex and sexuality are a "technology of power" in Tucson, Arizona. I am utilizing Michel Foucault's concept of "technology of power" to explain how sex is mobilized at the turn of the century to control prostitutes, which I define and explain later in the chapter. Foucault's notion of "technology of power" analyzes the methods and procedures used for governing human beings. More importantly, I am using "technology of power" as a concept that describes the phenomenon behind power, sex, and labor in the borderlands and how certain bodies are utilized and accounted for; first, by how the U.S. nation-state uses power to map racialized sex onto foreign bodies. Second, how photography uses bodies to account for their presence in society. The racialized body having sex and the body through photography tread a dreadfully similar path that operates through hierarchies of power: Who gets to use what bodies in the creation of the nation, and to what end? A photograph documents how certain bodies are staged according to discursive and material conditions that structure society. In other words, bodies are accounted for according to discursive and material construction. The Schneider archive documents prostitution, but it also tells an interesting story about racialized sex and sexuality that frames Mexican prostitutes through tropes of sexual excess. This narrative has cemented Mexican women as sexually excessive throughout history. The prostitute photographs, taken in Tucson, exemplify what visual scholar Tina M. Campt says "opens up the radical interpretative possibilities of images and state archives . . . by engaging the paradoxical capacity of identity photos to rupture the sovereign gaze of the regimes that created them by refusing the very terms of photographic subjection they were engineered to produce."[9] As Campt reminds us though, the prostitution archival photographs may center Schneider's gaze as he intends to see the prostitutes, but that gaze is ruptured through the subversive refusal of the prostitutes, as I will explain later in this chapter. Following Ariella Azoulay's proposal to "watch" rather than look at photographs and, by extension, Tina M. Campt's suggestion to "listen to" photographs rather than just look, I examine these photographs as part of the Latinx historical archive. I interrogate the visual property of Mexican prostitution in relation to the economy of prostitution in Tucson and Arizona and the moments that prostitution straddled the line between willful and dangerous.[10]

Shifting Economies in the Arizona Borderlands: Sex, Capital, and National Prostitution Laws

Now part of Pima County and north of the border town Nogales, Tucson was its own type of "border town" as borders moved and maps shifted throughout the nineteenth century. The Gila River separated the lands the United States would cede in 1848 after the Mexican-American War and the signing of the Treaty of Guadalupe Hidalgo. All the territory to the north of the Gila River was ceded in 1848, but the land to the south, including Tucson, was added when the Gadsden Purchase was ratified by the U.S. Congress in 1854. But before that, the Spanish colonized Tucson in 1775 as a *presidio*, and it became part of the state of Sonora during Mexican Independence in 1821. The Mexican presence was forceful in Tucson, and even after the Gadsden Purchase, soldiers continued to protect the frontier garrison until 1856. Located about fifty-five miles north of the new international border, Tucson was isolated and conflicted until the 1850s.[11] Arizona became a U.S. territory in 1863, and in 1867 Tucson became its territorial capital. Between 1860 and 1880, prostitution and the red-light district(s) in Tucson became a focal point of newspapers, Anglo settlers, and moral-reform national politics.

As the United States pushed westward and life transformed itself at the end of the nineteenth century, the move from agriculture, cattle ranching, and mercantile capital to industrialism and global capital shifted the material utilization of racialized sex and sexuality. As discussed in the introduction, Deena Gonzalez reminds us that merchant capitalism opened up new markets and modes of economy that would change the landscape of the frontier. While Mexicans and Mexican Americans were navigating the large-scale trade market, a new economic system was taking hold: monopoly capitalism and industrialism. The railroad undermined merchant and trade business when it came to Tucson in 1880, which had provided "goods and food to Southern Arizona through linkages with Sonora" for decades.[12] This economic revolution was a "furious expansion of railroad networks, fueled by government loans and land grants, [which] opened a vast continental market."[13] The industrial juggernaut demanded a labor workforce that could only be met by immigration. Fifteen million immigrants arrived in the United States between 1890 and 1914.[14] In 1870, the U.S. economy output had surpassed each of the German, French, and Japanese empires.[15] Where there was once a need for specialized labor and farmers, deflation hit hard with the new technological advances of the day, and by 1920, only one-quarter of American workers remained on the land.[16] What was once a liberal framework of laissez-faire during industrialism, centered on Anglo-American individualism and a "well-ordered society [that] channeled self-interested market behavior into socially beneficial outcomes," began to shift to an illiberal model of economic balance during the Gilded Age (1870–1900) that needed to be regulated because of the chaos that industrial capitalism had brought to the nation. Before, the economic systems of the early and mid-nineteenth century in the borderlands utilized poor, brown female bodies for labor and sex, as in the case of debt peonage in New Mexico, as discussed in chapter 3.

Sex and sexuality were closely tied to economics in the nineteenth century; as I argue in this chapter, this is particularly true in the Southwest borderlands throughout the different economic shifts in the region. Early scholarship of twentieth-century sexuality has argued that there was a transition from Victorian repressiveness to modern liberation. Of course, Michel Foucault interrupts this line of thinking by interrogating how, "rather than repressing sexuality, Victorians and their successors encouraged the proliferation of discourses and institutions concerned with the management of bodies and bodily processes."[17] Moderns then transformed the discreet function of sexuality as body management to a form of liberation that centered sexuality through subjectivity.[18] However, neither of these theorizations takes into consideration the material realities of sex and sexuality as tied to race and class. On the border, sexuality is a historically contingent condition, one that is neither repressed nor liberated. As Catherine Cocks reminds us, sexuality cannot have one universal identity and speculative theory; rather, "historians [must] . . . challenge ahistorical and singular models of how people come to 'have' sexuality by offering alternatives forged in colloquy with the voices and silences of the past."[19] Cocks also expresses that for all the "Victorian" talk of withholding sex, such was not actually the case among white, middle-class Americans. By the turn of the century, Black and brown women had sex and sexuality projected onto their bodies.

Many Anglo-American settlers arrived in Arizona after the California Gold Rush in 1849. As capital shifted in Arizona, so did the use for racialized sex. In 1862, there was not one saloon in the town of Tucson; however, by 1877,

Tucson had ten saloons and around five municipal buildings that governed the city by day and catered to the settler population in the evenings. Thomas C. Leonard reminds us, "The transformation from an agricultural to an industrial economy—and from rural communities to a metropolitan society—produced social dislocations so unprecedented as to require new words, such as *urbanization*, a term coined in Chicago in 1888 to describe the migration from farm to factory and the explosive growth of America's industrial cities."[20] The "frontier" was not much different. The push and pull between residual modes of economy and emergent modes had many *ricos* and middle- to lower-class people on the borderlands flailing and trying to maintain their existence while monopolies, Anglo settlers, and big business pushed west. In addition, the discourse that surrounded racialized sex at the turn of the century was still narrated as excessive, and life for Arizona prostitutes became dangerous in the 1900s.

While prostitution was legal in Mexico, U.S. Progressive reformers "countered that prostitution could never be truly voluntary due to an element of compulsion that compromised women's moral authority."[21] However, women on the border were never and would never be "moral" for the U.S. nation-state, and "moral" was a relative term in relation to whiteness. There were distinct and disparate approaches to prostitution on the border in different locations, and "the U.S.-Mexico border, easily traversed as it was, made El Paso and the territories of Arizona and New Mexico particularly desirable destinations for pimps [and prostitutes], because of the potential for quick financial gain that crossing into the United States could bring, and women who might have worked as prostitutes in Mexico, where prostitution was legal."[22] Mexican people outnumbered Anglo settlers in Tucson throughout the nineteenth century and up to the 1920s, but there were not many domestic homes or wives on the border because of the difficult conditions. Given the many settlers moving west, the prostitute became a "necessary evil" that men in the West depended on to sustain their life as laborers. Thus, Tucson became particularly well known for the presence of multiple red-light districts and prostitution on the borderlands.

This chapter centers Tucson, Arizona, in the conversation about Mexican prostitution and racialized sex and sexuality, yet it also considers the U.S.–Mexico border in a more material way than the other chapters of the book. In earlier chapters, I looked at the material effects of discursive ideology in the borderlands; this section historicizes the porous U.S.–Mexico border in terms of migration and deportation policy regarding prostitution. It wasn't until 1924, with the advent of the National Origins Act, that Mexican migrants became racially inferior, undesired, and targeted by nativists, and by the beginning of the 1930s Border Patrol began policing Mexicans nationally.[23] Additionally, at the end of the nineteenth century and into the twentieth century, Mexican prostitutes in Arizona were not necessarily targeted for their ethnic "foreign" makeup, unlike Chinese women. However, it was approximately within the first decade of the twentieth century that Mexican prostitutes in Arizona began experiencing the negative effects of nativist discourse; this is when the profession of prostitution became dangerous and racially pathologized. As stated earlier, Border Patrol in Arizona targeted unsanctioned border crossers and took a harsh stance against racialized prostitutes (Asians, Europeans, and Mexicans) as tied to national cleansing and statehood. However, before this time, prostitution was an economy of movement. Mexican prostitutes would travel back and forth across the U.S.–Mexico border.

During the presidency of Porfirio Díaz (1876–1911), a period known as "el Porfiriato," the history of Mexico changed through his programming, which modernized the country. Díaz expanded Mexico's railroad system, allowed wealthy and rich (outside) investors to purchase large swaths of land, and incorporated wage labor into Mexico's economic system. Kelly Lyttle Hernández reminds us that he also began a campaign for "order and progress" that released approximately five million Mexican campesinos from debt peonage.[24] There was a 6.1 percent rise in exports between 1876 and 1910, and the population went from nine million to fifteen million during that same time period and under the campaign of "order and progress." However, rural and Indigenous populations in Mexico suffered dispossession and poverty because of the land accumulation of wealthy Mexicans and foreigners and their need for free wage laborers. Migration during this time was high and intense, and those being displaced were looking for work up north. There were an estimated five hundred thousand border crossings in to the United Sated between 1900 and 1910.[25] While modernizing Mexico was good for some and bad for many, prostitution in Mexico began to rise because of the rise of commercial crops and land dispossession. The influx of Mexican prostitutes to the city centers and border towns exemplifies the sexual commerce of modernization. Before this, in 1872, the "Reglamento para el ejercicio de la prostitutución en México" stated that a prostitute was "any woman over the age of fourteen who was not a virgin, who habitually has sexual relations with more than one man, and who expressed a specific desire to engage in sexual commerce."[26] While this law placed the onus of disease on the sexually excessive Mexican women, prostitution was legal and regulated according to European standards established four decades earlier. Mexican health authorities, under the Restored Republic, adopted public health regulations of sexual commerce in 1867.[27] Between 1873 and 1898, the age in the "Reglamento" was modified only slightly from fourteen to sixteen. Prostitution picked up during the Mexican Revolution because of the chaos many people experienced as a result of the economic system. There was a crackdown on prostitution in the United States, but it was legal in Mexico, so prostitution on the border was an ideal situation for women to go back and forth; it allowed them to stay with their families and have a higher income.

On the other side of the border, federal immigration law and moral purity legislation merged in 1907, but before that, on July 12, 1891, "the Bureau of Immigration began operation in the Department of the Treasury, twenty-four border inspection stations were set up, and a system of medical inspection was implemented."[28] This selective immigration process was a modification of the Immigration Act of 1882, which "banned all lunatics, idiots, convicts, and those liable to become public charges, and those suffering from contagious disease."[29] This act defined the concept of deportation and excluded the sexually excessive, such as those with charges against them for adultery, bigamy, rape, sodomy, and polygamy. The earliest immigration laws were concerned with banning all Asians and curbing immigration from eastern and southern Europe, as well as "prostitutes, illiterates, criminals, contract laborers, unaccompanied children, idiots, epileptics, the insane, paupers, the diseased and defective, alcoholics, beggars, polygamists, [and] anarchists," among others.[30] The Immigration Act of 1903 solidified the bridge between morals and immigration, which only strengthened with the Immigration Act of 1907. The Immigration Act of 1903 prohibited alien women and girls from engaging in prostitution and stipulated that anyone who kept or supported prostitutes faced felony charges. The Immigration Act of 1903 made explicit reference to all prostitutes; if found guilty, the defendant faced felony charges, between one and five years in jail, and a fine not exceeding five thousand dollars.[31] When looking at the evolution of immigration law in relation to sexual prohibition and surveillance, it becomes clear that the discourse of immigration in the United States tied foreigners to cleansing of the nation because they were considered "dirty". However, for the prostitutes in Arizona, this meant utilizing their sex as productive until a discourse of foreignness set in to the borderlands.[32] What becomes even clearer is that sex and sexuality for Mexican prostitutes in Arizona made them fall outside of heteronormativity in relation to the conventional family unit: a mother, father, and children. What also becomes clear in a close reading of the Arizona archive of prostitution is that racialized women are no longer needed to reproduce for an outgoing economic system, such as debt peonage, and become a threat to the U.S. nation-state. The Page Act of 1875 foreshadowed the next one hundred years of immigration law and beyond and solidified the connection between the interchangeability of xenophobic national projects and the sexuality of women of color.

The Page Act of 1875, which prohibited the first-time entry of convicts, contract laborers, and Asian women coming to work in prostitution, foreshadowed the Immigration Act of 1903.[33] However, the Page Act targeted all Asian women, "even when other women of other nationalities were significantly involved in prostitution work too," according to Eithne Luibhéid.[34] The threat to white supremacy, the nation as tied to the heteronormative family, and white proper femininity intersected with the ways that race and sex/sexuality influenced immigration law; however, Mexican women were not at the forefront of the threat at first. And while prostitutes have always been excluded from entering the United States based on their nonnormative sexuality, at the turn of the century and through Progressive Era politics the sexual racialization of Mexican women living and practicing on the border became tied to who they were *not*: proper, white, feminized victims of male sexual exploitation. Conflating the voluntary practice of prostitution (or any reason for the voluntary entry into sex work—for example, single parenthood, divorce, abandonment on the border) with the involuntary sex trafficking of moral white women and girls, the Mann Act in 1910 made it a crime to "transport women and girls across international and interstate lines to prostitute them, to have sex with them, or to cohabitate with them."[35] Between 1907 and 1909 immigration officials turned heavily to the site of the border to curtail white slavery, but in fact ended up deporting more Mexican women than "saving" virtuous white women who were held against their will for sex. This set the tone for the racialized sex and sexuality of the women on the border.

The Local Prostitution Ordinances in Tucson and Their Economic Power

While national moral reform legislation and federal immigration law were beginning to merge to regulate entry in 1907, local prostitution in Tucson's Gay Alley was thriving. Gay Alley was a two-block-long, dusty, unpaved street named for pioneer settler Mervin Gay. It ran between McCormick Street and Ochoa Street (north/south) and Meyer Street and Convent Street (west/east). It was a bustling, vibrant business district and a distinctly Mexican place where prostitution in Tucson flourished between the 1870s to around 1915. Gay Alley does not exist as a street anymore. Today, because of urban renewal in the 1960s and the Pueblo Center Redevelopment Project, which bulldozed eighty acres of city streets, it lies buried beneath the Leo Rich Music Hall, sandwiched between the Tucson Convention Center to the west and the police and fire stations bordering the east side of Church Avenue. In fact, Meyer Street, originally named Callejon de las Flores (Flower Alley), bordered Gay Alley and was changed to Meyer Street to honor German-born soldier and politician Charles H. Meyer (1829–1907). Meyer came to Arizona with the U.S. Army as part of the Hospital Corps and settled in Tucson in 1858.[36] During his judgeship and justice of the peace tenure he implemented chain-gang labor in the area to "clean" the city streets. The area of La Calle and south, including El Hoyo, Membrillo, and Barrio Libre, which one could argue encompassed Gay Alley, was a place where racialized Mexican Americans "fled" to avoid law enforcement and freely engage in vice.[37] Not only did the naming of this part of Tucson involve racist and essentialist notions of Mexicans, but it also linked the process of racialization with sexual excess and thus racialized sexuality through zoning and segregation. As Mexicans moved south of the city center, their desirability as subjects of the U.S. nation-state was questioned many times over; the excess of their very lives intersected with the sexual excess of prostitutes, whether they approved of it or not. Exiling the "excess" to the margins allowed for the unseen to negotiate what public and private space meant because the city of Tucson wanted these populations eliminated. Many of the prostitutes sat outside of their "cribs" every day, making Gay Alley a topic of many political discussions at the end of the nineteenth century and into the twentieth. Most of the newspaper headlines often referred to the brawls and deaths in the red-light district of Tucson, but the newspaper stories either called for it to be closed or explained the discussion that the city Common Council was having in regard to keeping it open, but with more surveillance and collection from prostitutes. On Monday, December 4, 1911, the *Tucson Citizen* reported, "Lights Are Extinguished in Restricted District of Tucson." Gay Alley was being cleaned up. However, it was not until 1917 that prostitutes left Gay Alley for other areas. By the 1920s, Gay Alley had lost its appeal because of the nationwide "clean-up."[38] But before this national moral "clean-up" of sexual excess, prostitutes in Tucson not only had political power, but they contributed to the growing economy in Tucson. All of these shifts occurred alongside statehood debates among federal leaders who were hesitant to allow Arizona into the Union. Anita Huizar-Hernández reminds us that Arizona's territorial leaders began a "rhetorical whitewashing campaign," insisting that the Mexican population "was quantitatively and qualitatively insignificant and would pose no political, cultural, or economic threat."[39] Through this whitewashing narrative, Arizona created a historical amnesia in which Indigenous and other ethnic minorities did not exist. Arizona became a state on February 14, 1912.

This "cleaning up" was not just happening in Tucson but was also the aim of the Progressive Era crusade that was waged between the collapse of Reconstruction in 1877 and the United States' entry into the First World War in 1917. While Progressive Era ideals were not unified, they were generally discontent with liberal individualism and disorder, sexual and otherwise, which they blamed on industrial and laissez-faire capitalism that occurred during the Gilded Age. While these seem like good reasons for reform, they were attached to "pure" race ideals.[40] And because of the great influx of immigration and migration to and within the United States as a result of the Industrial Revolution, wars, and modernizing projects abroad, reformers saw the need to tighten immigration law. The Progressive Era, coupled with national immigration and border policies, solidified the militarized border when the Border Patrol was created in 1924. Irving Fisher, economist and Progressive social campaigner, noted that the new economic order required the leadership of "superior men."[41] He stated that "the world consists of two classes—the educated and the ignorant—and it is essential for progress that the former should be allowed to dominate the latter."[42] This "protection" of economy, society, labor, and restrictions was sold as human betterment, which came in the form of moral-reform politics.

The most influential moral reformer against prostitution in Tucson and against Gay Alley was Josephine Hughes, wife of Louis C. Hughes—founder of the *Arizona Daily Star*, Civil War veteran, and state governor—and mother of state senator John Hughes. Josephine Brawley Hughes was the cofounder of the Women's Christian Temperance League and the major reason the Tucson Common Council passed Ordinance No. 72, the city's first anti-prostitution statute that relocated *all* residents of Maiden Lane to Gay Alley in 1883.[43] Both from Philadelphia, Louis and Josephine came to Tucson because Louis Hughes needed to be in a warm climate due to an injury he sustained during the Civil War. When the Hugheses arrived in Tucson in 1872, there were only two other homemakers established in the area.[44] While Josephine was educated at Edinboro Normal in Pennsylvania and qualified to teach, moral-reform efforts in Tucson took center stage for her. In 1876, Hughes was appointed commissioner for Arizona's women's department for the Centennial Exposition in Philadelphia. Because of Josephine's distinguished role, Reverend George E. Adams, pioneer missionary to Arizona, appointed her one of the leaders in organizing Methodism in Tucson, which became the center for many reform movements in Arizona.[45] As Davis Montejano recounts, by the turn of the century, Mexican Americans, even the wealthy, were impacted by Anglo-American settlers and shifting economics, which "signified a collapsing of the internal class structure. With few exceptions, the propertied classes of the Mexican settlements did not reproduce themselves."[46] And how could they? The productive economic systems backed by reproduction (of the labor force) and trade were a residual mode of economy. By the end of the nineteenth century, the tension between local officials and national moral-reform politics was intense; "women of ill repute" were paying fines and license fees that went toward municipal funds, and female Anglo settlers from the east were contriving ways to put an end to prostitution, tying the political economy of sex in the borderlands to statehood.

While Josephine Hughes was ramping up her moral-reform platform in Tucson, one year after the Sunday closing law (passed in 1887 to restrict Sunday vice activities for religious reasons), Hughes and her Women's Christian Temperance League urged the Tucson City Common Council to clear up Maiden Lane (which would later be moved to Gay Alley) and compel the prostitutes of the dens to seek housing in some distant quarter of the city.[47] The national temperance movement found a home in moral-reform politics and suffrage during the Progressive Era and, interestingly enough, it was not all rooted in religious discourse. The intersection of eugenics, the savior complex, and purist movements were at the core of the eradication of prostitution nationwide. In 1885, there were many unsuccessful attempts to require that Gay Alley not be within four hundred feet of any respectable neighborhood or school.[48] One of the bordering streets of Gay Alley was Convent Street, named in 1869 for the convent located adjacent to San Augustín Cathedral and built to house seven Sisters of St. Joseph of Carondelet. The sisters arrived in 1870 and opened the city's first parochial school for girls next to San Augustín, called St. Joseph's Academy for Young Ladies. During the same time period, they opened a boarding school for Indigenous children (called American Indian Boarding Schools), San Xavier Mission, and lastly St. Augustine's Parochial School for Boys.[49] These schools were within the four-hundred-foot range of Gay Alley, and some revenue from the prostitutes' weekly health checkups, license fees, and misdemeanor ordinance fines went to these schools. Prostitution in Tucson subsidized the economy. The tension between prostitution as a thriving political and economic system and the moral reform legislation that Hughes was attempting to implement was palpable. Hughes had the ear of the mayor at the time, Mayor Henry Buehman, who published his views on Tucson in the *Arizona Weekly* and fabricated the position of prostitutes when he wrote, "Place yourselves in the position of those whose property has become valueless on account of a set of people who do not add one cent in taxes to our treasury."[50] As a Republican who had control of the city, state, and senate seats, this was a political tactic to rally those who did not know how municipal funds were garnered or spent to vote for stricter fines and licensing fees that would then go toward the needs of the city or be pocketed by city officials in Tucson. Though the prostitutes were anything but valueless, the citizens of Tucson bought into the moral discourse of the day and labeled these women unproductive members of society. Many of the headlines from 1873 to 1911 in the local Tucson newspapers represented the power of prostitutes in Tucson but exemplified the shift in hatred for sexual excess.[51] They also frequently commented on the growing tensions between different groups of prostitutes and strict political lines that either wanted to eradicate the profession from the territory or make prostitutes pay more fees for their practice. But like it or not, the madams held a significant amount of political power, and many in the community considered them businesswomen.

With the pressure of moral reformers in Tucson calling for a ban of prostitution, the political power of prostitutes in Tucson won the day in 1898, when Ordinance 117 did not ban lewd or bawdy houses at all, but instead implemented a fine of between ten dollars and fifty dollars for any open front door or window of a prostitute's house. However, their actual house could remain open for any amount of time during the day or night.[52] Before that, on May 8, 1883, "Ordinance 48 required a monthly health exam of all prostitutes and workers in 'bawdy houses' and levied a five-dollar fee per exam for a certificate stating that they were free of venereal disease."[53] On December 12, 1903, the *Arizona Daily Citizen*, a left-leaning newspaper, ran a story titled "The Present Administration in Partnership with Vice and an Immoral Tax Collected Monthly from Fallen Women." Targeting the local Republican Party, the newspaper article reads, "The disgraceful attitude of the Republican administration in its partnership with prostitutes also comes in for stern condemnation."[54] The article "exposed" the local Republican officials who were benefiting from the tax that was being collected from the prostitutes, when in reality Ordinance 169 banned all houses of prostitution in Tucson. In 1903, Ordinance 169 stated, "Be it ordained by the Mayor and Common Council of the City of Tucson ... it shall be unlawful for any person to open, keep or maintain within the limits of the City of Tucson, any bawdy house or place of ill-fame or room for prostitution, or reside or live in any such house, place, or room for the purpose of carrying on the business of prostitution or to practice the trade of a prostitute in any manner."[55] But, in the same year, the red-light district was still going strong and the police were not enforcing arrests, though they were still enforcing fines and license fees ranging from five dollars to fifty dollars. These fees were called an "immoral tax," and once the prostitutes paid them, the cops would turn a blind eye and not interfere with their business. In 1903, the City of Tucson was making more than two hundred dollars a month in "immoral taxes."[56] By 1907, none of the ordinances were being upheld, except to collect money from the prostitutes.

With their efforts failing, national moral-reform movements took a different stance; rather than ask for the complete closing of Gay Alley, they petitioned for an ordinance that prohibited alcohol sales to prostitutes and then prohibited saloons from selling alcohol. The ordinance was passed on January 11, 1909, and then repealed by January 30, 1909. In 1912, a corrugated metal fence was built around Gay Alley, separating it from the rest of Tucson.[57] This was the result of a petition signed by mostly women to move Gay Alley to the outskirts of the city. In 1911, twenty-eight years from the passage of the first ordinance in 1883, Gay Alley was "officially" closed, and in 1912, the City of Tucson outlawed prostitution. However, it was not until 1917 that prostitutes began to scatter from the locale of Gay Alley because of harsh police enforcement.

Simultaneously, while Tucson prostitutes were intertwined in local politics, national Progressive Era ideology was being coupled with discussion of Arizona entrance into the union. In 1902, when the red-light district of Gay Alley was going strong, the Subcommittee of the Committee on Territories on House Bill 12543 was considering Arizona, New Mexico, and Oklahoma for statehood, under the direction of Chairman Senator Beveridge (Indiana). While the committee asked many different questions in its investigation on whether Arizona was fit to become a state, it focused a large portion of its questioning on the racial makeup of the territory and the economy of vice that was prevalent at that time. In the first instance of explaining prostitution in Arizona, the mayor of Phoenix, J. C. Adams, stated, "Five or six years ago in this town bawdyhouses were public, and were practically licensed by the collection of fines. Women without license were allowed to sing in saloons and allowed to go around to the games and hang over the bars, and do things of that kind, without any ordinance."[58] In linking the propriety of the state with the inherently negative reputation of prostitution, Adams was feeding in to the "clean up" discourse. Directly after his statement, Adams stated that the bawdy houses had been driven out of the city of Phoenix because of the continual redistricting/rezoning of the city limits, which would ultimately continue to push prostitution to the margins of the city, where it would one day become invisible because of the constant movement of the profession. He ended his testimony saying that prostitution had been "driven out of existence, and today there are absolutely no bawdyhouses, licensed or otherwise absolutely none—as I am informed, and I believe that my information on that is reliable. The women in the saloons were gradually gotten rid of."[59]

What became distinctly clear from those testifying on behalf of Arizona statehood (all Anglo) were the lengths that all the testifiers went to establish Arizona as an "American" place. On November 17, 1902, Senator Beveridge asked the census data collector, Henry Hartin, if there were more Americans or Mexicans in the territory of Arizona. Hartin answered that there were mostly Americans with few Mexicans and some Basque French.[60] Hartin reminded Beveridge that he did not remember what district he was collecting information from, but he did state that his district went from Prescott down to Agua Fria. This question became tied to economics and class when Beveridge asked Hartin what was the nature of the occupation of people in the places where Hartin took the census. Hartin made sure to name mining as the biggest industry, with settlers coming in to invest in the mines. However, Hartin did not state who the laborers were in relation to their race and ethnic makeup. Two days later at the trial in Tucson, the question of sexual excess and vices came up. This time Senator Dillingham asked census enumerator, John E. Magee, at least three times if his enumeration of districts in South Arizona was complete and accurate. Magee answered yes every time Dillingham asked him. Senator Burham pushed the issue once more to ask W. L. G. Soule, another census enumerator, *how* careful the census was in getting a full enumeration.[61] Soule slipped up and said, "I was very careful. They were nearly all Spanish there, and I had an interpreter along and I was very careful, and I think I got everybody that was living in the district."[62] Burnham asked Soule if his enumeration included everyone in the district. Soule responded yes. We can see here the high anxiety toward Spanish-speaking peoples, but more importantly, the placement of racial questioning came directly before the questioning of sexual excess and vice, which inextricably linked race and sex together in ways the nation was attempting to do at the same exact time.

The Arizona statehood hearing in 1902 was focused on asking about the economy, the racial makeup of the territory, the education system, environmental resources and issues, banking, and the workforce. These issues seem to be conventional concerns not only for the time period, but also with respect to the ideology that was swarming regarding a "pure" nation. However, a huge part of the hearings that became tied to race and class were the sexual practices that were ongoing in Arizona at the turn of the century. James

Flynn, Tucson City tax and license collector, testified that the main license and revenue sources in Tucson were saloons and gambling. This was something the subcommittee on territories frowned upon immediately. Flynn continued that saloons and gambling houses were open twenty-four hours a day, seven days a week, and brought in a total income from licenses of $12,000 a year, which equals approximately half a million today. He stated that in 1902 there were forty-five saloons that employed prostitutes and six gambling establishments. Similarly, E. B. Moden, census enumerator, testified that Prescott, Arizona, derived around $6,000 a quarter from fines levied on saloons and dance halls, all knowingly connected to prostitution in the territory.[63] Chairman Beveridge became angry with Moden when he didn't necessarily indict the profession of prostitution as the main source of income that was supporting the municipality of Prescott. There was a definite intersection of race and sex that came to fruition during the hearings, which racially sexualized the prostitutes in the region. On December 10, 1902, Senator Beveridge delivered his majority report the Subcommittee of the Committee on Territories to the U.S. Senate, favoring statehood for Indian Territory and Oklahoma, but opposing statehood for New Mexico and Arizona. Racial politics and sexually excessive economy were the major reasons for Arizona not attaining statehood in 1902.

Arizona statehood hearings mirrored the "national cleansing" rhetoric that had its roots in the evangelical compulsion to set the world straight. Progressives not only attempted to educate people of color and the poor (which as we know are co-constitutive) to realize not what they lacked but what they *should* want; they also "provided essential intellectual support to the cause of race-based immigration restriction" to temper race suicide, a theory promoted by Richard T. Ely, John R. Commons, and Edward A. Ross that "racially inferior immigrants, by undercutting American workers' wages, outbred and displaced their Anglo-Saxon betters."[64] Even at the height of the "melting pot" discourse in the United States, the overwhelming material reality for foreign migrants was steeped in "Protestant self-improvement and [the] new scientific field of race nationalism—one that rebranded old assumptions of the superiority of Northern European whiteness with a veneer of intellectual legitimacy."[65] Eugenic discourse, moral reform legislation, and immigration laws collided in 1917 when the El Paso Disinfection Plant opened its doors to quarantine and disinfect Mexican subjects upon entry to the United States, and the Immigration Act of 1917 put strict restrictions on any immigrant (mostly Eastern and Southern Europeans) entering from Mexico.[66] This came after inspections of Chinese (enforcing the Chinese Exclusion Act of 1882), Jewish, Italian, and Slavic immigrants turned to focusing on people crossing the U.S.–Mexico border. Inspection and quarantine were tied to eugenic thinking, as the former were methods for "cleansing" a "tainted" group of people, while simultaneously knowing very well that "scientific" sensibility would "prove" that these populations were unfit in the first place.[67] But before the mobilizing of inspection and quarantine that targeted all immigrants coming from Mexico, "human defectives" was the phrase tied to prostitutes crossing the border. Before Mexicans became negatively racialized on the border, prostitutes on the border were marked as silent carriers of disease and death. Local Tucson politicians utilized the political economy of prostitution to build the city, while immigration law and racial taint were simultaneously ousting them. This foreshadowing of global capital and border industrialization secured Mexican women on the border as dirty, under constant threat of violence and death, and "too sexual" for entrance to the "pure" U.S. nation-state.

Sex and Race Collide: Sexual "Foreignness" and Deportation in Arizona

There are very few records in the National Archives that deal specifically with Arizona because they did not get forwarded from the Los Angeles and El Paso headquarter districts. Most of the records focus on prostitution activity in Texas, but the Arizona records that do exist exemplify a material shift from the political and economic power of Arizona prostitutes to the dangerous conditions of deportation that marked Mexican prostitutes as sexually excessive. The archive tells an interesting story of how Mexican prostitutes in Arizona were vulnerable to deportation as secondary subjects to the primary focus of deportation, which were male procurers and Asian female subjects. While Mexican prostitutes were not the primary focus of immigration officers and law at the turn of the century, their safety was still very much at risk. This section interrogates immigration memos from the acting immigration inspector stationed in Douglas, Arizona, named Charles Cornell. Additionally, this chapter examines archival newspapers and a court case for traveling immigration inspector Brown McDonald. Together, these archival documents show how Mexican prostitutes in Arizona lost power while simultaneously experiencing violence. They are also invisible in the archive because they are not the primary subjects of law and policy, but they still felt the effects of racialized sexuality.

At the beginning of the twentieth century, negative attitudes toward Mexican prostitutes were beginning to cement themselves along the border. For example, in an *El Paso Daily Times* article there was a salacious headline that read "Wile of Mexican Girls" in 1908.[68] This was becoming a common sentiment along the border, and these types of newspaper articles served as a warning for Anglo men to stay clear of the women they found so sexually appealing. Charles Cornell, the acting immigration inspector stationed in Douglas, Arizona, was known for targeting male procurers in his quest to enforce the law.

Immigration inspector Cornell, who was employed as a federal immigration inspector in 1903 with headquarters in Douglas, Arizona, and later was placed in charge of Arizona with headquarters in Tucson, was tasked with solidifying the connection between immigration law and the anti-white-slavery movement to protect white femininity.[69] Cornell and other inspectors working on the border shifted their focus from rescuing white women from sex trafficking to targeting males who, as he stated, accompanied female workers from across the border as concubines before being deserted and moving into the occupation of prostitution. This criminalized binational prostitution, but more importantly, it devalued brown women for their choices and bodies, heightening the discourse of sexual excess. On December 26, 1909, Cornell penned a memo that laid out the terms of his investigation, which related to the "prosecution of importers and harborers of alien immoral women and the deportation of such women from the United States."[70] The verbs used in the sentence are telling. The main objective for Cornell is to locate and prosecute the male procurers of "alien immoral" women. The way this sentence is written puts the onus of moral sexual excess on the women themselves and only seeks to punish the males for breaking the law. The memo suggests that the women are too far from saving and will be deported immediately, while the males will serve their punishment.

Evident in the memo is that Cornell focused on Mexican prostitutes who were border crossing from the Juárez, Chihuahua, Nogales, Cananea, Naco, Aqua Prieta, and Sonora areas. He prepared a list of approximately 150 registered who were threatening to cross international lines with male procurers. Cornell states that he personally arrested fourteen "aliens," two males and twelve females. Eleven of those twelve females were deported. Out of the eleven deported, eight women were Mexican prostitutes. The procurers were Spanish and French. Richard Bosch, Spanish procurer, was sentenced to three years in prison, and Alfredo Bernardin, French procurer, was held for an unknown time by U.S. authorities for violation of section 3 of the Immigration Act. Cornell admits that he was originally tasked with investigating the felonies of foreign commerce for immoral purposes, but instead "personally interested himself in the investigation of alien prostitutes who were illegally in the United States" for the purposes of deportation and not necessarily moral ethics.[71] The memo was intended to convey the good work Cornell had done in arresting the male procurers of prostitution, but if you read closer, it is clear that his strategy was to attack racialized and excessive sexuality on the border.

The fact that this memo was allegedly centered on the male procurers of prostitution in Arizona but in fact ends up unveiling the dangerous and pathologizing ways in which immigration law and moral reform policy were geared more toward Mexican prostitutes is very telling. While there were unknown numbers of deportations of foreign prostitutes made by Cornell throughout his tenure at the Douglas, Arizona, district, he clearly states in the memo that he made five arrests for violation of section 3 of the Immigration Act, which prohibits harboring, maintaining, keeping, or controlling an alien prostitute within three years after she enters the United States.[72] The men arrested were Manuel Salazar (Mexican, but U.S. citizen), Francisco Villescas (Mexican, but U.S. citizen), Fileto Lorenzo (Italian, but U.S. citizen), Alfredo Bernardin (French), and Ricardo Bosch (Spanish). Of the five male procurers, four of them served a prison term in the Territory of Arizona, and one was acquitted but arrested again in Tucson, Arizona. The mandate given to the immigration inspectors on the border was to put a stop to white slavery; however, their focus wasn't on the safety of foreign women, as seen by the deep investment in deporting the women and only arresting and charging the men, even if they were foreign as well. Arizona was still a territory at this time, and conversations about statehood were at the forefront of enforcing federal law, so local officials allowed national immigration inspectors to enforce the immigration law. Cornell even has a section in his memo that addresses the lax laws and consequences for procurers, pimps, and prostitutes in the Territory of Arizona. He states, "Through my investigation, a large number of pimps and procurers were brought to my notice and I suggested to the several local officers in the different cities that steps be taken to harass this class of residents and I am pleased to note that prompt action was taken by the local officer in the different cities."[73] In his memo, Cornell establishes that Arizona is a lawless territory that needs some structure in terms of morals and ethics. The political and economic power of prostitutes in Arizona was dwindling. Cornell ends his memo by stating that the prostitutes most commonly found in the mining towns of Arizona are Mexican prostitutes brought across the border by males who "promise marriage or lucrative employment."[74] He talks about Russian-Jewish and French prostitutes, but he generalizes all Mexican prostitutes when he says, "Mexican prostitutes are not of the highest order.

They are usually brought into the United States by Mexicans for immoral purposes, that is, to live with them as their concubines, and eventually are deserted and thereafter drift into dance halls and houses of prostitution."[75] Taking all volition out of the profession of prostitution for Mexican women, Cornell depicts Mexican women as overly and overtly sexual, with no real moral compass or agency in their decisions to have sex. Local Mexican prostitutes in Arizona were some of the most powerful people around, and whether they chose their lifestyle or were forced into it because of the dire economic shifts in the borderlands, the focus on their dangerous removal marks their bodies as unproductive at the turn of the century.

Alternatively, in 1909, the *Arizona Daily* ran weekly stories on deported prostitutes, mostly from Mexico, though some were from Germany and France. The immigration inspector in all of the stories was Brown McDonald. Not much is known of immigration inspector Brown McDonald, but what we can gather from the archive is that he was very invested in tracking down prostitutes who were "aliens." On August 27, 1909, there was a story that ran in the *Arizona Daily* titled "Prominent Merchant Held to Grand Jury: Women Waiting at Detention Quarters to Appear against Nogales Man." Brown McDonald returned from Nogales, Arizona, where "he took two Mexican women, mother and daughter, and the latter's three infant children" as witnesses against Ruchard T. Rogers, a well-known candy manufacturer in Nogales, for allowing the younger of the two women to live in his house for sex.[76] The *Arizona Daily* calls the two women and children "aliens" and states that McDonald returned with the "aliens to Tucson . . . and [they] are now detained as witnesses." Meanwhile, Rogers made bond and was released from custody. A couple months later, Brown McDonald was in the *Arizona Daily* again, this time in a story titled "To Be Deported" that ran on October 3, 1909. Brown McDonald arrested Rita Avilez in a house of prostitution and immediately deported her.

While Brown McDonald was the immigrant inspector in almost all of the deportation stories of Mexican prostitutes in Arizona, a case that was brought upon him by the United States Circuit Court of Appeals, Eighth Circuit, in 1915 exposes his xenophobic deportation practices but also allows us to witness how he utilized all the deportation laws to create havoc. In *McDonald, Immigrant Inspector, v. Siu Tak Sam*, Brown McDonald illegally utilized the Chinese Exclusion Act to deport Su Tak Sam, who was a Chinese merchant living in Hibbing, a village in St. Louis County, Minnesota, and was at his cousin's laundry ironing his clothes. Brown McDonald stated that "the said alien is a member of the excluded classes in that he was a person likely to become a public charge . . . and he is unlawfully within the United Stated [and] he has found therein violation of the Chinese Exclusion Laws and is, therefore, subject to deportation."[77] Brown McDonald did not ask if Siu Tak Sam was a laborer and interviewed him and his cousins as the documented authority, even though he was not a lawyer and did not have authority to do so. He broke all protocol when he arrested Siu Tak Sam to be deported. It turned out that Siu Tak Sam was a wealthy merchant who was only ironing his own clothes in the laundry when he was arrested. The appeal ruled that he could not be lawfully deported and ordered him to be discharged from Brown McDonald's custody. This example shows the precarious nature of immigration law to begin with, but it also exemplifies how immigration inspectors functioned under an umbrella protocol of arresting racialized populations under any circumstances. Brown McDonald particularly carried out illegal deportation tactics, and he serves as just one example of the effects of systemic violence and institutional racism.

Technology of Power: Prostitution, Hierarchies of Power, and Sex

The political economy of prostitution in Arizona, and particularly in Tucson, was undeniable at the turn of the century. The power that the madam portrayed in enunciating her needs, as exemplified at the beginning of this chapter, was not an anomaly. Outside women were messing with her economic stability, and it was not uncommon in Tucson for prostitutes to state their political needs. It was also not uncommon for their licensure fees, health-screening checkup fees, and policing fees to go back into the municipal funds for the city, growing a needed area on the borderlands. However, that power became fleeting in 1909 when immigration policy began targeting Mexican prostitutes. With this shift in the sexual economy in Arizona, history shifted as well. This last section traces the history of prostitution in Arizona through the visual representation of Mexican prostitutes in the Gustav Schneider archive.

Gustav van Hemert Schneider was born in Contra Costa County, California, on January 9, 1885. He studied art and architecture at Mark Hopkins Art School before moving from Oakland, California, to Tucson, Arizona, in 1902, where he worked for the Southern Pacific Railroad (SPRR) Engineering Department from 1903 to 1948. During his career, he designed bridges for the railroad, including the Rio Fuerte bridge in Mexico. Schneider was also a cultural consultant and Arizona historian. In fact, he served as technical consultant to Columbia Pictures during the filming of the movie *Arizona* (1940) and assisted the *Tucson Daily Citizen* with preparation of its "Arizona Album" column by identifying historic photographs and providing historical information. While collecting information for the film and drawing maps of old Arizona, he began taking pictures of local prostitutes between 1912 and 1913, when Arizona became a state. This was an important time for Arizona prostitutes because statehood changed their status and position of power. He also kept a written roster with their given name, sex name, and ethnicity; many of the women were from Mexico. The visual representation of prostitutes in Gay Alley by Schneider portrays the contours of racialized prostitution on the borderlands by visually exemplifying the prostitution hierarchy and representing the shift from the power of prostitution to pathology.

Within the Schneider archive, there is a roster of prostitutes that gives their names, many times their nicknames, and their ethnicity. The sixty-nine prostitutes that Schneider comes into contact with include American, Mexican, French, Japanese, German, Jewish, Polish, Irish, Dutch, Belgian, and Texan women. He even lists a Yaqui Indian named Maria Sanchez, also known as Haroun al Raschid's girl.[78] However, Schneider's ethnic breakdowns seem to be surface, at best. Many of the American women on his list have Spanish surnames and might only have been telling him they were American because of fear of deportation. Regardless of the narrative authority, almost half of the women on the roster have Spanish surnames.

In Tucson, prostitutes worked different areas depending on race and class. At the top of the prostitute hierarchy in Tucson were courtesans. These were women who lived far away from Gay Alley, the most populated area for prostitution in Tucson, in the north, northwest, and northeast areas of the city.[79] They rarely worked out of saloons and charged exponentially more than other prostitutes who did not have the means to work out of their home. Typically, courtesans dressed lavishly, donned expensive jewelry, and had wealthy men as their customers. Below them were prostitutes who operated out of "boardinghouses," another word for brothels. These women conducted their service in prime locations that had servants and/or bouncers.[80] There were cheaper versions of boardinghouses called parlors and bawdy houses that were located on Maiden Lane, also known as *Calle de la India Triste*, near downtown Tucson, known as the Sporting District, which was located off the Wedge on Congress Street. The local stories surrounding *Calle de la India Triste* claim that it was named during Tucson's Mexican period in reference to an unmarried Indian girl who lived with a Mexican officer in the presidio. She was shunned and exiled from her own family and his. In the 1870s the street name was changed to Maiden Lane (which is no longer in existence).[81] Maiden Lane was made up of "cribs" that were "single-story adobe framed buildings with several rooms aligned in a row" and was predominantly Mexican.[82] The location of the "cribs" along Maiden Lane was significant because it "indicated the importance of this route as a connector to the rest of Southern Arizona, as well as Sonora and Mexico as a whole."[83] But as the Anglo settlers came to Tucson, they pushed the historical Mexican community south. Still, the women on Maiden Lane remained and would spend their time outside or at the threshold of their doors or windowsills, luring men into their small space. Many more "cribs" popped up on Gay Alley because they were the fastest and most economically efficient way to get customers. At the bottom of the prostitution hierarchy were streetwalkers, transient and racialized women who performed sexual acts in the alleyways because they were not groomed for or could not afford a "crib."

Schneider's first batch of prostitute photos speaks to this hierarchy and the technology of power, not only within the prostitute community but using the camera as a technology of power as well. These two photographs are stylized and aestheticized. The ornate and courtesan-like portraits register lightness for two reasons. While the first portrait is light because of the actual photography lighting, the second portrait registers light in the gentle clasp of the handbag, the soft smile on her face, and the sweeping luminosity of her perfectly molded hair. Even as portraits of prostitutes, these photos symbolize a coming into modernity, with the regal dress, the ornate props, the posturing of class, and the distinct gaze into the camera. The women are staged and stylized to evoke a high-class sensibility that was not uncommon in prostitute hierarchies in Tucson. Both photographs center the prostitute as powerful, but at the same time their bodies are centered on the self. Said differently, even while these prostitutes have political power within the city of Tucson and they aid in the building of the City of Tucson through their sex, they are still unproductive in their construction of family through children or properness. Yet, however stylized these photographs are, there is a still an air of spectacle about them. The overly large hats that both of the prostitutes wear lead the eye straight to the face and head in the photographs.

Portraits at the turn of the century were meant to capture the "living quality of the subject" and the soul of individuality.[84] However, this proved difficult because any instantaneous click of the camera would be distorted visually, so the photographer had to stylize the sitter for the photograph. Through this stylization, the generalization of certain "types" of people begins within photography.[85] Schneider's stylized photographs of Arizona prostitutes don't necessarily get to the core of the prostitutes' soul; rather, they provide a general representation of what prostitutes on the higher end of the hierarchy were supposed to look like. Orvell reminds us that the typical studio photographer entertained all social classes, from the aristocratic to the uncouth.[86] However, what becomes so interesting in the Schneider prostitute photography archive is the way he stylizes the prostitutes to seem to belong to a higher class. But his "type" and generalizations come to the forefront through racialization and through his technology of power over the prostitutes.

Technology of power, realized through sex and the photograph—as Foucault employed it and its French translation, *"technique"*—is a theorizing of "methods and procedures for governing human beings."[87] Technologies of power extend beyond complex socio-technological systems that signify modern society and are a way to control populations. According to Foucault, "Political power, before acting on ideology, on the consciousness of individuals, exerts itself in a much more physical way of their bodies. The way in which gestures, attitudes, usages, allotments in space . . . are imposed—this physical, spatial distribution of people belongs, it seems to me, to a political technology of the body."[88] The racialized sex and sexuality of Mexican prostitutes in Arizona was willful at the turn of the century. However, local and national moral and immigration laws not only started to pathologize their sex, but they racialized it as well and used it for control. Aside from the local and national political powers clashing in Tucson over the prostitute debate, there were also tensions in the ways that discourse about sexual excess was mapped on different (racialized) bodies.

Not only were the above two photographs *real photo postcards*, which was a new technology that was introduced in 1903 by Kodak, we can read the history of immigration reform through the Schneider photography as a technology of power as well. In the late nineteenth century into the early twentieth century, the photograph took many forms, which included the stereograph card, the print, and the printed portfolio. By the 1900s, photographs had become a major commodity in the American marketplace, and selling the American voyeuristic experience, either through American landscape photography or industrial and city scenes, became something desirable in American homes.[89] In 1894, William Biel advertised his photograph exposition of Chicago's World Fair as "better" than the real thing.[90] The replication of the photograph kept people safe from the dangers of the outside world but included them enough to feel as if they were experiencing it firsthand. This type of photographic realism models the literary realism of the time, but at what point are the photograph and the photographer aggressively conquering natural constraints? Said differently, how are the Schneider prostitute photographs not just a body in front of a camera but also a constellation of

Bettie (facing page) and unnamed woman (above). Arizona Historical Society, Gustav van Hemert Schneider Archive, 1912, MS 0715, Schneider, Gustav van Hemert, 1885–1951, Collection, 1867–1868, 1903–1951, Box 1, f 11–12. These photographs were taken in Gay Alley, Tucson, Arizona, a known street where prostitution flourished.

histories rather than a single object? Through the realist lens of photography and the technology of power, I read Schneider's prostitute photography through a constellation of historical moments that exemplify the hierarchy of the prostitutes and racialized sex. I read these photographs through a realist photography lens while simultaneously building off of A. D. Coleman's formulation of the "directorial mode," where the photographer manipulates the subject in front of the camera, in contrast to Victorian photography, which records the image in its untouched reality.[91] The ways in which these photographs convey meaning reach far beyond the bodies in the photograph. To read these images through what is familiar in them, while simultaneously reading them for what is *not* present in the photograph, we can get a better story of the material conditions of the excessive, brown, overly sexual woman living on the border.

The third photograph from the Schneider archive is labeled "Carmen." The photographic archive begs the audience to question who she is because the Carmen photo is elusive and mocking. We do not know anything about Carmen. The back of her photo reads, "Carmen?" In looking for information about Carmen, I came across three records that could possibly be her. However, this does not matter. What matters about the Carmen photograph is the spectral presence of border crossing, sexual leveraging, and racialized sex. Carmen did not want me to figure out exactly who she was because, whether she was Carmen Calles of Hermosillo, Sonora; Carmen Verdugo, the Mexican woman who ended up marrying a miner by the name of Henry Barmore; or Carmen Riuteria, she did not need to be found, and everything I needed to know about her was in her photo. The Carmen photograph is, as Miles Orvell states, an accepted representation because it is convincing, not more truthful.[92] This convincing representation becomes what is "real" in the imagination of society. Carmen, a Mexican woman, stands in for all other Mexican prostitutes through the dark, murky photograph that becomes representative of how Mexican prostitutes look in this space.

The photo is dark, almost as if the positive space of the photograph had been transferred to negative space. Carmen has a dismal look on her face. She sits on a bed and there is a mirror vanity in the background that never catches her in its reflection. The absence in the vanity set mirrors, quite literally, the ghostly haunting of the lives lost and affected by the intersection of empire, sex, and race. In contradistinction to the posed studio photos, this is the fugitive photo of the bunch—the one that seems like it does not belong. Though her gaze is still, she never arrives at stillness because of the position she occupies on her bed. Our gaze goes right to her leg, which is half off and half on the bed, as if she will be stepping off soon to continue her day. The lens provides a soft focus that juxtaposes the dark lighting. This photograph is not stylized, and while Carmen is not frozen in time, the symbolism of her photo represents the technology of power that many Mexican prostitutes experienced crossing the border at the turn of the century. Her visual representation is justification for the stories that ran in the territorial newspapers above. Her visual representation lends itself to a *politics of reading*, as Stuart Hall suggests, "a strategy of reading that engages an image; perpetual inscription in multiple historical contexts, their implication in existing systems, and the impossibility of former truths."[93] Reading Carmen's photograph in the darkness of her "crib" evokes the discursive meaning of Mexican prostitutes crossing the border: the excess of the negative, the darkness, the emptiness, and the absence. Carmen makes meaning across time, even at the very same time that we know very little about her.

The last three photographs in the Schneider archive are of a Mexican American prostitute named Molly León. These three photos close this chapter because they visually reflect the history of prostitution in Arizona. According to the Arizona Department of Health Services, Molly was born in Arizona on July 9, 1882, and died on March 6, 1956, in Pima County. Her parents were Jesús León and Dolores Márquez from Mexico. Other than what is on Molly León's death certificate, not much is known about her history, except for the fact that Schneider took a liking to her and photographed her the most out of all the prostitutes he recorded. These three photographs sum up (1) the political power, however fleeting, that prostitutes had in Arizona, (2) the turn-of-the-century Progressive Era politics that influenced pathologizing discourse of the "alien" in Arizona, and (3) a turn to "unproductive" sex and the dangerous ousting of prostitution in Arizona. These photographs correlate historically with the sexual climate on the border at the turn of the century. This chapter highlights, through the cultural case study of prostitution, how Mexican women crossing the border began to occupy a space of "unproductive" sex and sexual practices where prostitution became dangerous for Mexicanas.

So why does the connection between sex, capital, and history remain unexplored? The answer is twofold. First, because as Rosemary Hennessy states, "sexual identity—in all of the varied ways it has been culturally differentiated and lived—has been fundamentally, though never simply, affected by several aspects of capitalism: wage labor, commodity production and consumption."[94] This means that while sex and sexual identity touch on all forms of capitalism, it is hidden in the way we ideologically speak about sex and

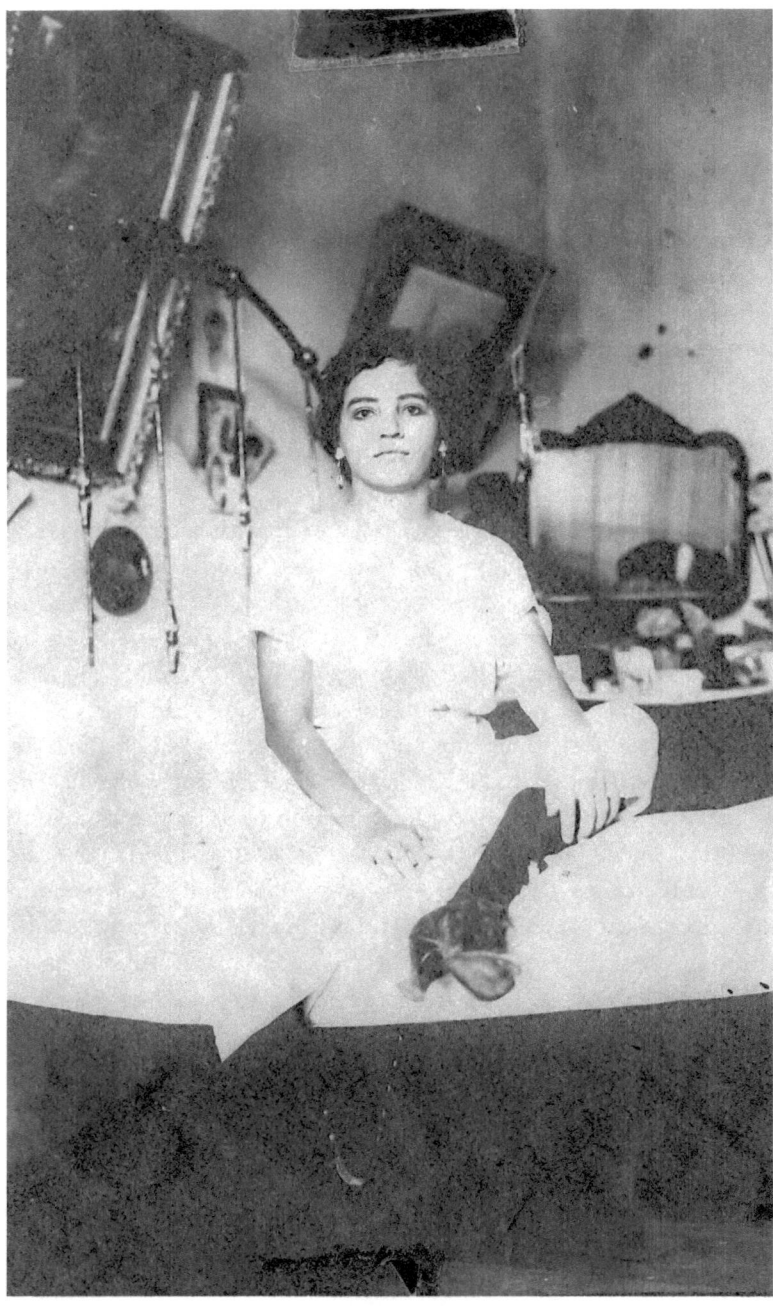

Carmen[?]. Arizona Historical Society, Gustav van Hemert Schneider Archive, 1912, MS 0715, Schneider, Gustav van Hemert, 1885–1951, Collection, 1867–1868, 1903–1951, Box 1, f 11–12.

sexuality. Sexuality cannot be merely an identity category, but a technology of power that shapes the organization of human relations.[95] U.S. empire used sex and the body to control how brown females on the border moved and existed. Heteronormativity stood as a pillar of what was "acceptable" in the ever-expanding U.S. nation-state, and heteronormative sex set the foundation for how the nation would progress and succeed. Sex and sexuality for Mexicanas on the border have always shaped the way their lives have been negotiated. Second, the meaning-making systems of hegemony make cultural signification sites of struggle because of their material connections to the capitalist modes of production.[96] But those systems of meaning are not always direct and oftentimes are concealed by what Antonio Gramsci refers to as "hegemony," which is the coupling of dominant ideas to a historical bloc that has acquired power over the means of production that ideological struggle is intended to secure.[97] The meaning-making and sense-making of sex and sexuality subordinate particular classes without question.

This capitalist patriarchal structure of hegemony secures and maximizes the appropriation of surplus labor through productive labor forces that utilize the sex of poor, brown women on the border as a dual capacity of production and reproduction; but these productive labor forces also formed racial constructions that historically involved a gendered and sexualized process that began to mark these women as unproductive through their sex and sexuality. It was at the turn of the century that poor brown women began to witness how their own racialized sex and sexuality operated as an absent presence that linked racial reform (or cleansing) and excessive sexual practices. Sexual deviance was the new language of sexual reform policy that shifted from productive bodies to unproductive bodies and sex. Marx misses how reproductive labor is imperative to surplus labor and, therefore, misses that brown females on the border had the dual capacity to produce and reproduce for the nation, while simultaneously becoming unproductive through a discourse of excessive sexuality. The sexual ideology of the nineteenth century and the turn of the twentieth century unraveled the notion of traditional womanhood and productive and reproductive capacities. For white women on the border and frontier, the domestic space was private and familial, but for women of color who were poor, sex was racialized and their sexual position was much different. The switch from productive to unproductive took hold at the turn of the century for Mexicana prostitutes on the border, and so began the discourse of excessive sexuality that legitimated the poor treatment of these very same women.

Molly 1. Arizona Historical Society, Gustav van Hemert Schneider Archive, 1912, MS 0715, Schneider, Gustav van Hemert, 1885–1951, Collection, 1867–1868, 1903–1951, Box 1, f 11–12.

Molly 2 (top) and Molly 3 (bottom). Arizona Historical Society, Gustav van Hemert Schneider Archive, 1912, MS 0715, Schneider, Gustav van Hemert, 1885–1951, Collection, 1867–1868, 1903–1951, Box 1, f 11–12.

The first picture of Molly Leon, Molly 1, shows her glancing to her left and smiling slightly, while two people are holding a backdrop for a "staged" photo look; however, the hands holding the backdrop show how cheaply made the entire staging is. Molly wears a white dress with a dark shawl draped over her shoulders. She is wearing modest jewelry, and her hands are crossed on her lap. Ostensibly, she sits outside of her "crib" on a wooden chair. This is the only picture in which Molly is smiling. The other two photographs show Molly sad, angry, or disinterested. What was Molly smiling at? It is less interesting to me to know what she was looking and smiling at than it is to mark this first panel as Molly holding her position historically, not only in Tucson as a racialized prostitute, but on the border, which she surely crossed time and time again. Her modest sitting position shows her confidence in her work and position in the city of Tucson. She is somewhat happy—whatever that signified at the time. I read this first photograph as powerful, and thus representing the political power of Tucson's prostitutes before sexual reform politics took hold.

Molly sitting for this portrait is counter to what studio portraits looked like at the turn of the century. First, she is not in a studio. Second, she is not posed with regal clothing or jewelry, like the earlier portraits. Molly sits outside of her crib, and the backdrop is supposed to hide the fact that she is outside. Molly is also Mexican American, so her fear of deportation at this time was not as high as that of her Mexican counterparts. However, she is still racialized in the construction of the photograph. She does not occupy the domestic space, nor does she occupy a space in the photograph that would fool us into thinking she was of a different class. Laura Wexler reads this as "tender violence" that separates the "races" through the management of how the domestic space is represented.[98] The separation of Molly from the domestics space as a racialized subject exemplifies the larger set of struggles that Mexican prostitutes on the borderlands experienced.[99] This not only allows us to read the work Schneider has done to stage or destage these prostitutes, but it also allows us to interrogate the familiar parts of the photograph and everything else that is not in the photograph. Just as the de la Guerra photograph archives serve as a representation of the absence in the photographs, so do Schneider's prostitute photographs.

The second photograph, Molly 2, shows Molly with a dark-skinned woman, a Mexican or Indigenous woman by all regards. The two stand in front of the black "backdrop," where Molly is not even looking at the camera. Her face is stoic, and I would even say that she is angry or upset in the photograph. Molly no longer has the shawl on her shoulders that she wore in the first sitting portrait, and the same black background that would be used to cover up the crib is visible by the hand holding it up. Her companion standing next to her has the slightest smile and looks directly into the camera lens. This second photograph represents the unstable and dangerous immigration practices that were sweeping the state of Arizona. The companion/friend next to Molly is not seen in any of the other photographs in the archive collection, and she disappears in the last photograph. The woman, who is dark-skinned with dark hair, vanishes from the frame. She represents the thousands of Mexicanas on the border who were deported back to Mexico after the staunch immigration crackdown was tied to the sexual politics of the day on the border. Molly loses her community and her friends and is angry at the transition from political power to pathology. I should briefly mention that my readings of these prostitute photographs are just that—mine. These readings are crafted from what Wexler states are our own "ignorance and blindness," which differ from individual to individual.[100] However, the reading of this photographic archive is informed by the social and historical context that surrounds these photographs: immigration reform and prostitution.

The last photograph, Molly 3, is Molly alone, sitting somberly on the same chair she was in in the first photograph. Her hands are crossed the same way over her lap, except this time she stares off into the distance. She is not as playful as she was in the first sitting portrait, and she has her shawl back over her shoulders. This photograph finalizes the historical position of Molly and Mexican women on the border. She is alone, childless, and in front of her crib, where she has sex for pay. This last photograph symbolizes a turn to "unproductive" sex and the ousting of prostitution for women on the border, which literally built the City of Tucson from prostitution money. Her friend is gone from the frame, and Molly is not moving, not glaring, not staring intently. Her gaze is empty and she is not focused on any one thing. Her unproductive nature in the photograph correlates with her position in society. In society, her worth is attached to her production; she means nothing to the U.S. imagination.

Coda

As I walked through the Women's Memorial Park in Albuquerque, New Mexico, on a cold winter day, I couldn't help but be struck by the sterility of the park. As soon as you enter the two-acre park, there is a large stone monument that has a tree etched with the inscription "In memory of the eleven women who were gone too soon." Directly underneath that inscription is a prayer by an unknown author that tells whoever comes into the park to continue their life and remember the eleven women until everyone can be together again. On the other side of the large stone monument, there is an inscription that takes up the whole side and reads, "In memory of Michelle Valdez's unborn angel," with an angel inscribed on the stone, leading a child by the hand. Around the large stone monument, there were painted rocks with religious sayings and verses, a pumpkin, and two vases with dead flowers that were knocked over.

The park was created to be a circular memorial. You can walk to eleven benches that are directly in front of the names of the women who have been murdered and buried in that mass gravesite before it was a park. The names of the women are etched into the concrete, and there are wooden crosses with name tags that were put into the grass behind each name. Each cross bears the name tag of one murdered woman, made out of what looks like cut-up milk jugs, with a printed name glued to the plastic jug remnant and tied with wire around the wooden crosses. The grass was turning yellow. Not one person was at the park. It is located on the outskirts of town, and the mesa lies directly west of it. Dirt bikes were roaring the entire time I was out there. It was windy and cold. I walked around a second time and I realized I had missed the two largest memorial sites at the entrance of the park. They were both etched into the concrete at the front. One read, "Thank you to Mr. Valdez for his support in this creation of this park." The other one read, "Thank you to 'Rucca the dog' for finding the eleven women." How odd, I thought. Nowhere did I see the actual stories of the eleven women. Nowhere did I see the story of the horrendous things that happened to them. Nowhere did I see them. Most of the fake flowers that were in the vases by the wooden crosses were sun damaged and had completely lost their vibrant colors. And I thought that was completely symbolic of how these women were being memorialized in that sterile, empty park. "We don't know anything about them," I stated as I walked back to my car.

And to be quite honest, we never will. I will never know the stories of Jamie Barela, Monica Candelaria, Victoria Chavez, Virginia Cloven, Syllania Edwards, Cinnamon Elks, Doreen Marquez, Julie Nieto, Veronica Romero, Evelyn Salazar, or Michelle Valdez. And honestly, I don't want their stories out in the public. I saw and read firsthand how these eleven women were treated and vilified by the Albuquerque Police Department and the surrounding community for being sex workers, drug addicts, and houseless. And airing their life stories will only make their murders more sensational. For the City of Albuquerque, the memorial park was the best way they could "honor" these eleven women. Honoring them meant depoliticizing their lives while simultaneously sanitizing their narratives from the park. Funding for the park included $350,000 from the city of Albuquerque and $50,000 from a state grant, for a total of $400,000. The land was deeded over to the City of Albuquerque from KB Homes. The memorial park was finished and opened to the public in 2020, ten years after the first body was unveiled by Rucca the dog. There are still two persons of interest in the case, but no arrests have been made.

I started this book with the West Mesa Murders, and I end with them as well. They bookend the entirety of my work here because they so clearly exemplify the connection between sex, capital, and violence. Sayak Valencia calls this *gore capitalism*, where the borderlands pay for adhering to the increasingly demanding logic of capitalism.[1] These eleven women were found on the land of the seventh top-grossing residential homebuilder in the United States, KB Homes. They were all sex workers. They were pathologized to be disposable to the nation-state because they were not wage laborers. They were selling their sex, their labor; however, it was outside of the realm of what counts as productive labor that produces commodities. They were part of an intercontinental struggle that desired consumption.[2] Lastly, they were not proper subjects of the state. In contradistinction to women who were upholding their homes for their families, as I examined in the de la Guerra archives and through the hemispheric turn to Ruiz de Burton, these women and their racialized sex were not productive for Albuquerque, and they were left to be unexamined for years and then erased in their own memorial.

Juana Maria Rodriguez examines the historical position of Latina sex when she states, "We who have been repeatedly colonized and violated, who have been tricked and traded, who have given ourselves over to the allure of erasure through assimilation or who have repeatedly lived up to the stereotype thrust upon us ... have had to live with the shame of it."[3] Chicanas and Latinas embody the histories of colonialism, enslavement, migration, and displacement/dispossession. These historical legacies of sexual violence are tied to positions of domination and servitude. This is not to say that there are not nuanced positions of power in history—as I exemplify in this book—that maintain white supremacy, patriarchy, and capital; however, representation and stereotypes procure the "excessive" Mexicana female body as voluptuous, open for sex, overproducing, and excessive. Racialized gender and sex denote the social construction and performativity of masculinity and femininity through the lens of race and law; thus the social construction of distinctions between white, Black, Native, and brown femininity. Gender and sex are always racialized and not universal, and they are structured through hegemonic repetition, which falls into gendered regulatory schemes.

The transnational economic context is central to the gender violence toward brown females on the borderlands. In order to think about how certain bodies—in this case, the women murdered on the West Mesa in Albuquerque, New Mexico—were treated upon their excavation and even before their deaths, we must examine how the social constructs of the U.S. national imaginary positions the women as a living commodity or "thing" to be consumed and discarded. To think of the women as a commodity in the Marxist sense is to think about how they are owned. For Karl Marx, the body is the mere appendage to capital, and its labor becomes a commodity external to being. However, in the case of the West Mesa murders, how can a body be a commodity if it is not really owned by anyone or anything? Julia Estela Monárrez Fragoso reminds us that "the different bodily qualities that are codified in gender, ethnicity, social class, and other means of valuing human men and women, including the degree of respect of bodily integrity and the dignity of the worker's body achieves in different places, exist in an environment that is made spatially competitive through the circulation of capital."[4] The women are represented and produced as signifiers of the racial, gender, and economic systems through a social process of value or who is worth what. These women, both before and after death, are "exterior object[s], a thing with its own properties satisfying needs of all kinds."[5] In this case, the patriarchal conditions the brown female lived under in the borderlands, as well as the global capital investment in her body, constitute these "needs." While she is not transactionally owned and has agency, she embodies social use and exchange value for the United States. This is not a new phenomenon, and it is not unique to brown female bodies; however, this book has traced a discourse of sexual capital that is needed and therefore requires violence in certain geopolitical spaces.

What the West Mesa murders exemplify are the "systematic patterns of violence" that shape the lives of pathologized women on the borderlands.

Poor, sexually excessive, improper, and unproductive are a recipe for death. Josefa (Chipita) Rodríguez's story unveils that her body was visible only through the economy of racially gendered violence, which is exemplified through her gendered racial formation in the slim archive of her life that remains. To this day, no one knows the location of Rodríguez's grave. The abstraction of her labor, her body, and her voice further complicates her racialized positionality and relationship to gender and sexuality in the borderlands. Similarly, the conversation the archives has concerning the economy of debt peonage exemplifies the position poor Nuevomexicanas were put in to build racialized civility and sexual capital through violence. While the U.S. empire did not want to accept New Mexico into the union because of anti-Mexican ethnocentrism and anti-Catholic nativism, the *ricos* utilized the racialized sexuality of poor Nuevomexicana women to attempt to maintain their power in the region. This book makes evident that these rich archives of the past are crucial for understanding the contemporary struggles of women of color.

Equally important was looking at the elite landholding Californiana and Hispana narratives, which enunciated the conditions for proper femininity in relation to racialized sex, sexuality, and gender. While there is no shortage of scholarship on Ruiz de Burton, my findings put her in conversation with hemispheric conditions of racialized sex, sexuality, and gender in Mexico. As a border subject who crossed into the United States permanently through war and land cessation, Ruiz de Burton merges U.S. and Mexican racial hierarchies by relying on racist feminine tropes circulating in the Americas during the colonial period. And while Ruiz de Burton's letters shows no connections to the de la Guerra daughters, their desire to hold on to a certain political economy is evident. The de la Guerras were part of a somatic and epistemological change in economy that brought in a new form of capitalism, which can now be understood as "displacing the categories of humanism with hedonistic ones that entail an absolute change in the conception and apprehension of reality."[6] This book is not a complete history of sexual and gender violence on the borderlands, but is a look at snapshots that provide information on how we work, are educated, live, and love. This means that while we are fighting for a safer and alternative world, living under capitalism has made us accustomed to violence. Sayak describes this as "violence as a tool to acquire money, which allows individuals to purchase both commercial goods and social status."[7]

The main argument of this book—that our past shapes our present—is nothing new. This book has attempted to uncover a history of gender and sexual violence. But more importantly, it has attempted to think critically about how sexual capital is mobilized at different historical moments for different projects

Women's Memorial Park cross, Albuquerque, New Mexico.
Photo by Bernadine Hernández, 2020.

on the U.S.–Mexico border and in the Southwest borderlands before and after annexation. Whether tied to racist colonial ideology, economic interests, or nation-building projects, racialized sex, gender, and sexuality utilize the extraction of sexual capital in violent ways. Law and order have never been lacking for Chicana, Latina, Mexicana, or Latin American women, but what has been lacking is how law and order have been upheld or negotiated because the brown female body is not perceived as important enough to attempt to combat brutalization and murder on the border.

There is much more work to be done in uncovering a history of violence toward brown females on the borderlands. Probably more important, there is much more work to be done in order to create a trans-feminist connection to keep each other safe. The violent systems and constructions of racialized sex, sexuality, and gender that inform sexual capital I have examined in this book present us with an opportunity to enter the fissures of that violence. These fissures can offer us new possibilities of collective action, mutual aid, and alternative worlds. Because as the saying goes: Another world is possible.

Notes

Introduction

1. CBS News, "Discovery Near Mass Gravesite Leads to Fears of More Victims in Unsolved Serial Killings."
2. Browman, "Albuquerque Journal Special Report: West Mesa Murders."
3. After an uproar by community members as to how the Albuquerque Police Department and the Albuquerque media were portraying the victims, these statements have been almost completely stricken from the records of the case. However, similar language can still be found—for instance, in an article by Fox News, "Five Years after Mass Grave Discovered, Albuquerque Killings Remain Unsolved," February 10, 2014 (accessed September 16, 2019), foxnews.com/us/five-years-after-mass-grave-discovered-albuquerque-killings-remain-unsolved.
4. I will also use the term "Mexicana" to refer to a Spanish-speaking woman residing in or traversing boundaries back and forth between the U.S.-Mexico boundary established in 1848/1853; most Mexicanas were mixed racially in some way, and some court documents utilize the Spanish *casta* system to describe their subjectivity. When the *casta* system racial terms are utilized in the archive, I will utilize them and explain in an endnote what they mean. I will use the term "Mexican American" for women who resided on the U.S. side after the invasion and annexation of Mexico in 1846 when the documents use that term; however, I will *always* use the women's regional territorial name, like "Nuevomexicana" and "Tejana," if "Mexican American" is absent in the documents. I will use the regional territorial name for elite landholding women, such as "Hispana" (New Mexican), "Californio," and "Tejana." I refer to women who were associated with tribes as "native/Indigenous."
5. The feminicides in Juárez took a steady upturn in May 1993. Since then, upwards of one thousand female bodies have been found in various forms and places, such as the desert, alleyways, water sources, and garbage dumps. Other women in Juárez and surrounding areas have gone missing and their bodies never recovered. According to the National Citizen Femicide Observatory, as of 2015, six women are killed each day in the border town of Juárez, and only approximately 1.6 percent of the murders investigated lead to sentencing (Aljazeera America, 2015).
6. I am defining the Southwest borderlands from Northern California to Colorado down to Houston, Texas.
7. Moñarrez Fragoso and Bejarano, "The Disarticulation of Justice," 44.
8. Cisneros, "Woman Hollering Creek."
9. Browman, "Albuquerque Journal Special Report: West Mesa Murders."
10. *Sexual capital* is a term mostly utilized in the field of sociology and a term explored by Pierre Bourdieu, a sociologist at the College de France. Bourdieu examines how structured sexual divisions of labor generate a *sexually* differentiated perspective on the world. He theorizes about sexual capital as a division of labor that is a dialectical relationship between

the body (made up of meaning, value gestures, postures, physical bearing, speech, and language) and a space structured on ritual oppositions (gender roles). This sexual capital becomes objectified in the caring labor of femininity and is institutionalized beyond the domestic space. This sociological theorizing of sexual capital examines gendered divisions of labor as universal. This definition studies sexual capital through social constructions that are symbolic, where no material exchange exists, and carries logics of desire and attractiveness. For a sociological study of sexual capital, please see Pierre Bourdieu's *Outline of a Theory of Practice* (1977) and *Logic of Practice* (1980), and John Levi Martin and Matt George, "Theories of Sexual Stratification" (2006).

11. Guidotti-Hernández, *Unspeakable Violence*, 3.

12. I am building off of foundational Chicana feminists who have shaped this book: Deena Gonzalez, *Refusing the Favor*; Antonia Castañeda, *Three Decades of Engendering History*; Rosaura Sánchez, *Telling Identities*; Miroslava Chávez-García, *Negotiating Conquest*; Erika Pérez, *Colonial Intimacies*; Vicki Ruiz, *From out of the Shadows*; María Cotera, *Native Speakers*; and Emma Peréz, *The Decolonial Imaginary*.

13. Castañeda, "Engendering the History of Alta California," 230.

14. Castañeda, "Engendering the History of Alta California," 231.

15. JanMohamed, "Sexuality on/of the Racial Border," 94.

16. JanMohamed, "Sexuality on/of the Racial Border," 97.

17. For more on racialized sexuality, see Emma Pérez's *The Decolonial Imaginary*; Sandy Soto's *Reading Chican@ Like a Queer: The De-Mastery of Desire* (Austin: University of Texas Press, 2010); and Juana Maria Rodriguez's *Sexual Futures, Queer Gestures, and Other Latina Longings* (New York: New York University Press, 2014).

18. Marx, "Economic and Philosophic Manuscripts of 1844," 82.

19. Marx, "Economic and Philosophic Manuscripts of 1844," 82.

20. Engels, "The Monogamous Family," 126.

21. In his *Economic and Philosophical Manuscripts of 1844*, Marx begins defining the terms he would later elaborate on in *Das Capital*, productive and reproductive labor being some of those very important definitions. Where productive labor produces value, and labor is a commodity that can be sold and exchanged, reproductive labor does not produce value and sees reproductive labor as household duties that reproduce the worker to go to work the next day. Marx also sees the commodity as the universal presence within the capitalist mode of production, where labor, a commodity that the worker can sell and exchange, makes commodities for value. Marx is essential in my understanding of sexual capital, because it is building off what Marx sees as wage productive labor and what he says is not.

22. Fortunati, *The Arcane of Reproduction*, 5.

23. Fragoso, "The Victims of Ciudad Juárez Feminicide," 63.

24. Questions that the special issue of *Radical History Review* took up in Benjamin A. Cowan, Nicole M. Guidotti-Hernández, and Jason Ruiz, eds., "Sexing Empire," *Radical History Review*. 123 (October 2015).

25. For gender performativity, see Judith Butler, *Gender Trouble*, and *Bodies That Matter: On the Discursive Limits of "Sex"* (New York: Routledge, 1996).

26. Lazo, "Introduction: Historical Latinidades and Archival Encounters," 9.

27. Tortorici, *Sins against Nature*, 3.

28. Barrera, *Race and Class in the Southwest*, 4.

Notes to Introduction 183

29. Chávez-García, *Negotiating Conquest*, 26.
30. *Los indios (bárbaros)*: barbarous Indians; *la cautiva*: the captive; *la mulata*: mixed-race girl.
31. Adam Smith, *An Inquiry into the Nature and Causes of the Wealth of Nations*.
32. Coronado, *A World Not to Come*, 113.
33. Coronado, *A World Not to Come*, 114.
34. González, *Refusing the Favor*, 20.
35. Mitchell, *Coyote Nation*, 12.
36. Turner, "The Significance of the Frontier in American History."
37. Kaplan, "Manifest Domesticity," 582.
38. Kaplan, "Manifest Domesticity," 582.
39. For more on domestic metaphors (i.e., "home" as nation, and "family" as the people who occupy the nation, but also through "woman" as the center of the domestic unit that keeps everything together though heteronormative relations), see Anne McClintock, *Imperial Leather: Race, Gender and Sexuality in the Colonial Contest* (New York: Routledge, 1995); Gopinath, "Nostalgia, Desire, Diaspora," 467–89.
40. Zink, *Fictions of Western American Domesticity*, 4.
41. González, "Lupe's Song," 255.
42. See Deena González, *Refusing the Favor*, especially chapter 2.
43. Fray Junipero Serra to Antonio Maria de Bucareli y Ursua, 21 May 1773, in Antonine Tibesar, ed., *Writings of Junipero Serra*, 1:363; Antonia I. Castañeda, "Sexual Violence in the Politics and Policies of Conquest: Amerindian Women and the Spanish Conquest of Alta California," in *Building with Our Hands: New Directions in Chicana Studies*, ed. Adela de la Torre and Beatriz M. Pesquera (Berkeley: University of California Press, 1993), 15–33.
44. Castañeda, "Anglo American Stereotypes of Californianas," 162.
45. Chávez-García, *Negotiating Conquest*, xiii.
46. Paz, *The Labyrinth of Solitude*, 16.
47. Cypess, *La Malinche in Mexican Literature*, 35.
48. Alarcón, "Traddutora, Traditora," 58.
49. For more scholarship on Malinche see Alarcón, "Traddutora, Traditora"; Cypess, *La Malinche in Mexican Literature*; and Godayol, "Malintzin/La Malinche/Doña Marina."
50. Guidotti-Hernández, *Unspeakable Violence*, 141.
51. Castañeda, "Gender, Race, and Culture," 9.
52. Valerio-Jiménez, *River of Hope*, 76.
53. Arrom, *The Women of Mexico City*, 56–64; Lavrin, "Sexuality in Colonial Mexico," 65.
54. For more on race, immigration, and disease, see Natalia Molina's *Fit to Be Citizens: Public Health and Race in Los Angeles, 1879–1939* (Berkeley: University of California Press, 2006).
55. Best and Marcus, "Surface Reading: An Introduction," 2.
56. Jameson, *Political Unconscious*, 60.
57. Valencia, *Gore Capitalism*, 36.
58. Hennessy, *Profit and Pleasure*, 6.
59. This book is taking cues from Rosemary Hennessy (2000), Lisa Lowe (1996), and David Roediger (1991) to argue that what seems to be an identity as "sexuality" is closely tied to the historical process of how sex was utilized in the nineteenth century. This produced what

we now know as *racial capitalism*, which pit "normative" categories of subjectivity against racialized difference. To view heteronormative, white sexuality as the pillar of U.S. national discourse is an understatement and a rhetoric of American exceptionalism that "built" the nation; however, by challenging this "norm," this book uncovers how the racialized sexual and gendered history of the borderlands was the abstracted labor that also built the nation. Sex and sexuality go hand in hand in this book, as Foucault states.

60. Hennessy, *Profit and Pleasure*, 15.

61. Hennessy, *Profit and Pleasure*, 2.

62. Hennessy, *Profit and Pleasure*, 40.

63. Hennessy, *Profit and Pleasure*, 42.

64. See Wilhelm Reich, *Sex-Pol: Essays 1929–1934*, ed. Lee Baxandall, trans. Anna Bostock, Tom DuBose, and Lee Baxandall (New York: Vintage Books, 1972).

65. Marcuse, *Eros and Civilization*, 166.

66. Hennessy, *Profit and Pleasure*, 10.

67. McClanahan, *Dead Pledges*, 12.

68. Bernes, *The Work of Art in the Age of Deindustrialization*, 140.

69. Bernes, *The Work of Art in the Age of Deindustrialization*, 2.

70. Denning, "Wageless Life," 79; Davis, *Planet of Slums*, 14; Standing, *The Precariat*; Bernes, *The Work of Art in the Age of Deindustrialization*, 182.

71. Quoted in Day, *Alien Capital*, 8.

72. Marx, *Capital*, 128.

73. Lowe, *Immigrant Acts*, 27–28.

74. Rosemary Hennessy blames structuralist Marxists, namely Louis Althusser, for identifying the mode of production (the abstract structural relations of capitalism) with the social formation (the specific historical instance of these structures). She looks at Ellen Wood and says she contends that even though Althusser distinguishes between a social formation and the capitalist mode of production, the tension between the abstract structures of capitalism's mode of production and the contingent or provisional and specific ways they are enacted in any social formation remains in his theory. The concept of "social formation" that Althusser and his collaborator Etienne Balibar come up with implies that no historically existing individual society represents the capitalist mode of production pure and simple. In other words, the abstract formal capitalist mode of production never exists in the strong sense in reality; it only exists in particular "social formations" or actually existing social forms at particular times. One of the issues involved in theorizing the relationship between the mode of production and the ways it is played out in a particular social formation is how we are to understand any causal relationship between social structures (like capitalism's exploitative division of labor) and the ways they are lived in any particular time and place. Wood contends that the distinction Althusser and Balibar draw between the mode of production and social formations, like the distinction they make between social relations that are determinate and those that are contingent or temporary, finally only drives a wedge between the concepts of mode of production and social formation rather than formulating a way to answer the challenge posed by Marx himself—that is, "how to encompass historical specificity, as well as human agency, while recognizing within it the logic of mode of production" (Wood 59). Wood reminds us that Marx's own account of the connection between economic and political-ideological forms suggests the complex vari-

ability of empirical reality and the operation within it of a logic derived from and organized by production relations. Here Marx is understanding "the innermost secret" of capitalist relations—the economic relationship of owner and producer—as a determining logic. But this determining logic is not abstract and monocausal, but rather a structure that is both necessary to capitalism and always historically inflected. The relationship of owner and producer is never unaffected by historical influences, among them cultural forms like race (and we might add gender and sexuality), which Marx mentions.

Chapter One

1. The de la Guerra Collection, Santa Barbara Mission Archive (SBMA).
2. Robinson to Don José de la Guerra y Noriega, New York, October 21, 1847.
3. Robinson to Don José de la Guerra y Noriega, New York, November 22, 1846; Robinson to Pablo de la Guerra, New York, September 20, 1846.
4. Robinson to Pablo de la Guerra, New York, September 20, 1846.
5. I will be using the term "Californiana" to talk about the elite women that were born in Alta California and spoke Spanish. I will be using the term "Californio" when I am talking about the entire population of elite Californians in Alta California in the nineteeth century.
6. Chávez-García, *Negotiating Conquest*, xiv, xv.
7. Mitropoulos, *Contract and Contagion*, 50
8. Mitropoulos, *Contract and Contagion*, 50.
9. Mitropoulos, *Contract and Contagion*, 50.
10. Mitropoulos, *Contract and Contagion*, 50.
11. Mitropoulos, *Contract and Contagion*, 56.
12. Casas, *Married to a Daughter of the Land*, 7.
13. González, *Refusing the Favor*, 114.
14. Mitropoulos, *Contract and Contagion*, 56.
15. Mitropoulos, *Contract and Contagion*, 49. "Family" is *genea* and connects to lineage and genealogy.
16. See Aristotle, *The Complete Works of Aristotle*, vol. 1.
17. Mitropoulos, *Contract and Contagion*, 58.
18. Xenophon, *The Economist*, 290.
19. Aristotle, *The Complete Works of Aristotle*, vol. 2, Politics, 1256b.26–1257a.4.
20. Aristotle, *The Complete Works of Aristotle*, vol. 1, Physics, II, I, 192b9–17; Aristotle, *The Complete Works of Aristotle*, vol. 2, Politics, 1254a4–18.
21. Mitropoulos, "Oikonomia," in *Philosophy Today*, 1027.
22. Marx, *Capital, Volume One*, 69.
23. Mitropoulos, "Oikonomia," in *Philosophy Today*, 1029.
24. Marx, *Capital, Volume One*, 42.
25. Mitropoulos, "Oikonomia," in *Philosophy Today*, 1033.
26. Mitropoulos, *Contract and Contagion*, 50.
27. Pubols, *The Father of All*, 14.
28. Pubols, *The Father of All*, 16. De la Guerra was part of the military salary and supply administration, which is the translation of the Habilitado General section.
29. Pubols, *The Father of All*, 16.

30. Pubols, *The Father of All*, 25.
31. Pubols, *The Father of All*, 25.
32. Pubols, *The Father of All*, 26.
33. Thompson, *El Gran Capitán*, 12.
34. Thompson, *El Gran Capitán*, 26.
35. Angustias de la Guerra, Journal, September 3, 1846.
36. Sánchez, *Telling Identities*, 8.
37. Sánchez, *Telling Identities*, 8.
38. López, "The Political Economy of Early Chicano Historiography," 876.
39. Angustias de la Guerra Ord to Thomas Savage, *The California Recollections*, 8.
40. Angustias de la Guerra Ord to Thomas Savage, *The California Recollections*, 24.
41. Angustias de la Guerra Ord, to Thomas Savage, *The California Recollections*, 24.
42. Angustias de la Guerra Ord, to Thomas Savage, *The California Recollections*, 24.
43. Angustias de la Guerra Ord, to Thomas Savage, *The California Recollections*, 24.
44. Angustias de la Guerra Ord, to Thomas Savage, *The California Recollections*, 24.
45. Pubols, *The Father of All*, 110.
46. Pubols, *The Father of All*, 112.
47. Pubols, *The Father of All*, 115.
48. The most informative and thorough study of de la Guerra and his life and wealth is Louise Pubols, *The Father of All: The de la Guerra Family, Power, and Patriarchy in Mexican California*.
49. Pubols, *The Father of All*, 115.
50. Alfred Robinson to María Antonia, Los Angeles, May 16, 1834.
51. Alfred Robinson to Jose de la Guerra y Noriega, Santa Barbara, December 28, 1834.
52. Ogden, "The Business Letters of Alfred Robinson," 315–16.
53. Ana María (de la Guerra) Robinson to José de la Guerra, her father, and to María Antonia (Carillo), her mother, Boston, June 11, 1838, DLG 836, Letter 1, SBMA.
54. Ana María (de la Guerra) Robinson to José de la Guerra, her father, New York, February 27, 1839, DLG 836, Letter 2, SBMA.
55. Ibid.
56. Fortunati, *Arcane of Reproduction*, 8.
57. Fortunati, *Arcane of Reproduction*, 8.
58. Fortunati, *Arcane of Reproduction*, 231.
59. Ana María (de la Guerra) Robinson to José de la Guerra, her father, New York, February 27, 1839, DLG 836, Letter 2, SBMA.
60. Ana María (de la Guerra) Robinson to José de la Guerra, her father, New York, February 27, 1839, DLG 836, Letter 2, SBMA.
61. Ana María (de la Guerra) Robinson to José de la Guerra, her father, New York (sent by way of the Sandwich Islands), April 15, 1839, DLG 836, Letter 3, SBMA.
62. Ana María (de la Guerra) Robinson to her parents, unknown location, September 30, 1840, DLG 836, Letter 5, SBMA.
63. Bernes, *The Work of Art in the Age of Deindustrialization*.
64. Deniz Kandiyoti. "Identity and Its Discontents: Women and the Nation," 429–43.
65. See chapter 1, "Gender and the Conquest and Colonization of California," of Miroslava Chávez-García's book, *Negotiating Conquest*.

66. Chávez-García, *Negotiating Conquest*, 6.
67. Chávez-García, *Negotiating Conquest*, 14.
68. Chávez-García, *Negotiating Conquest*, 14.
69. Chávez-García, *Negotiating Conquest*, 17.
70. Chávez-García, *Negotiating Conquest*, 15.
71. Chávez-García, *Negotiating Conquest*, 26.
72. Zink, *Fictions of Western American Domesticity*.
73. Pérez, *Colonial Intimacies*, 120.
74. Pérez, *Colonial Intimacies*, 122.
75. Pérez, *Colonial Intimacies*, 122.
76. Pubols, *The Father of All*, 113.
77. Pubols, *The Father of All*, 107.
78. Beebe and Senkewicz, "Teresa de la Guerra," in *Testimonios*, 51.
79. Beebe and Senkewicz, "Teresa de la Guerra," in *Testimonios*, 58.
80. Beebe and Senkewicz, *Testimonios*, 58.
81. Angustias de la Guerra Ord, to Thomas Savage, *The California Recollections*, 44.
82. Angustias de la Guerra Ord, to Thomas Savage, *The California Recollections*, 44.
83. Beebe and Senkewicz, *Testimonios*, 62.
84. Lopez, "Picturing Mexican America in the Age of Realism," 270.
85. Lopez, "Picturing Mexican America in the Age of Realism," 265.
86. Henning, "The Subject as Object: Photography and the Human Body," 164.
87. Henning, "The Subject as Object: Photography and the Human Body," 221, 223.
88. Prosser, *Light in the Dark Room*, 1.
89. Wexler, *Tender Violence*, 54.
90. Wexler, *Tender Violence*, 54.
91. Wexler, *Tender Violence*, 53.
92. Wexler, *Tender Violence*, 53.

Chapter Two

1. Coronado, *A World Not to Come*, 8.
2. Coronado, *A World Not to Come*, 10.
3. Coronado, *A World Not to Come*, 17.
4. Coronado, *A World Not to Come*, 12.
5. Ruiz, "Captive Identities," 118.
6. Ruiz de Burton, *Who Would Have Thought It?*, 173.
7. Sánchez and Pita, "Introduction," xxxi.
8. Arce, *Mexico's Nobodies*, 4.
9. Ramos, "'I Am Not the Mulata de Córdoba,'" 92.
10. Orozco y Berra, *Apéndice al Diccionario universal de historia y de geografía*, 935.
11. For a more in-depth look at Blackness in Mexico, please see Marco Polo Hernandez Cuevas, "Modern National Discourse and La Muerte de Artemio Cruz: The Illusory 'Death' of African Mexican Lineage," *Afro-Hispanic Review* 23, no. 1 (Spring 2004): 10–16; Marco Polo Hernandez Cuevas, *African Mexicans and the Discourse of Modern Nation* (New York: Oxford University Press, 2004); José Ortiz Monasterio, *México Eternamente: Vicente Riva Palacio ante*

la escritura de la historia (Mexico: Instituto de Investigaciones Dr. José María Luis Mora, Fondo de Cultura Económica, 2004); Ramos, "'I Am Not the Mulata de Córdoba,'" 90–101; and Arce, *Mexico's Nobodies*.

12. Ruiz de Burton, *Who Would Have Thought It?*, 200.
13. Ruiz de Burton, *Who Would Have Thought It?*, 200.
14. Ruiz de Burton, *Who Would Have Thought It?*, 200.
15. Salas, *In the Shadow of the Eagles*, 104–5.
16. Irwin, "Early Paradoxes," 1.
17. Irwin, "Early Paradoxes," xxix.
18. Ruiz de Burton, *Conflicts of Interest*, 7.
19. Aranda, "Returning California to the People," 11–26.
20. See Jesse Alemán, "Historical Amnesia and the Vanishing Mestiza: The Problems of Race in *The Squatter and the Don* and *Ramona*," *Aztlán* 27, no. 1 (2005): 59–93; and Jesse Alemán, "'Thank God, Lolita Is Away from Those Horrid Savages,'" 95–111.
21. Ruiz, "Captive Identities," 112–32.
22. Ruiz de Burton, *Conflicts of Interest*, 4.
23. Ruiz de Burton, *Conflicts of Interest*, 17.
24. Rosaura Sánchez and Beatrice Pita have done extensive research on Ruiz de Burton and her family in *Conflicts of Interest: The Letters of María Amparo Ruiz de Burton*. See chapter 1, "Baja California," in the book for a more in-depth examination of her life.
25. Martha Menchaca states in her book *Recovering History, Constructing Race: The Indian, Black, and White Roots of Mexican Americans*, "Though by law the *criollo* racial category was reserved for whites, it was common for parish priests to register mestizo children of means as *criollo* by including in the baptismal registry only the race of the father" (65).
26. "MARB to M. G. Vallejo. 15 February 1869, New York," in Sánchez and Pita, eds., *Conflicts of Interest: The Letters of María Amparo Ruiz de Burton*, 280.
27. Letters from December 6, 1857, and September 1, 1857. In Sánchez and Pita, eds., "MARB to Prudenciana Moreno. 1 September 1857, Jamul" and "MARB to Prudenciana Moreno. 6 December 1857, Jamul," in *Conflicts of Interest: The Letters of María Amparo Ruiz de Burton*.
28. Ruiz de Burton, *Conflicts of Interest*, 149.
29. Ruiz de Burton, *Conflicts of Interest*, 280.
30. Ruiz de Burton, *Conflicts of Interest*, 105.
31. Ruiz de Burton, *Conflicts of Interest*, 235.
32. Spain instituted a racial order called the *casta* system through which Mexico's population came to be legally distinguished based on race. The categories included *peninsulares*, individuals of full European descent who had been born in Spain, and *criollos*, who were also of full European descent but had been born in the New World. *Mestizos* were other persons of mixed blood who enjoyed higher social prestige than *indios* but were considered inferior to Spaniards. The *indio* category included only people of full Indigenous descent. *Afromestizos* were accorded the same legal privileges as mestizos; however, because they were of African descent, they were stigmatized and considered socially inferior to *indios* and mestizos. For more on the institutionalization of the *casta* system in eighteenth-century New Spain, see Menchaca, *Recovering History, Constructing Race*.

33. For more on how Latin American historians think about race in Mexico, please see María Elena Martínez's *Genealogical Fictions*, Ben Vinson's *Before Mestizaje*, Peter Guardino's *The Dead March*, Juan Mora-Torres's *The Making of the Mexican Border*, Gonzalo Aguirre Beltrán's *La Población Negra de México*, Claudio Lomnitz-Adler's *Exits from the Labyrinth*, and Ann Twinam's *Purchasing Whiteness*.
34. Lomnitz-Adler, *Exits from the Labyrinth*, 274.
35. Lomnitz-Adler, *Exits from the Labyrinth*, 275.
36. Lomnitz-Adler, *Exits from the Labyrinth*, 276.
37. Lomnitz-Adler, *Exits from the Labyrinth*, 276.
38. Goldman, "Beasts in the Jungle," 89.
39. Alemán, "'Thank God, Lolita Is Away from Those Horrid Savages,'" 103.
40. Murphy, "Geographic Morality," 99.
41. Ruiz de Burton, *Who Would Have Thought It?*, 197.
42. Ruiz de Burton, *Who Would Have Thought It?*, 197.
43. Sánchez and Pita, "(Shifting) Frames of Reference: Southwest by East," *Conflicts of Interest* 182.
44. Murphy, "Geographic Morality," 103.
45. "MARB to Matías Moreno, 9 March 1967, Fortress Monroe," in Sánchez and Pita, eds., *Conflicts of Interest: The Letters of María Amparo Ruiz de Burton*, 268–70.
46. Rosaura Sánchez and Beatrice Pita categorize Ruiz de Burton as a Francophile. She bases the fusion of the Austrian Mexican character of Lola on the works of Michel Chevalier, who was a spokesman for Napoleon III and expressed his support for official French recognition of the Confederacy.
47. Murphy, "A Europeanized World," 138.
48. Aranda, "Contradictory Impulses," 573.
49. Ramos, "'I Am Not the Mulata de Córdoba,'" 90.
50. Tinnemeyer, "Rescuing the Past," 181.
51. Arce, *Mexico's Nobodies*, 147.
52. Arce, *Mexico's Nobodies*, 91.
53. Arce, *Mexico's Nobodies*, 4.
54. Arce, *Mexico's Nobodies*, 148.
55. Arce, *Mexico's Nobodies*, 148.
56. Arce, *Mexico's Nobodies*, 148.
57. Ruiz de Burton, *Who Would Have Thought It?*, 27.
58. Ruiz de Burton, *Who Would Have Thought It?*, 18.
59. Ruiz de Burton, *Who Would Have Thought It?*, 16.
60. Arce, *Mexico's Nobodies*, 156.
61. Ruiz de Burton, *Who Would Have Thought It?*, 16.
62. Ruiz de Burton, *Who Would Have Thought It?*, 17.
63. Ruiz de Burton, *Who Would Have Thought It?*, 25.
64. Ruiz de Burton, *Who Would Have Thought It?*, 17.
65. Ruiz de Burton, *Who Would Have Thought It?*, 17.
66. Palacio, *Tradiciones y Leyendas Mexicanas*, 214.
67. Arce, *Mexico's Nobodies*, 156.
68. Arce, *Mexico's Nobodies*, 25.

69. Arce, *Mexico's Nobodies*, 30.
70. Palacio, *Tradiciones y Leyendas Mexicanas*, 214.
71. Ruiz de Burton, *Who Would Have Thought It?*, 42.
72. Ruiz de Burton, *Who Would Have Thought It?*, 49.
73. Ruiz de Burton, *Who Would Have Thought It?*, 78.
74. Ruiz de Burton, *Who Would Have Thought It?*, 100.
75. Ruiz de Burton, *Who Would Have Thought It?*, 286.
76. Ruiz de Burton, *Who Would Have Thought It?*, 35.
77. Cabezut, "Cuatro palabras al bello sexo," 3.
78. Goldman, "Who Ever Heard of a Blue-Eyed Mexican?," 65.
79. Cabezut, "Cuatro palabras al bello sexo," 3.
80. "República Mexicana," *La Estrella de Occidente*, column 3, page 1.
81. "Noticia de Apaches," *La Estrella de Occidente*, column 1.
82. "Editorial," *La Estrella de Occidente*, column 1, page 3.
83. Saldaña-Portillo, "Adjudicating Exception," 8.
84. Saldaña-Portillo, "Adjudicating Exception," 8.
85. "Situacion de Sonora y los Apaches," column 1, page 3.
86. Saldaña-Portillo, "Adjudicating Exception," 154.
87. For more in-depth discussions on the "whitening" Mexican immigration policies, see Moisés González Navarro, *La política Colonizadora del Porfiriato* (México: Separata de Estudios Históricos Americanos, 1953); Moisés González Navarro, *La colonización en México, 1877–1910* (México: 1960); Ignacio González-Polo, "Ensayo de una bibliografía de la colonización en México durante el siglo XIX," *Boletín del Instituto de Investigaciones Bibliográficas* 4 (1960): 179–91; George Dieter Berninger, "Mexican Attitudes towards Immigration, 1821–1857" (PhD diss., Department of History, University of Wisconsin, 1972); Ignacio González-Polo y Acosta, "Colonización e inmigración extranjera durante las primeras décadas delsiglo xix," *Boletín bibliográfico de la Secretaria de Hacienda y Crédito* 412 (1973): 4–7; Nancy N. Barker, "The French Colony in México, 1821–1861," *French Historical Studies* 9, no. 4 (Fall 1976): 596–618; Dieter Berninger, "Immigration and Religious Toleration: A Mexican Dilemma, 1821–1860," *The Americas* 32, no. 4 (April 1976): 549–65; José B. Zilli Mánica, "Proyectos liberales de colonización en el siglo XIX," *La palabra y el hombre* 52 (Octubre–Diciembre 1984): 129–42; Jan de Vos, "Una legislación de graves consecuencias: El acarpamiento de tierras baldías en México con el pretexto de colonización, 1821–1910," *Historia Mexicana* 34, no. 1 (Julio–Septiembre 1984): 76–113; Moisés González Navarro, *Los extranjeros en México y los mexicanos en el extranjero, 1821–1970*, 3 vols. (México: El Colegio de México, Centro de Estudios Históricos, 1993); David K. Burden, "La idea salvadora: Immigration and Colonization Politics in México, 1821–1857" (PhD article, Department of History, University of California–Santa Barbara, 2005); Luz María Martínez Montiel, *Inmigración y diversidad cultural en México: Una propuesta metodológica para su estudio* (México: Universidad Autónoma de México, 2005).
88. Saldaña-Portillo, "Adjudicating Exception," 155.
89. Weber, *The Mexican Frontier*, 103.
90. Gutiérrez de Lara, *Proyecto de Ley General de Colonización*, 54, quoted in Burden, "La idea salvadora."
91. Arce, *Mexico's Nobodies*, 2.

92. Ruiz de Burton, *Who Would Have Thought It?*, 35.
93. Ruiz de Burton, *Who Would Have Thought It?*, 35.
94. "Apaches," *La Estrella de Occidente*, column 1.
95. "Apaches," *La Estrella de Occidente*, column 1.
96. Ruiz de Burton, *Who Would Have Thought It?*, 28, 36.
97. Ruiz de Burton, *Who Would Have Thought It?*, 28.
98. Sánchez and Pita, "Introduction," lxi.
99. Cabezut, "Cuatro palabras al bello sexo," 3.
100. Ruiz de Burton, *Who Would Have Thought It?*, 35.
101. Cabezut, "Cuatro palabras al bello sexo," 35
102. Ruiz de Burton, *Who Would Have Thought It?*, 30.
103. Krivulskaya, "The Itinerant Passions of Protestant Pastors," 77.
104. Krivulskaya, "The Itinerant Passions of Protestant Pastors," 78.
105. Douglas, *The Feminization of American Culture*, 97.
106. Douglas, *The Feminization of American Culture*, 97.
107. "The Pastor of Illinois Church Convicted as a Despicable Thief," *Petersburg Index and Appeal*.
108. "The Rev. Alfred Thompson," *Chicago Daily Tribune*.
109. Douglas, *The Feminization of American Culture*, 100.
110. Ruiz de Burton, *Who Would Have Thought It?*, 149.
111. Ruiz de Burton, *Who Would Have Thought It?*, 151.
112. Ruiz de Burton, *Who Would Have Thought It?*, 171.
113. Ruiz de Burton, *Who Would Have Thought It?*, 173.
114. Ruiz de Burton, *Who Would Have Thought It?*, 120.
115. Foster, "The Contest for the Laws of Reform in Mexico," 526.
116. Ruiz de Burton, *Who Would Have Thought It?*, 11.

Chapter Three

1. In this chapter, I use "Tejano" as a term to describe peoples who were generationally from Spanish colonization—with long ties to land because of family history—but were racially constructed as Mexicans and shifted as citizens as the geographical location of and power over Texas changed throughout history. I use "Texas Mexicans" to describe Mexicans who settled in Texas during the Texas Revolution. I use the term "Anglo-American" to describe U.S. settlers from the East Coast.
2. McDaniel, "The Day They Hanged Chipita."
3. Lazo, "Introduction: Historical Latinidades and Archival Encounters," 9.
4. Conner, "Foreword."
5. It is unclear how Rachel Bluntzer Hebert was related to Kate McCumber.
6. Bluntzer Hebert, "Shadow on the Nueces," 17.
7. Bluntzer Hebert, "Shadow on the Nueces," 17.
8. Bluntzer Hebert, "Shadow on the Nueces," 23, 24.
9. Bluntzer Hebert, "Shadow on the Nueces," 24.
10. Bluntzer Hebert, "Shadow on the Nueces," 25, 27.
11. Bluntzer Hebert, "Shadow on the Nueces," 20.

12. Bluntzer Hebert, "Shadow on the Nueces," 33.
13. Bluntzer Hebert, "Shadow on the Nueces," 35.
14. Bluntzer Hebert, "Shadow on the Nueces," 47.
15. Bluntzer Hebert, "Shadow on the Nueces," 48.
16. Bluntzer Hebert, "Shadow on the Nueces," 62.
17. Bluntzer Hebert, "Shadow on the Nueces," 63.
18. Guthrie, *The Legend of Chipita*, 14–15.
19. By all legal accounts, Judge Benjamin F. Neal was not a hanging judge, but his clean record on capital punishment did not speak to his political opinions on race relations in Texas. Judge Neal was born in Virginia sometime in the early 1790s, and he went to Texas seeking fortune on the frontier. He started a newspaper called the *Galveston News* and was not only involved in the Mexican Federalist cause but also served in a Confederate military unit during the start of the Civil War. In 1863, when Judge John F. McKinney passed away, Neal turned in his commission to the Confederate forces and ran for the office. Judge Neal's involvement with Rodríguez's case was always risky, because for one, federal authorities constantly received complaints about the competence and conduct of ex-Confederate judges in Texas. Randolph B. Campbell, in "The District Judges of Texas in 1866–1867," states that "Judge Thomas Harrison of Waco "had been a member of the vigilance committee that came to [Nathan Patten's] home in an unsuccessful attempt to hang him for unionism at the outset of the Civil War." Judge Neal functioned along the same vigilante legal lines. He ordered Rodríguez to be hung against the jury's recommendation for a lenient sentence because of her age. The future governor of Corpus Christi described Judge Neal as an "ignorant, prejudicial, bitter fellow" and called for his removal.
20. Guthrie, *The Legend of Chipita*, 28.
21. Keith Guthrie states in *The Legend of Chipita* that grand jury members were as follows: Pat Henry, John Welder, Juan Leal, Thos. Redmond, G. W. McCown, George Williams, F. B. Means, R. H. Bass, J. L. Gilbert, John Choate, George Allen, John Henderickson, John Cofhan, and John E. A. Randolph.
22. San Patricio County District Court Records, Volume 2, Monday, October 5–Saturday, October 10, 1863, 113.
23. Bluntzer Hebert, "Shadow on the Nueces," 36.
24. San Patricio County District Court Records, Volume 2, Monday, October 5–Saturday, October 10, 1863, 113.
25. San Patricio County District Court Records, Volume 2, Monday, October 5–Saturday, October 10, 1863, 113.
26. According to Keith Guthrie in *The Legend of Chipita* (34–35), John Silvera was a member of Captain Aldrete's division of Jeff Davis's Home Guards. He was listed in the 1850 census as a resident of San Patricio County and was forty years old with a wife and daughter.
27. Kandaswamy, "Gendering Racial Formation," 23–24.
28. In thinking about gender racial formations, I build off of Priya Kandaswamy's chapter in *Racial Formation in the Twenty-First Century* titled "Gendering Racial Formation," where she extends Omi and Winant's work on race through an intersectional analysis. Omi and Winant define race not as a category of biological difference but rather in what perceived bodily difference comes to mean in the context of social construction. They further argue

that race is in contrast to gender, which is a social construction that is grounded in natural biological divisions between the sexes, relegating gender politics to sexual difference. Kandaswamy argues that there is a deep problem with this analysis. First, by stating that sex is static and natural, they miss the opportunity to think about how sex is always in relation to gender and therefore always a social construction. Second, Kandaswamy calls out Omi and Winant for positioning race and gender as distinct categories to be compared rather than imbricated categories that are constructed simultaneously and gain their meaning in and through each other (24–26).

29. Bluntzer Hebert, "Shadow on the Nueces," 24.
30. Davis, *Land!*, 76.
31. Davis, *Land!*, 73.
32. Davis, *Land!*, 73.
33. Refugio County Commissioner's Court minutes, 1:186, 195, 196, 197, 444, 452, 461.
34. Guthrie, *The Legend of Chipita*, 7–8.
35. Marx, "Theories of Surplus Value," 391.
36. Kurz, "Marx and the 'Law of Value,'" 49.
37. Kurz, "Marx and the 'Law of Value,'" 49.
38. Day, *Alien Capital*, 9.
39. "The Logic of Gender on the Separation of the Spheres and the Process of Abjection," https://endnotes.org.uk/issues/3/en/endnotes-the-logic-of-gender.
40. For a more in-depth explanation of gendered labor through the lens of productive and reproductive labor, see "The Logic of Gender on the Separation of the Spheres and the Process of Abjection," https://endnotes.org.uk/issues/3/en/endnotes-the-logic-of-gender.
41. Smylie, *A Noose for Chipita*, 8–9.
42. Smylie, *A Noose for Chipita*, 9.
43. Smylie, *A Noose for Chipita*, 9.
44. Smylie, *A Noose for Chipita*, 9.
45. Bluntzer Hebert, "Shadow on the Nueces," 31.
46. Bluntzer Hebert, "Shadow on the Nueces," 31.
47. Bluntzer Hebert, "Shadow on the Nueces," 33.
48. Jane Eklins was the first woman hanged by capital punishment in 1853 and was a female slave who killed her master with an ax.
49. Bluntzer Hebert, "Shadow on the Nueces," 62.
50. Bluntzer Hebert, "Shadow on the Nueces," 63.
51. To read about Chipita Rodríguez and her life, see Keith Guthrie, *The Legend of Chipita*; Ruel McDaniel, "The Day They Hanged Chipita"; Vernon Smylie, *A Noose for Chipita*; Rachel Herbert Bluntzer, *The Forgotten Colony*; and Keith Guthrie, *The History of San Patricio County*.
52. Kandaswamy, "Gendering Racial Formation," 33.
53. Carrigan and Webb, *Forgotten Dead*, 1.
54. Carrigan and Webb, "The Lynching of Persons of Mexican Origin," 411–38.
55. Martinez, *The Injustice Never Leaves You*, 6.
56. Martinez, *The Injustice Never Leaves You*, 20.
57. *Ranchero*, November 29, 1863, in Corpus Christi Library.
58. Martinez, *The Injustice Never Leaves You*, 6.

59. Weigman, "The Anatomy of Lynching," 445.
60. Weigman, "The Anatomy of Lynching," 446.
61. Weigman, "The Anatomy of Lynching," 446.
62. Freud, "Fetishism," 198–204.
63. Eng, *Racial Castration*, 2.
64. Weigman, "The Anatomy of Lynching," 449.
65. Keith Guthrie, *The Legend of Chipita*, 63. Almost all the books I consulted have drawings of Chipita Rodríguez. This turn to hand-sketched drawings to humanize Rodríguez is understandable. However, all of the drawings portray Rodríguez as visibly masculine. To see drawings by Iris Guthrie, please see Keith Guthrie's book *The Legend of Chipita*.
66. Guthrie, *The Legend of Chipita*, 60.
67. Robinson, *Black Marxism*, xiii.
68. Marx, *Capital (Volume 1)*, 462.
69. Marx, *Capital (Volume I)*, 45.
70. Taylor, *The Archive and the Repertoire*, 142.
71. Weiner, *Chipita Rodríguez*, 2.
72. Weiner, *Chipita Rodríguez*, 8.
73. Weiner, *Chipita Rodríguez*, 7.
74. Weiner, *Chipita Rodríguez*, 4.
75. Weiner, *Chipita Rodríguez*, 9.
76. Weiner, *Chipita Rodríguez*, 10.
77. Paz, *The Labyrinth of Solitude*, 87.
78. Weiner, *Chipita Rodríguez*, 10.
79. Weiner, *Chipita Rodríguez*, 11.
80. Weiner, *Chipita Rodríguez*, 12.
81. Weiner, *Chipita Rodríguez*, 16.
82. Weiner, *Chipita Rodríguez*, 13.
83. Weiner, *Chipita Rodríguez*, 16.
84. Acosta, "Chipita," 90.
85. Acosta, "Chipita," 90.
86. Acosta, "Chipita," 90.
87. Acosta, "Chipita," 90.
88. Acosta, "Chipita," 91.
89. Acosta, "Chipita," 92.
90. Acosta, "Chipita," 92.
91. Senate Concurrent Resolution 14, 1.
92. Senate Concurrent Resolution 14, 2.
93. Senate Concurrent Resolution 14, 2.
94. Senate Concurrent Resolution 14, 4.

Chapter Four

1. "Hispanas," "New Mexicans," "Nuevomexicanas," and later "Mexican Americans" are all terms used to describe the people of New Mexico who occupied (genealogical) spaces during Spanish colonialism, Mexican rule, and finally U.S. empire. For the purposes of this

chapter, I will be utilizing "Nuevomexicana" when I refer to lower-class, racialized New Mexican women because "Hispana" was a term reserved for the elite landholding New Mexican women of the nineteenth century, and New Mexico was still a territory, so "Mexican American" does not apply.

2. Boyle, *Los Capitalistas*, xi.

3. Later in the chapter, I will explain how these trading relations set the stage for the way New Mexicans got involved in monopoly capitalist endeavors like the railroad. While more elite landholding New Mexicans were fighting for their space and agency during Anglo encroachment than not, wealthy New Mexicans valued the *system* of class and capital that hierarchized people against one another. The *patrones* utilized the bodies of the poor Nuevomexicana women to their full capacity to situate themselves within the burgeoning monopoly capitalist relations that they were ousted from with the arrival of Anglo homesteaders.

4. Sánchez, *Telling Identities*, 188.

5. Marx, *Capital: Critique of Political Economy (Volume 1)*.

6. Fortunati, *Arcane of Reproduction*.

7. Fortunati, *Arcane of Reproduction*, 99.

8. Fortunati, *Arcane of Reproduction*, 106.

9. Fortunati, *Arcane of Reproduction*, 106.

10. Marx, *Capital: Critique of Political Economy (Volume 1)*, 59.

11. Adrienne Davis first coins the term "sexual economy" in "Don't Let Nobody Bother Yo' Principle: The Sexual Economy of American Slavery." She explains that under slavery, reproduction was integral to the plantation economy. Black reproduction yielded economic profits, creating value for the slaveholding class. Enslaved Black women gave birth to white wealth. Masters established enslaved women as sexual outlets to perform sexual and productive labor. Davis notes that Black women's sexuality and reproductive capacity were for white pleasure and profit. Black women could be sexually terrorized in order to coerce economic work or discipline enslaved men. The unrapabilty of Black women (there were militaristic codes of law during slavery that made the Black female "owned" body incapable of claiming rape by a master) within the institution of slavery was all part of the sexual economy of chattel slavery. Davis defines sexual economies as "reproducing the slave workforce through giving birth and serving as forced sexual labor to countless men of all races" (105). The sexual and reproductive exploitation of the institution of slavery helps us understand that it was a violent economic structure that was gendered and sexualized as well as a racial institution for economic and market relations. I am also building off of Jennifer Morgan and Kristen Fischer's definition of sex in the colonies in "Sex, Race, and the Colonial Project" (197–98).

12. I am speaking of colonial rule under Spain and Northern Mexican governance in what is now the U.S. Southwest. In *American Sensations*, Shelley Streeby states, "Although 'Southern [Mexican] plantations' were the 'great bastions' of classic, coercive debt peonage, 'traditional peonage,' in which the worker was not necessarily tied to the hacienda by extra economic coercion and in which debt did not always function as a bond, was more common, especially in Northern Mexico" (192).

13. *Repartimientos* involved the Spanish crown distributing Native labor, so they could regulate labor relations more specifically. *Encomiendas* were the granting of land and the

use of the people on it by the Spanish crown, which was formally abolished in 1730 but was ineffective much earlier.

14. Meyers and Carlson, "Peonage, Power Relations, and the Built Environment," 226.
15. Meyers and Carlson, "Peonage, Power Relations, and the Built Environment," 226.
16. Rebolledo, "Las Hijas de la Malinche," 132.
17. Brooks, *Captives and Cousins*.
18. Kiser, *Borderlands of Slavery*, 65.
19. For current scholarship on Indigenous captivity and slavery, see William S. Kiser, *Borderlands of Slavery*, and Andrés Reséndez, *The Other Slavery: The Uncovered Story of Indian Enslavement in America* (Boston: Mariner Books, 2016).
20. Menchaca, *Recovering History, Constructing Race*, 226.
21. The old order under Mexican governance abolished Black slavery in 1834, but not Native slavery.
22. Hays, "The Curious Case of New Mexico's Pre–Civil War Slave Code," 255.
23. Hays, "The Curious Case of New Mexico's Pre–Civil War Slave Code," 261.
24. Streeby, *American Sensations*, 192.
25. Knight, "Mexican Peonage," 45–46.
26. Kiser, "A 'Charming Name for a Species of Slavery,'" 171.
27. Weber, *The Mexican Frontier, 1821–1846*, 212.
28. See Miguel A. Otero's letter to the editor printed on January 12, 1861, in the *Santa Fe Weekly Gazette*.
29. Kiser, "A 'Charming Name for a Species of Slavery,'" 171. Kiser, "A 'Charming Name for a Species of Slavery,'" 173.
30. Kiser, "A 'Charming Name for a Species of Slavery,'" 175.
31. *Mariana Jaremillo v. José de la Cruz Romero*, 194.
32. *Mariana Jaremillo v. José de la Cruz Romero*, 194.
33. In her book *Recovering History, Constructing Race*, Marta Menchaca states, "Though by law the *criollo* racial category was reserved for whites, it was common for parish priests to register mestizo children of means as *criollo* by including in the baptismal registry only the race of the father" (65).
34. *Mariana Jaremillo v. José de la Cruz Romero*, 256.
35. Kiser, "A 'Charming Name for a Species of Slavery,'" 182.
36. This is a play on the acronym "WPA" and the white women who collected the stories, Annette Hesch Thorp and Lou Sage Batchen, the devil on foot.
37. Annette Hesch Thorp and Lou Sage Batchen were both long-term residents of New Mexico when they started collecting stories for the WPA. Neither woman was fluent in Spanish and both used translators; however, as Rebolledo points out, neither collector no translator shaped the final version of the narratives.
38. Rebolledo and Márquez, "Introduction: The Federal Writers Project," xix.
39. Rebolledo and Márquez, "Introduction: The Federal Writers Project," xix.
40. Rebolledo and Márquez, "Introduction: The Federal Writers Project," xxii.
41. Rebolledo and Márquez, "Introduction: The Federal Writers Project," xl.
42. "The Panic of 1862," 396–491.
43. "The Panic of 1862," 396–491.
44. "The Panic of 1862," 396–491.

45. "The Panic of 1862," 396–491.
46. "The Panic of 1862," 400.
47. Sánchez, *Telling Identities*, 6.
48. Sánchez, *Telling Identities*, 13.
49. Rebolledo and Márquez, "Introduction: The Federal Writers Project," xxii.
50. "Mateo y Raquel," *Museum of New Mexico History Library*, 1.
51. "Mateo y Raquel," *Museum of New Mexico History Library*, 2.
52. "Mateo y Raquel," *Museum of New Mexico History Library*, 6.
53. "Mateo y Raquel," *Museum of New Mexico History Library*, 6.
54. Radden and Kovecses. "Towards a Theory of Metonymy," 19.
55. González, "Lupe's Song," 251–64.
56. Lazo, "Migrant Archives," 36.
57. Fortunati, *Arcane of Reproduction*.
58. Fortunati, *Arcane of Reproduction*, 2.
59. Fortunati, *Arcane of Reproduction*, 2.
60. Fortunati, *Arcane of Reproduction*, 5.
61. In the 1970s, significant debates among Marxist feminists (and anti-Marxist feminists) attempted to make clear the precise relationship between reproductive labor and the value it contains. See Ellen Malos, *The Politics of Housework* (Cheltenham, UK: New Clarion Press, 1995); Lise Vogel, *Woman Questions: Essays for a Materialist Feminism* (Hove, UK: Psychology Press, 1995); Mariarosa Dalla Costa and Selma James, *The Power of Women and the Subversion of the Community* (London: Falling Wall Press, 1975); Silvia Federici, *Caliban and the Witch* (Brooklyn, NY: Autonomedia, 2004); and Maria Mies, *Patriarchy and Accumulation on a World Scale: Women in the International Division of Labour* (New York: Palgrave Macmillan, 1998).
62. Bernes, *The Work of Art in the Age of Deindustrialization*, 214.
63. Bernes, *The Work of Art in the Age of Deindustrialization*, 214.
64. "Mateo y Raquel," *Museum of New Mexico History Library*, 358–64.
65. "José Librado Gurulé's Recollections, 1867," 120–34.
66. "José Librado Gurulé's Recollections, 1867," 124.
67. New Mexico State Record Center and Archives, with film at Center for Southwest Research. Mexican Archive of New Mexico, CD3394.N413 c.1. Roll 24, Frame 799.
68. Boyle, *Los Capitalistas*, 94.
69. Boyle, *Los Capitalistas*, 94.
70. Cabeza de Baca, *We Fed Them Cactus*, 139–40.
71. Cabeza de Baca, *We Fed Them Cactus*, 6.
72. Padilla, *My History, Not Yours*, 4.
73. For more on the perceptions of Spanish Hispanos/Nuevomexicanos, please see John Nieto Phillips, *The Language of Blood: Making of Spanish-American Identity in New Mexico, 1880s–1930s* (Albuquerque: University of New Mexico Press, 2004); and for gendered perceptions of Cabeza de Baca, see Melina Vizcaíno-Alemán's *Gender and Place in Chicana/o Literature: Critical Regionalism and the Mexican American Southwest* (London: Palgrave MacMillian, 2017).
74. Padilla, *My History, Not Yours*, 44.
75. Padilla, *My History, Not Yours*, 44. The Native "I" is not Indigenous, but rather *criollo*.

76. Rebolledo, "Narrative Strategies of Resistance in Hispana Writing," 136.
77. Reed, "Making Homes in a Changing Land," 122.
78. Rebolledo, "Las Escritoras: Romances and Realities," 201.
79. Cabeza de Baca, *We Fed Them Cactus*, 15.
80. Roybal, *Archives of Dispossession*, 103.
81. Roybal, *Archives of Dispossession*, 104.
82. Roybal, *Archives of Dispossession*, 105.
83. Cabeza de Baca, *We Fed Them Cactus*, 31.
84. Cabeza de Baca, *We Fed Them Cactus*, 59.
85. Gopinath, "Nostalgia, Desire, Diaspora," 468.
86. McClintock, "No Longer in a Future Heave," 89–112.
87. Cabeza de Baca, *We Fed Them Cactus*, 1.
88. Cabeza de Baca, *We Fed Them Cactus*, 1.
89. Cabeza de Baca, *We Fed Them Cactus*, 8.
90. Massey, *For Space*, 10–11.
91. Cabeza de Baca, *We Fed Them Cactus*, 6.
92. Sheridan, *Landscapes of Fraud*, 143.
93. Mexican Archives of New Mexico, New Mexico State Records Center, roll 24, frame 799.
94. In *Captives and Cousins*, James F. Brooks states that 60 percent of those animals were owned by the Chávez, Otero, and Sandoval families. The same families, with the Pereas and Yrrissarris, also dominated transshipment of foreign (American) goods—predominantly cotton textiles, Chinese silks, and small manufactures like cutlery (46–47).
95. Brooks, *Captives and Cousins*, 46.
96. Brooks, *Captives and Cousins*, 49.
97. Foucault, "Of Other Spaces," 25.
98. Cabeza de Baca, *We Fed Them Cactus*, 11, 41.
99. Cabeza de Baca, *We Fed Them Cactus*, 59.
100. Brady, *Extinct Lands, Temporal Geographies*, 5.
101. Cabeza de Baca, *We Fed Them Cactus*, 89, 147.
102. Klein, "On the Emergence of Memory in Historical Discourse," 128.
103. Klein, "On the Emergence of Memory in Historical Discourse," 129.
104. Maylei Blackwell coins the term "retrofitted memory" in *Chicana Power!*
105. Cabeza de Baca, *We Fed Them Cactus*, 81.
106. Cabeza de Baca, *We Fed Them Cactus*, 81.
107. Cabeza de Baca, *We Fed Them Cactus*, 160.

Chapter Five

1. Smalley, "Arizona Album."
2. Smalley, "Arizona Album."
3. Smalley, "Arizona Album."
4. Smalley, "Arizona Album."
5. For a review of the most notorious case on mining fraud that occurred in journalism, see Harold Herbert, "Geroge Smalley," 135–60.
6. Delgado, "Border Control and Sexual Policing," 160.

7. This chapter adds to the growing scholarship on how sex, sexuality, and sexual excess were coupled with border and immigration policy. Whether it was through moral reform policy, nativist movements, or Progressive Era politics, the border was a contested space that contained race, sex, gender, and class. See Martha Gardner, *The Qualities of a Citizen*, and Eithne Luibhéid, *Entry Denied*. On the development of the U.S. Bureau of Immigration and the sweeping power of its policies in determining national belonging, see Erika Lee and Judy Yung, *Angel Island*, and Anna Pegler-Gordon, *In Sight of America*; see also Grace Peña Delgado, "Border Control and Sexual Policing," 157–78.

8. Hernández, "The Specter of Statehood," 55.

9. Campt, *Listening to Images*, 5.

10. Azoulay, *The Civil Contract of Photography*, 16; Campt, *Listening to Images*, 6.

11. Thomas E. Sheridan states in *Los Tucsoneses: The Mexican Community in Tucson, 1854–1941* that for the first half of the nineteenth century, Tucson was an isolated outpost of Sonora. Tucson was never part of the military struggle between Mexico and Spain, but Mexican Independence had disastrous effects on the northwestern frontier of Mexico. The war had depleted the Mexican treasury, and as Sheridan explains, "destroyed the colonial silver mining industry" (21). The battle for who would control the Mexican state was in full force in Tucson. While Anglo settlement and westward expansion were bringing change to the northern Mexican frontier in the 1820s, Tucson remained free from these types of settlements. This began to change in the 1840s. By 1845, Mexico and the United States were headed toward war, and Tucson became a place gold rushers passed through while traversing Northern Mexico, which brought an end to the Mexican period. After the Gadsden Purchase, mining dominated Southern Arizona's economy; however, Tucson was mostly a mercantile economy and not extractive. Sheridan states, "Tucson eventually functioned as a supply depot and service center for the mines, [but] those functions were underdeveloped in 1860" (37). Between 1860 and the arrival of the Southern Pacific Railroad in 1880, Tucson was a combination of Sonoran and territorial. Those two decades were a transition period.

12. Otero, *La Calle*, 43.

13. Leonard, *Illiberal Reformers*, 3.

14. Leonard, *Illiberal Reformers*, 3.

15. Leonard, *Illiberal Reformers*, 3.

16. Leonard, *Illiberal Reformers*, 3.

17. Cocks, "Rethinking Sexuality in the Progressive Era," 95.

18. Cocks, "Rethinking Sexuality in the Progressive Era," 95.

19. Cocks, "Rethinking Sexuality in the Progressive Era," 97.

20. Leonard, *Illiberal Reformers*, 3.

21. Delgado, "Border Control and Sexual Policing," 163.

22. Delgado, "Border Control and Sexual Policing," 163.

23. Hernandez, *Migra!*, 63.

24. Hernandez, *Migra!*, 35.

25. Hernandez, 36.

26. Bliss, *Compromised Positions*, 29. Also see "Reglamento para el ejercicio de la prostitución," 1872, article 1, in Archivo Histórico de la Secretaría y Asistencia, México, D.F., Salubridad Pública, IAV, box 1, file 1. Franco-Guzmán in "El régimen jurídico" gives an overview of the history of regulations in Mexico.

27. Bliss, *Compromised Positions*, 29.

28. Luibhéid, *Entry Denied*, 8–9.

29. Immigration Act of 1882, 47th Congress, 1st session (18 *Stat.* 477), March 3, 1875. See also Hernandez, *Migra!*, and Luibhéid, *Entry Denied*.

30. Hernandez, *Migra!*, 27.

31. Ch. 1012, section 3, 32 Stat. 1213, 1214 (1903).

32. The border was a different space economically and environmentally than the eastern and southern United States. The terrain was rough, and settlers populated it sporadically by uprooting Indigenous populations. Women on the border were shifting from agrarian and mercantile trade to corporate and monopoly capital, so there were limited job opportunities. The competing economic interests of the Industrial Revolution (between 1820 and 1840) and slavery made the domestic landscape different in terms of race and gender. However, while the ability to earn a living in agriculture (for white women) decreased because of migration and industrialization, women had to find work outside of the domestic space.

33. This chapter cannot possibly contend with all the nuances of Asian female sexuality (particularly Chinese and Japanese) and the interchangeability of xenophobic national projects and the sexuality of Mexican and Asian women. Without going into great detail, the intersection of patriarchy (family, social, and government structures) with American capitalism and racism enunciates the ways in which Asian female migrants and Mexican female migrants became part of an overarching structure to pathologize them outside of proper white femininity. For more on Chinese and Japanese women and their sexuality as tied to American Empire, see Yung, *Chinese Women of America*; Hirata, "Chinese Women Immigrants in Nineteenth Century California," 223–44; and Glenn, *Issei, Nisei, War Bride*.

34. Luibhéid, *Entry Denied*, 31.

35. Delgado, "Border Control and Sexual Policing," 177.

36. Lockwood and Page, *Tucson the Old Pueblo*.

37. Otero, *La Calle*, 22–23.

38. "Lights Are Extinguished in Restricted District of Tucson," *Tucson Citizen*, December 6, 1911.

39. Huizar-Hernández, "The Specter of Statehood," 54.

40. Leonard, *Illiberal Reformers*, 9.

41. Leonard, *Illiberal Reformers*, 53.

42. Leonard, *Illiberal Reformers*, 53.

43. Wilson and Wilson, "From Maiden Lane to Gay Alley," 177.

44. Louis Hughes journeyed to Tucson alone in 1871 to make money to send for his wife in 1872; upon arrival, only Mrs. Charles Lord (wife of Dr. Lord) and Mrs. C. Scott (wife of Judge C. Scott) were established in Tucson, Arizona. The adobe house Louis C. and Josephine Hughes lived in was built on the site of the presidio (old fort) that marked the first settlement by the Anglo settlers. This settlement was called Court Plaza and, as Lydia R. Otero states in *La Calle: Spatial Conflicts and Urban Renewal in a Southwest City*, "As Anglos arrived, they appropriated the most commercially desirable, developed, and established sections that had evolved during the Spanish and Mexican periods. By 1862, Anglos owned twenty-one (64 percent) of the thirty-three residences within the crumbling walls of the presidio" (13).

45. Boehringer, "Josephine Brawley Hughes: Crusader, State Builder," 98–107.

46. Montejano, *Anglos and Mexicans in the Making of Texas, 1836–1986*, 74.
47. *Arizona Daily Star*, August 3, 1888.
48. "Petition to Close Houses," *Tucson Citizen* (Tucson, AZ, Territory), September 14, 1907.
49. Sheridan, *Los Tucsonenses*.
50. "Mayor Buehman Gives His Views on the City and Its Conditions," *Arizona Weekly Citizen*, (Tucson, AZ, Territory), July 6, 1895.
51. The newspapers that followed the issue of prostitution in Arizona and that this chapter has consulted closely are as follows: *Arizona Daily Citizen, Arizona Daily Star, Arizona Weekly Citizen, Arizona Weekly Star, Daily Arizona Citizen*, and *Tucson Citizen*.
52. "Ordinance No. 117," *Arizona Daily Citizen* (Tucson, AZ, Territory), October 4, 1898.
53. Wilson and Wilson, "From Maiden Lane to Gay Alley," 179.
54. "The Present Administration in Partnership with Vice and an Immoral Tax Collected Monthly from Fallen Women," *Arizona Daily Citizen*, December 12, 1903.
55. "Ordinance No. 169," *Arizona Daily Citizen*, July 6, 1903.
56. Wilson and Wilson, "From Maiden Lane to Gay Alley," 183.
57. Wilson and Wilson, "From Maiden Lane to Gay Alley," 182.
58. U.S. Congress, Senate, *New Statehood Bill*, 57th Cong., 2nd sess., 1902, 161.
59. U.S. Congress, Senate, *New Statehood Bill*, 57th Cong., 2nd sess., 1902, 161.
60. U.S. Congress, Senate, *New Statehood Bill*, 57th Cong., 2nd sess., 1902, 122.
61. U.S. Congress, Senate, *New Statehood Bill*, 57th Cong., 2nd sess., 1902, 163.
62. U.S. Congress, Senate, *New Statehood Bill*, 57th Cong., 2nd sess., 1902, 163.
63. *New Statehood Bill*, 57th Cong., 2nd sess., 1902, 131.
64. Leonard, *Illiberal Reformers*, xii.
65. Chen, "Fit for Citizenship?," 73.
66. Stren, "Buildings, Boundaries, and Blood," 41–81.
67. Charles McCarthy, *The Wisconsin Idea* (New York: Macmillian, 1912), 28–29.
68. "Wile of Mexican Girls," *El Paso Daily Times*, January 30, 1908.
69. Delgado, "Border Control and Sexual Policing," 169.
70. Charles Cornell to Commissioner-General of Immigration, December 26, 1909, File: 5248418-A, RG 85, Entry 9, National Archives and Records Administration, 1.
71. Charles Cornell to Commissioner-General of Immigration, December 26, 1909, 4.
72. Charles Cornell to Commissioner-General of Immigration, December 26, 1909, 5.
73. Charles Cornell to Commissioner-General of Immigration, December 26, 1909, 11.
74. Charles Cornell to Commissioner-General of Immigration, December 26, 1909, 12.
75. Charles Cornell to Commissioner-General of Immigration, December 26, 1909, 12.
76. "Prominent Merchant Held to Grand Jury: Women Waiting at Detention Quarters to Appear against Nogales Man," *Arizona Daily*, August 27, 1909.
77. "McDonald, Immigrant Inspector, v. Siu Tak Sam," No. 4356, *United States Circuit Courts of Appeals Reports. Reports Containing the Cases Determined in All the Circuits from the Organization of the Courts: Fully Reported with Numerous Annotations*, Vol. 140 (West Publishing Company, 1916), 585.
78. Schneider, Gustav van Hemert, 1885–1951 Collection, 1867–1868, 1903–1951. MS 0715. f.12. Arizona Historical Society.
79. Wilson and Wilson, "From Maiden Lane to Gay Alley," 167–86.

80. Wilson and Wilson, "From Maiden Lane to Gay Alley," 171.
81. Woosley, *Early Tucson*; Carmony, *Whiskey, Six-Guns and Red-Light Ladies.*
82. Wilson and Wilson, "From Maiden Lane to Gay Alley," 175.
83. Otero, *La Calle*, 16.
84. Orvell, *The Real Thing*, 89.
85. Orvell, *The Real Thing*, 89.
86. Orvell, *The Real Thing*, 91.
87. Behrent, "Foucault and Technology," 55.
88. Foucault, "'Prisons et asiles dans le mécanisme du pouvoir,'" 523.
89. Orvell, *The Real Thing*, 73.
90. Orvell, *The Real Thing*, 75.
91. Coleman, "The Directorial Mode," 58.
92. Orvell, *The Real Thing*, 85.
93. Hall, "Reconstruction Work," 106–13.
94. Hennessy, *Profit and Pleasure*, 4.
95. Foucault states that power can be summed up through a "battery of multifarious techniques concerning the education of children, assistance to the poor, and the institution of workers' tutelage [that are] coordinated through psychiatric order. This kind of method entails going behind the institution and trying to discover in a wider and more overall perspective what we can broadly call a technology of power" (162). He further expands on the notion of how power comes to have different institutional backing and techniques in *Security, Territory, Population*.
96. Hennessy, *Profit and Pleasure*, 20.
97. Hennessy, *Profit and Pleasure*, 20.
98. Wexler, *Tender Violence*, 57.
99. Wexler, *Tender Violence*, 57.
100. Wexler, *Tender Violence*, 57.

Coda

1. Valencia, *Gore Capitalism*.
2. Valencia, *Gore Capitalism*, 76.
3. Rodriguez, *Sexual Futures, Queer Gestures, and Other Latina Longings*, 139.
4. Fragoso, "The Victims of Ciudad Juárez Feminicide," 63.
5. Marx, *Capital: A Critique of Political Economy (Volume 1)*, 46.
6. Marx, *Capital: A Critique of Political Economy (Volume 1)*, 92.
7. Marx, *Capital: A Critique of Political Economy (Volume 1)*, 79.

Bibliography

Unpublished Sources

Alfred Robinson to Don José de la Guerra y Noriega, New York, November 22, 1846. DLG 833, Letter 6, SBMA and Alfred Robinson to Pablo de la Guerra, New York, September 20, 1846. DLG 834, Letter 1, SBMA.
Alfred Robinson to Don José de la Guerra y Noriega, New York, October 21, 1847. DLG 833, Letter 7. Santa Barbara Mission Archive (cited hereinafter as SBMA).
Alfred Robinson to Jose de la Guerra y Noriega, Santa Barbara, December 28, 1834, DLG 833, Letter 15, SBMA.
Alfred Robinson to María Antonia, Los Angeles, May 16, 1834. DLG 831, Letter 2, SBMA.
Alfred Robinson to Pablo de la Guerra, New York, September 20, 1846. DLG 834, Letter 1, SBMA.
Ana María (de la Guerra) Robinson to de la Guerras, New York (sent by way of the Sandwich Islands), April 15, 1839, DLG 836, Letter 3, SBMA.
Ana María (de la Guerra) Robinson to her parents, unknown location, September 30, 1840, DLG 836, Letter 5, SBMA.
Ana María (de la Guerra) Robinson to José de la Guerra, her father, and to María Antonia (Carillo), her mother, Boston, June 11, 1838, DLG 836, Letter 1, SBMA.
Ana María (de la Guerra) Robinson to José de la Guerra, her father, New York, February 27, 1839, DLG 836, Letter 2, SBMA.
Angustias de la Guerra, Journal, September 3, 1846, DLG 725, SBMA.
Charles Cornell to Commissioner-General of Immigration, December 26, 1909, File: 5248418-A, RG 85, Entry 9, National Archives and Records Administration.

Published Primary Sources

Acosta, Teresa Paloma. "Chipita." *Nile and other Poems*. Austin: Red Salmon Press, 1999.
Alarcón, Norma. "Traddutora, Traditora: A Paradigmatic Figure of Chicana Feminism." *Cultural Critique* 13, no. 3 (Autumn 1989): 57–87.
Alemán, Jesse. "'Thank God, Lolita Is Away from Those Horrid Savages': The Politics of Whiteness in *Who Would Have Thought It?*" In *María Amparo Ruiz de Burton: Critical and Pedagogical Perspectives*, ed. Amelia María de la Luz Montes and Anne Elizabeth Goldman. Lincoln: University of Nebraska Press, 2004.
———. "Historical Amnesia and the Vanishing Mestiza: The Problems of Race in *The Squatter and the Don* and *Ramona*." *Aztlán* 27, no. 1 (2005): 59–93.
Anzaldúa, Gloría. *Borderlands/La Frontera: The New Mestiza*. San Francisco: Aunt Lute Books, 1987.
"Apaches." *La Estrella de Occidente*, July 27, 1860, column 1.

Aranda, José. "Contradictory Impulses: María Amparo Ruiz de Burton, Resistance Theory, and the Politics of Chicano/a Studies. *American Literature* 70, no. 3 (September 1998).

Aranda, José F. "Returning California to the People: Vigilantism in *The Squatter and the Don*." In *María Amparo Ruiz de Burton: Critical and Pedagogical Perspectives*, ed. Amelia María de la Luz Montes and Anne Elizabeth Goldman. Lincoln: University of Nebraska Press, 2004.

Arce, Christina. *Mexico's Nobodies: The Cultural Legacy of the Soldadera and Afro-Mexican Women*. Albany: SUNY Press, 2017.

Aristotle. *The Complete Works of Aristotle: The Revised Oxford Translation*. New Jersey: Princeton University Press, 1984.

Arrom, Silvia Marina. *The Women of Mexico City, 1790–1857*. Palo Alto, CA: Stanford University Press, 1985.

Azoulay, Ariella. *The Civil Contract of Photography*. Cambridge: MIT Press, 2008.

Barrera, Mario. *Race and Class in the Southwest: A Theory of Racial Inequality*. Indiana: University of Notre Dame Press, 1979.

Barthes, Roland. *Camera Lucida: Reflections on Photography*. New York: Hill and Wang, 1981.

Barthes, Roland. *Image, Music, Text*. Translated by Stephen Heath. New York: Hill and Wang, 1977.

Beebe, Rose Marie, and Robert M. Senkewicz. *Testimonios: Early California through the Eyes of Women, 1815–1848*. Norman: University of Oklahoma Press, 2006.

Behrent, Michael C. "Foucault and Technology." *History and Technology: An International Journal* 29, no. 1 (2013): 54–104.

Beltrán, Gonzalo Aguirre. *La Población Negra de México: Estudio Etnohistórico*. Mexico City: Fondo de Cultura Económica, 1946.

Bernes, Jasper. *The Work of Art in the Age of Deindustrialization*. Stanford: Stanford University Press, 2018.

Best, Stephen, and Sharon Marcus. "Surface Reading: An Introduction." *Representation* 108, no. 1 (Fall 2009): 1–21.

Blackwell, Maylei. *Chicana Power!: Contested Histories of Feminism in the Chicano Movement*. Austin: University of Texas Press, 2011.

Bliss, Katherine Elaine. *Compromised Positions: Prostitution, Public Health, and Gender Politics in Revolutionary Mexico City*. University Park: Pennsylvania State University Press, 2001.

Bluntzer Hebert, Rachel. "Shadow on the Nueces: The Story of Chepita Rodríguez." In *Shadow on the Nueces*. Atlanta: Banner Press, 1942.

Boehringer, C. "Josephine Brawley Hughes: Crusader, Sate Builder." *Arizona Historical Review* 2, no. 4 (January 1930): 98–107.

Bolton, Herbert Eugene. *The Spanish Borderlands: A Chronicle of Old Florida and the Southwest*. Albuquerque: University of New Mexico Press, 1996.

Bourdieu, Pierre. *Outline of a Theory of Practice*. Cambridge: Cambridge University Press. 1977.

Bourdieu, Pierre. *The Logic of Practice*. Translated by Richard Nice. Stanford: Stanford University Press, 1980.

Boyle, Susan. *Los Capitalistas: Hispano Merchants and the Santa Fe Trade*. Albuquerque: University of New Mexico Press, 1997.
Brady, Mary Pat. *Extinct Lands, Temporal Geographies: Chicana Literature and the Urgency of Space*. Durham: Duke University Press, 2002.
Brooks, James F. *Captives and Cousins: Slavery, Kinship, and Community in the Southwest Borderlands*. Chapel Hill: University of North Carolina Press, 2002.
Browman, Robert. "Albuquerque Journal Special Report: West Mesa Murders." *Albuquerque Journal*. Accessed September 16, 2019. https://www.abqjournal.com/community-data/west-mesa-murders.
Burden, David K. "La idea salvadora: Immigration and Colonization Politics in México, 1821–1857." Ph.D. Diss., Department of History, University of California-Santa Barbara, 2005.
Butler, Judith. *Gender Trouble: Feminism and the Subversion of Identity*. New York: Routledge, 1990.
Cabeza de Baca, Fabiola. *We Fed Them Cactus*. Albuquerque: University of New Mexico Press, 1954.
Cabeza de Baca, Luis María. "Guia Records." Mexican Archives of New Mexico, New Mexico State Records Center, roll 24, frame 799.
Cabezut, Manuel. "Cuatro palabras al bello sexo—Lo que pueden hacer las mexicanas en favor de nuestra independencia." *La Estrella Occidente*, November 12, 1863.
Campbell, Randolph B. "The District Judges of Texas in 1866–1867: An Episode in the Failure of Presidential Reconstruction." *The Southwestern Historical Quarterly* 93, no. 3 (January 1990).
Campt, Tina. *Image Matters: Archive, Photography, and the African Diaspora in Europe*. Durham, NC: Duke University Press, 2012.
Campt, Tina M. *Listening to Images: An Exercise in Counterintuition*. Durham, NC: Duke University Press, 2017.
Carmony, Neil. *Whiskey, Six-Guns and Red-Light Ladies: George Hand's Diary, Tucson 1875–1878*. Silver City, NM: High Lonesome Books, 1994.
Carrigan, William D., and Clive Webb. *Forgotten Dead: Mob Violence against Mexicans in the United States, 1848–1928*. New York: Oxford University Press, 2013.
Carrigan, William D., and Clive Webb. "The Lynching of Persons of Mexican Origin or Descent in the United States 1848 to 1928." *Journal of Social History* 37, no. 2 (Winter 2003): 411–38.
Casas, Raquél Maria. *Married to a Daughter of the Land: Spanish-Mexican Women and Interethnic Marriage in California, 1820–80*. Reno: University of Nevada Press, 2007.
Castañeda, Antonia I. "Anglo American Stereotypes of Californianas." In *Major Problems in Mexican American History: Documents and Essays*, ed. Zaragoza Vargas, 162–67. Boston, MA: Cengage Learning, 1999.
Castañeda, Antonia I. "Engendering the History of Alta California, 1769–1848: Gender, Sexuality, and the Family." *California History* 76, no. 2–3 (Summer/Fall 1997): 230–59.
Castañeda, Antonia I. "Gender, Race, and Culture: Spanish-Mexican Women in the Historiography of Frontier California." *Frontiers: A Journal of Women Studies* 11, no. 1 (1990): 8–20.

Castañeda, Antonia I. "Malinche, Calafía y Toypurina." In *Three Decades of Engendering History: Selected Works of Antonia I. Castañeda.* Denton: University of North Texas Press, 2014.

Casteñeda, Antonia I. "Political Economy of Nineteenth-Century Stereotypes." *Three Decades of Engendering History: Selected Works of Antonia I. Castañeda,* ed. Linda Heindenreich and Antonia I. Castañeda, 37–63. Denton: University of North Texas Press, 2014.

Caswell, Michelle. "'The Archive' Is Not an Archive: On Acknowledging the Intellectual Contributions of Archival Studies." *Reconstruction: Studies in Contemporary Culture* 16, no. 1 (2016).

CBS News. "Discovery near Mass Gravesite Leads to Fears of More Victims in Unsolved Serial Killings." *CBS News,* July 4, 2018. Accessed September 16, 2019. https://www.cbsnews.com/news/albuquerque-discovery-near-mass-grave-leads-to-fears-of-more-victims-in-unsolved-serial-killings/.

Chávez, Thomas E. *New Mexico: Past and Future.* Albuquerque: University of New Mexico Press, 2006.

Chávez-García, Miroslava. *Negotiating Conquest: Gender and Power in California, 1770s to 1880s.* Tucson: University of Arizona Press, 2004.

Chen, Michelle. "Fit for Citizenship?: The Eugenics Movement and Immigration." *Dissent* 62, no. 2 (Spring 2015): 73–86.

Cisneros, Sandra. "Woman Hollering Creek." In *Woman Hollering Creek, and Other Stories.* New York: Random House, 1991.

Cocks, Catherine. "Rethinking Sexuality in the Progressive Era." *The Journal of the Gilded Age and the Progressive Era.* 5, no. 2 (2006): 93–118.

Coleman, A. D. "The Directorial Mode: Notes toward a Definition." *ArtForum* 15, no. 1 (September 1976): 55–61.

Conner, J. E. Foreword to *Shadows on the Nueces,* by Rachel Bluntzer Hébert, 11. Atlanta: Banner Press, 1942.

Coronado, Raúl. *A World Not to Come: A History of Latino Writing and Print Culture.* Cambridge, MA: Harvard University Press, 2013.

Cowan Benjamin A., Nicole M. Guidotti-Hernández, and Jason Ruiz, eds. "Sexing Empire." Special Issue, *Radical History Review* 123, (October 2015).

Cypess, Sandra Messinger. *La Malinche in Mexican Literature: From History to Myth.* Austin: University of Texas Press, 1991.

Davis, Adrienne. "Don't Let Nobody Bother Yo' Principle: The Economy of American Slavery." In *Sister Circle: Black Women and Work,* ed. Sharon Harley, 103–27. New Brunswick, NJ: Rutgers University Press, 2002.

Davis, Graham. *Land!: Irish Pioneers in Mexican and Revolutionary Texas.* College Station: Texas A&M University Press, 2002.

Davis, Mike. *Planet of Slums.* New York: Verso, 2007.

Day, Iyko. *Alien Capital: Asian Racialization and the Logic of Settler Colonial Capitalism.* Durham, NC: Duke University Press, 2016.

de la Guerra Ord, Angustias. *The California Recollections of Angustias de la Guerra Ord.* Washington, DC: Academy of American Franciscan History, in collaboration with the Santa Barbara Trust for Historic Preservation, 2004.

Delgado, Grace Peña. "Border Control and Sexual Policing: White Slavery and Prostitution along the U.S.–Mexico Borderlands, 1903–1910." *Western Quarterly* 43, no. 2 (Summer 2012): 157–78.
Denning, Michael. "Wageless Life." *New Left Review* 66 (November/December 2010): 79–97.
Derrida, Jacques. *Archive Fever: A Freudian Impression*. Translated by Eric Prenowitz. Chicago: University of Chicago Press, 1995.
Douglas, Ann. *The Feminization of American Culture*. New York: Noonday Press, 1998.
"Editorial." *La Estrella de Occidente*, August 30, 1867, column 1, page 3.
Eng, David. *Racial Castration: Managing Masculinity in Asian America*. Durham, NC: Duke University Press, 2001.
Engels, Friedrich. "The Monogamous Family." In *The Origin of the Family, Private Property, and the State*, ed. Eleanor Leacock. New York: International Publishers, 1972.
Federici, Silvia. *Caliban and the Witch: Women, the Body and Primitive Accumulation*. Brooklyn, NY: Autonomedia, 2004.
Fischer, Kirsten, and Jennifer Morgan. "Sex, Race, and the Colonial Project." *Sexuality in Early America*, special issue of *William and Mary Quarterly* 60, no. 1 (2003): 197–98.
Fisher, Beth. "The Captive Mexicana and the Desiring Bourgeois Woman: Domesticity and Expansionism in Ruiz de Burton's *Who Would Have Thought It?*" *Legacy* 16, no. 1 (1999): 59–69.
Foley, Neil. *The White Scourge: Mexicans, Blacks, and Poor Whites in Texas Cotton Culture*. Berkeley: University of California Press, 1997.
Fortunati, Leopoldina. *Arcane of Reproduction: Housework, Prostitution, Labor, and Capital*. Translated by Hilary Creek. Edited by Jim Fleming. Brooklyn, NY: Autonomedia, 1995.
Foucault, Michel. *The History of Sexuality*. Vol. 1, *An Introduction*. Translated by Robert Hurley. New York: Vintage Books, 1990.
Foucault, Michel. "Of Other Spaces." *Diacritics* 16 (Spring 1986): 22–27.
Foucault, Michel. "'Prisons et asiles dans le mécanisme du pouvoir.'" In *Dits et Ecrits*, Vol. 11. Paris: Gallimard, 1974.
Foucault, Michel. *Security, Territory, Population: Lectures at the Collège de France 1977–1978*. New York: Palgrave Macmillan, 2009.
Foster, John W. "The Contest for the Laws of Reform in Mexico." *The American Historical Review* 15, no. 3 (April 1910): 526–46.
Fragoso, Julia E. Moñarrez, and Cynthia Bejarano. "The Disarticulation of Justice: Precarious Life and Cross-Border Feminicides in the Paso del Norte Region." In *Cities and Citizenship at the U.S.-Mexico Border: The Paso del Norte Metropolitan Region*, ed. Kathleen Staudt, César M. Fuentes, and Julia E. Monárrez Fragoso, 43–70. New York: Palgrave Macmillan, 2010.
Fragoso, Julia Estela Monárrez. "The Victims of Ciudad Juárez Feminicide: Sexually Fetishized Commodities." In *Terrorizing Women: Feminicide in the Américas*, ed. Rosa-Linda Fregoso and Cynthia Bejarano, 59–69. Durham, NC: Duke University Press, 2010.
Franco-Guzmán, Ricardo. "El regimen jurídico de la prostitución en México." *Revista de la Facultad de Derecho en México*, 85–86 (1972): 85–134.

Freud, Sigmund. "Fetishism." In *Miscellaneous Papers, 1888–1938*. Vol. 5, *Collected Papers*. London: Hogarth and Institute of Psycho-Analysis, 1927.

Gardner, Martha. *The Qualities of a Citizen: Women, Immigration, and Citizenship, 1870–1965*. Princeton, NJ: Princeton University Press, 2005.

Glenn, Evelyn Nakano. *Issei, Nisei, War Bride: Three Generations of Japanese American Women in Domestic Service*. Philadelphia, PA: Temple University Press, 1986.

Godayol, Pilar. "Malintzin/La Malinche/Doña Marina: Re-Reading the Myth of the Treacherous Translator." *Journal of Iberian and Latin American Studies* 18, no. 1 (2012): 61–76.

Goldman, Anne Elizabeth. "Beasts in the Jungle: Foreigners and Natives in Boston." In *María Amaparo Ruiz de Burton: Critical and Pedagogical Perspectives*, ed. Amelia María de la Luz Montes and Anne Elizabeth Goldman. Lincoln: University of Nebraska Press, 2004.

Goldman, Anne Elizabeth. "Who Ever Heard of a Blue-Eyed Mexican?: Satire and Sentimentality in María Amparo Ruiz de Burton's *Who Would Have Thought It?*" In *Recovering the U.S. Hispanic Literary Heritage*, Vol. 2, ed. Erlinda Gonzales-Berry and Charles M. Tatum. Houston: Arte Publico Press, 1996.

González, Deena J. "Lupe's Song: On the Origins of Mexican Woman-Hating in the U.S." In *Velvet Barrios: Popular Culture & Chicana/o Sexualities*, ed. Alicia Gaspar de Alba, 251–64. New York: Palgrave Macmillan, 2003.

González, Deena J. *Refusing the Favor: The Spanish-Mexican Women of Santa Fe, 1820–1880*. New York: Oxford University Press, 1999.

Gopinath, Gayatri. "Nostalgia, Desire, Diaspora: South Asian Sexualities in Motion." *positions* 5, no. 2 (Fall 1997): 467–89.

Guardino, Peter. *The Dead March: A History of the Mexican-American War*. Cambridge, MA: Harvard University Press, 2017.

Guidotti-Hernández, Nicole Marie. *Unspeakable Violence: Remapping U.S. and Mexican National Imaginaries*. Durham, NC: Duke University Press, 2011.

Guthrie, Keith. *The Legend of Chipita: The Only Woman Hanged in Texas*. Austin, TX: Eakin Press, 1990.

Gutiérrez, Ramón A., and Elliott Young. "Transnationalizing Borderlands History." *Western Historical Quarterly* 41 (Spring 2010): 27–53.

Gutiérrez de Lara, José. *Proyecto de Ley General de Colonización*. Mexico; En la oficina de D. José Maria Ramos Palomera 1822.

Hall, Stuart. "Reconstruction Work." In *The Critical Decade: Black Photography in the 1980's*, ed. David Bailey and Stuart Hall, *Ten-8*, no. 16 (1984): 106–13.

Harris, Cheryl. "Whiteness as Property." *Harvard Law Review* 106, no. 8 (June 1993): 1710–91.

Harris, Verne. "The Archival Sliver: A Perspective on the Construction of Social Memory in Archives and the Transition from Apartheid to Democracy." In *Refiguring the Archive*, ed. Carolyn Hamilton, Verne Harris, Jane Taylor, Michele Pickover, Graeme Reide, and Razia Saleh. Dordrecht: Kluwer Academic Publishers, 2002.

Hartman, Saidiya. "Venus in Two Acts." *Small Axe* 26 Volume 12, no. 2 (June 2008): 1–14.

Hartman, Saidiya V. *Scenes of Subjection: Terror, Slavery, and Self-Making in Nineteenth-Century America*. New York: Oxford University Press, 1997.

Hays, John P. "The Curious Case of New Mexico's Pre–Civil War Slave Code." *New Mexico Historical Review* 92, no. 3 (Summer 2017).
Hennessy, Rosemary. *Profit and Pleasure: Sexual Identities in Late Capitalism*. New York: Routledge, 2002.
Henning, Michelle. "The Subject as Object: Photography and the Human Body." In *Photography: A Critical Introduction*. London: Routledge, 2000.
Herbert, Harold. "Geroge Smalley, Territorial Journalism, and the Spenazuma Mining Fraud." *The Journal of Arizona History* 46, no. 2 (Summer 2005): 135–60.
Hébert Bluntzer, Rachel. *The Forgotten Colony: San Patricio de Hibernia*. Burnet, Texas: Eakin Press, 1981.
Hernández, Anita Huizar. "The Specter of Statehood: Inventing Arizona in Charles D. Poston's *Building a State in Apache Land* and Marie Clara Zander's "The Life of an Arizona Pioneer."" *MELUS*. 42, no. 2. (Summer 2017): 53–78.
Hernandez, Kelly Lytle. "Borderlands and the Future History of the American West." *Western Historical Quarterly* 42 (Autumn 2011): 325–30.
Hernandez, Lytle Kelly. *Migra!: A History of the U.S. Border Patrol*. Berkeley: University of California Press, 2010.
Hirata, Lucy Cheng. "Chinese Women Immigrants in Nineteenth Century California." In *Women of America*, ed. Carol Ruth Berkin and Mary Beth Norton, 223–44. Boston: Houghton Mifflin, 1979.
Huizar-Hernández, Anita. "The Specter of Statehood: Inventing Arizona in Charles D. Poston's *Building a State in Apache Land* and Marie Clara Zander's 'The Life of an Arizona Pioneer.'" *MELUS* 42, no. 2 (2017): 53–78.
Immigration Act of 1882, 47th Congress, 1st session (18 *Stat*. 477), March 3, 1875.
Irwin, Robert. "Early Paradoxes of Masculinity and Male Homosocial Bonding: The Nineteenth Century." In *Mexican Masculinities*. Minneapolis: University of Minnesota Press, 2003.
Jameson, Fredric. *The Political Unconscious: Narrative as a Socially Symbolic Act*. Ithaca, NY: Cornell University Press, 1982.
JanMohamed, Abdul. "Sexuality on/of the Racial Border: Foucault, Wright, and the Articulation of 'Racialized Sexuality.'" In *Discourses of Sexuality: From Aristotle to AIDS*, ed. Domna Stanton, 94–116. Ann Arbor: University of Michigan Press, 1992.
Jiménez Ramos, Marisela. "'I Am Not the Mulata de Córdoba': The Cultural Meaning of Blackness in Nineteenth-Century Mexico." *The Journal of Pan African Studies* 6, no. 1 (July 2013).
"José Librado Gurulé's Recollections, 1867." In *On the Santa Fe Trail*, ed. Marc Simmons. Lawrence: University of Kansas Press, 1986.
Kandaswamy, Priya. "Gendering Racial Formation." In *Racial Formation in the Twentieth Century*, ed. Daniel Martinez HoSang, Oneka LaBennett, and Laura Pulido. Berkeley: University of California Press, 2012.
Kandiyoti, Deniz. "Identity and Its Discontents: Women and the Nation." *Millennium* 20 (1991).
Kaplan, Amy. "Manifest Domesticity." *American Literature* 70, no. 3 (1998): 581–606.
Katz, Jonathan Ned. *Gay/Lesbian Almanac: A New Documentary*. New York: Harper and Row, 1983.

Kiser, William S. *Borderlands of Slavery: The Struggle over Captivity and Peonage in the American Southwest*. Philadelphia: University of Pennsylvania Press, 2017.

Kiser, William S. "A 'Charming Name for a Species of Slavery': Political Debate on Debt Peonage in the Southwest, 1840s–1860s." *Western Historical Quarterly* 45, no. 2 (2014): 169–89.

Klein, Kerwin Lee. 2000. "On the Emergence of Memory in Historical Discourse." *Representations* 69 (Winter): 127–50.

Knight, Alan. "Mexican Peonage: What Was It and Why Was It?" *Journal of Latin American Studies* 18, no. 1 (1986): 41–74.

Krivulskaya, Suzanna. "The Itinerant Passions of Protestant Pastors: Ministerial Elopement Scandals in the Gilded Age and Progressive Era Press." *The Journal of the Gilded Age and Progressive Era* 19, no. 1 (January 2020): 77–95.

Kurz, Heinz D. "Marx and the 'Law of Value': A Critical Appraisal of the Occasion of His 200th Birthday." *Investigación Económica* 77, no. 304 (Abril–Junio 2018).

Lavrin, Asunción. "Sexuality in Colonial Mexico: A Church Dilemma." In *Sexuality and Marriage in Colonial Latin America*, ed. Asunción Lavrin. Lincoln: University of Nebraska Press, 1989.

Lazo, Rodrigo. "Introduction: Historical Latinidades and Archival Encounters." In *The Latino Nineteenth Century*, ed. Rodrigo Lazo and Jesse Alemán, 1–19. New York: New York University Press, 2018.

Lazo, Rodrigo. "Migrant Archives: New Routes in and out of American Studies." In *States of Emergency: The Object of American Studies*, ed. Russ Castronovo and Susan Gillman, 36–54. Chapel Hill: University of North Carolina Press, 2009.

Lee, Erika, and Judy Yung. *Angel Island: Immigrant Gateway to America*. New York: New York University Press, 2010.

Leonard, Thomas. *Illiberal Reformers: Race, Eugenics and American Economics in the Progressive Era*. Princeton, NJ: Princeton University Press, 2016.

Leshem, Dotan. "Retrospectives: What Did the Ancient Greeks Mean by *Oikonomia*?" *Journal of Economic Perspectives* 30, no. 1 (Winter 2016): 225–31.

"Lights Are Extinguished in Restricted District of Tucson." *Tucson Citizen*, December 6, 1911.

Lockwood, Frank C., and Donald W. Page. *Tucson the Old Pueblo*. Tucson: Santa Cruz Valley Press, 1930.

"The Logic of Gender on the Separation of the Spheres and the Process of Abjection." *Endnotes 3: Gender, Race, and Class and Other Misfortunes* (September 2013). Accessed October, 7, 2019. https://endnotes.org.uk/issues/3/en/endnotes-the-logic-of-gender.

Lomnitz-Adler, Claudio. *Exits from the Labyrinth: Culture and Ideology in the Mexican National Space*. Berkeley: University of California Press, 1992.

López, Marissa. "Introduction: Nuevo Fronteras/New Frontiers." In *Chicano Nations: The Hemispheric Origins of Mexican American Literature*. New York: New York University Press, 2011.

López, Marissa. "Picturing Mexican America in the Age of Realism." *American Literary Realism* 49, no. 3 (Spring 2017).

López, Marissa. "The Political Economy of Early Chicano Historiography: The Case of Hubert H. Bancroft and Mariano G. Vallejo." *American Literary History* 19, no. 4 (Winter 2007): 874–904.

Lowe, Lisa. *Immigrant Acts: On Asian American Cultural Politics*. Durham, NC: Duke University Press, 1996.
Luibhéid, Eithne. *Entry Denied: Controlling Sexuality at the Border*. Minneapolis: University of Minnesota Press, 2002.
Marcellina Bustamento v. Juana Analla (1857). In *Reports of Cases Argued and Determined in the Supreme Court of the Territory of New Mexico, January Term 1852 to January Term, 1879*. Vol 1., Extra Annotated Edition, 255–62. Ed. Charles Gildersleeve. Chicago: Callaghan & Co., 1911.
Marcuse, Herbert. *Eros and Civilization: A Philosophical Inquiry into Freud*. Boston: Beacon, 1974.
Mariana Jaremillo v. José de la Cruz Romero (1857). In *Reports of Cases Argued and Determined in the Supreme Court of the Territory of New Mexico, January Term 1852 to January Term, 1879*. Vol 1., Extra Annotated Edition, 190–208. Ed. Charles Gildersleeve. Chicago: Callaghan & Co., 1911.
Martin, John Levi, and Matt George. "Theories of Sexual Stratification: Toward an Analytics of the Sexual Field and a Theory of Sexual Capital." *Sociological Theory* 24, no. 2 (June 2006): 107–32.
Martínez, María Elena. *Genealogical Fictions: Limpieza de Sangre, Religion, and Gender in Colonial Mexico*. Stanford, CA: Stanford University Press, 2008.
Martinez, Monica Muñoz. *The Injustice Never Leaves You: Anti-Mexican Violence in Texas*. Cambridge: Harvard University Press, 2018.
Matloff, Judith. "Six Women Murdered Each Day as Femicide in Mexico Nears a Pandemic." *Aljazeera America*. January 4, 2015. http://alj.am/1DbdWJV.
Marx, Karl. *Capital*. Vol. 1, *A Critique of Political Economy*. Translated by Samuel Moore and Edward Aveling. Edited by Friedrich Engels. Mineola, NY: Dover Publications, 2011.
Marx, Karl. *Capital*. Vol. 1, *A Critique of Political Economy*. Translated by Ben Fowkes. London: Penguin Publishing, 1982.
Marx, Karl. "Economic and Philosophic Manuscripts of 1844." In *The Marx-Engels Reader*. 2nd ed. Ed. Robert C. Tucker. New York: W. W. Norton & Company, 1978.
Marx, Karl. *Marx Engels Collected Works*. Vol. 31, *Economic Manuscripts of 1861–63*. London: Lawrence and Wishart, 1989.
Marx, Karl. "Theories of Surplus Value," In *Marx Engels Collected Works*, vol. 31: Economic Manuscripts of 1861–63. London: Lawrence and Wishart, 1989.
Marx, Karl. "Wage Labour and Capital." In *Wage Labour and Capital*. Neue Rheinische Zeitung pamphlet, 1891.
Massey, Doreen. *For Space*. London: Sage Publications, 2005.
"Mateo y Raquel." In *Women's Tales from the New Mexico WPA: La Diabla a Pie*, ed. Tey Diana Rebolledo, 358–64. Houston, TX: Arte Público Press, 2000.
"Mateo y Raquel." *Museum of New Mexico History Library*, file no. WPA 5-5-49 @ 12.
"Mayor Buehman Gives His Views on the City and Its Conditions." *Arizona Weekly Citizen* (Tucson, AZ, Territory), July 6, 1895.
McCarthy, Charles. *The Wisconsin Idea*. New York: Macmillan, 1912.
McClanahan, Annie. *Dead Pledges: Debt, Crisis, and Twenty-First-Century Culture*. Stanford, CA: Stanford University Press, 2017.

McClintock, Anne. *Imperial Leather: Race, Gender and Sexuality in the Colonial Contest.* New York: Routledge, 1995.
McClintock, Anne. "No Longer in a Future Heave: Gender, Race, and Nationalism." In *Dangerous Liaisons: Gender, Nation, and Postcolonial Perspectives,* ed. Anne McClintock, Aamir Mufti, and Ella Shohat, 89–112. Minneapolis: University of Minnesota Press, 1997.
McDaniel, Ruel. "The Day They Hanged Chipita." In *San Patricio County in 1976: A Bicentennial Perspective.* Sinton, TX: Sinton Bicentennial Celebrations, 1976.
McDonald, Immigrant Inspector, v. Siu Tak Sam. No. 4356. *United States Circuit Courts of Appeals Reports. Reports Containing the Cases Determined in All the Circuits from the Organization of the Courts: Fully Reported with Numerous Annotations.* Vol. 140. West Publishing Company, 1916.
Menchaca, Martha. 2010. *Recovering History, Constructing Race: The Indian, Black, and White Roots of Mexican Americans.* Austin: University of Texas Press.
Meyers, Allan D., and Davis L. Carlson. "Peonage, Power Relations, and the Built Environment at Hacienda Tabi, Yucatan, Mexico." *International Journal of Historical Archaeology* 6, no. 4 (December 2002).
Milian, Claudia. *Latining America: Black Brown Passages and the Coloring of Latino/a Studies.* Athens: University of Georgia Press, 2013.
Mitchell, Pablo. "Introduction: Bodies on Borders." In *Coyote Nation: Sexuality, Race, and Conquest in Modernizing New Mexico, 1880–1920.* Chicago: University of Chicago Press, 2005.
Mitropoulos, Angela. "Oikonomia." In *Contract and Contagion: From Biopolitics to Oikonomia.* Brooklyn, NY: Minor Compositions, 2012.
Mitropoulos, Angela. "Oikonomia." *Philosophy Today* 63, no. 4 (Fall 2019): 1027.
Montejano, David. *Anglos and Mexicans in the Making of Texas, 1836–1986.* Austin: University of Texas Press, 1987.
Mora-Torres, Juan. *The Making of the Mexican Border: The State, Capitalism, and Society in Nuevo León, 1848–1910.* Austin: University of Texas Press, 2001.
Murphy, Gretchen. "A Europeanized World: Colonialism and Cosmopolitanism in *Who Would Have Thought It?*" In *María Amparo Ruiz de Burton: Critical and Pedagogical Perspectives,* ed. Amelia María de la Luz Montes and Anne Elizabeth Goldman. Lincoln: University of Nebraska Press, 2004.
Murphy, Gretchen. "Geographic Morality and the New World." In *Hemispheric Imaginings: The Monroe Doctrine and Narratives of U.S. Empire.* Durham, NC: Duke University Press, 2005.
Nora, Pierre, and Lawrence D. Kritzman, eds. *Realms of Memory: Conflicts and Divisions.* Vol. 1. New York: Columbia University Press, 1996.
"Noticia de Apaches." *La Estrella de Occidente,* November 20, 1863, column 1.
Oberste, William H. *Texas Irish Empresarios and Their Colonies.* Austin: Von Boeckmann-Jones Co., 1953.
Ogden, Adele. "The Business Letters of Alfred Robinson." *California Historical Society Quarterly* 23, no. 3 (September 1944).
Olcott, Jocelyn. *Revolutionary Women in Postrevolutionary Mexico.* Durham, NC: Duke University Press, 2005.

Olguín, B. V. "*Caballeros* and Indians: Mexican American Whiteness, Hegemonic Mestizaje, and Ambivalent Indigeneity in Proto-Chicana/o Autobiographical Discourse, 1858–2008." *MELUS: Multi-Ethnic Literature of the United States* 38, no. 1 (2013): 30–49.

Omi, Michael, and Howard Winant. *Racial Formation in the United States: From the 1960s to the 1990s.* New York: Routledge, 1994.

"Ordinance No. 117." *Arizona Daily Citizen* (Tucson, AZ, Territory), October 4, 1898.

"Ordinance No. 169." *Arizona Daily Citizen*, July 6, 1903.

Orozco y Berra, Manuel. *Apéndice al Diccionario universal de historia y de geografía.* Tomo II, Vol. IX. México: Imprenta de J. M. Andrade y F. Escalante, 1856.

Orvell, Miles. *The Real Thing: Imitation and Authenticity in American Culture, 1880–1940.* Chapel Hill: University of North Carolina Press, 2014.

Osselaer, Heidi J. "The Battle Begins: The Early Woman Suffrage Movement, 1883 to 1903." In *Winning Their Place: Arizona Women in Politics, 1883–1950.* Tucson: University of Arizona Press, 2009.

Otero, Lydia R. *La Calle: Spatial Conflicts and Urban Renewal in a Southwest City.* Tucson: University of Arizona Press, 2010.

Otero, Miguel. "Letter to the Editor." *Santa Fe Weekly Gazette*, January 12, 1861.

Padilla, Genaro. "Imprisoned Narrative? Or Lies, Secrets, and Silence in Mew Mexico Women's Autobiography." In *Criticism in the Borderlands: Studies in Chicano Literature, Culture, and Ideology*, ed. Hector Calderon and José David Saldívar, 43–60. Durham, NC: Duke University Press, 1991.

Padilla, Genaro. *My History, Not Yours: The Formation of Mexican American Autobiography.* Madison: University of Wisconsin Press, 1993.

Palacio, Vicente Riva. *Tradiciones y Leyendas Mexicanas.* Mexico City: J. Ballesca y Compañía, 1880.

"The Panic of 1862." 2000. *Women's Tales from the New Mexico WPA: La Diabla a Pie.* Ed. Tey Diana Rebolledo. Houston: Arte Público Press, 396-491.

"The Pastor of Illinois Church Convicted as a Despicable Thief." *Petersburg Index and Appeal* (Petersburg, Virginia) 24, no. 70 (October 23, 1877), column 5.

Paz, Octavio. *The Labyrinth of Solitude: The Other Mexico, Return to the Labyrinth of Solitude, Mexico and the United States, the Philanthropic Ogre.* New York: Grove Press, 1994.

Pegler-Gordon, Anna. *In Sight of America: Photography and the Development of U.S. Immigration Policy.* Berkeley: University of California Press, 2009.

Perea, José Leandro. New Mexico State Record Center and Archives, with film at Center for Southwest Research. Mexican Archive of New Mexico. CD3394.N413 c.1. Roll 24, Frame 799.

Pérez, Emma. "Beyond the Nation's Maternal Bodies: Technologies of Decolonial Desire." In *The Decolonial Imaginary: Writing Chicanas into History.* Bloomington: Indiana University Press, 1999.

Pérez, Erika. *Colonial Intimacies: Interethnic Kinship, Sexuality, and Marriage in Southern California, 1769–1885.* Norman: University of Oklahoma Press, 2018.

"Petition to Close Houses." *The Tucson Citizen* (Tucson, AZ, Territory), September 14, 1907.

"The Present Administration in Partnership with Vice and an Immoral Tax Collected Monthly from Fallen Women." *Arizona Daily Citizen*, December 12, 1903.
"Prominent Merchant Held to Grand Jury: Women Waiting at Detention Quarters to Appear Against Nogales Man." *Arizona Daily*, August 27, 1909.
Prosser, Jay. *Light in the Dark Room: Photography and Loss*. Minneapolis: University of Minnesota Press, 2005.
Pubols, Louise. "'A Thing of Honor and Profit': The Creation of California's Elite Families." In *The Father of All: The de la Guerra Family, Power, and Patriarchy in Mexican California*. Berkeley: Huntington-USC Institute on California and the West by UC Press, 2009.
Radden, Gunter, and Zoltan Kovecses. "Towards a Theory of Metonymy." In *Metonymy in Language and Thought*. Amsterdam: John Benjamins Publishing Company, 1999.
Ramos, Marisela Jiménez. "'I Am Not the Mulata de Córdoba': The Cultural Meaning of Blackness in Nineteenth-Century Mexico." *The Journal of Pan African Studies* 6, no. 1 (July 2013): 92.
Ranchero, November 29, 1863, in Corpus Christi Library.
Rebolledo, Tey Diana. "Las Escritoras: Romances and Realities." In *Pasó Por Aquí: Critical Essays on the New Mexican Literary Tradition 1542–1988*, ed. Erlinda Gonzales-Berry. Albuquerque: University of New Mexico Press, 1989.
Rebolledo, Tey Diana. "Las Hijas de la Malinche: Mexicana/India Captivity Narratives in the Southwest, Subverting Voices." In *Nuevomexicano Cultural Legacy: Forms Agencies & Discourse*, ed. Francisco A. Lomelí, Víctor A. Sorell, and Genaro M. Padilla, 129–50. Albuquerque: University of New Mexico Press, 2002.
Rebolledo, Tey Diana. "Introduction: The Federal Writers Project." In *Women's Tales from the New Mexico WPA: La Diabla a Pie*, xix–liv. Houston: Arte Público Press, 2000.
Rebolledo, Tey Diana. "Narrative Strategies of Resistance in Hispana Writing." *The Journal of Narrative Technique* 20, no. 2 (Spring 1990): 134–46.
Reed, Maureen. "Making Homes in a Changing Land: Fabiola Cabeza de Baca and the Double-Edged Present." In *A Woman's Place: Women Writing New Mexico*, 121–69. Albuquerque: University of New Mexico Press, 2005.
Refugio County Commissioner's Court minutes, 1:186, 195, 196, 197, 444, 452, 461.
Reich, Wilhelm. *Sex-Pol: Essays 1929–1934*. Translated by Anna Bostock, Tom DuBose, and Lee Baxendall. Edited by Lee Baxandall. New York: Vintage Books, 1972.
"República Mexicana." *La Estrella de Occidente*, April 11, 1862, column 3, page 1.
"The Rev. Alfred Thompson." *Chicago Daily Tribune*, October 19, 1877.
Robinson, Cedric. *Black Marxism: The Making of the Black Radical Tradition*. Chapel Hill: University of North Carolina Press, 2005.
Rodríguez, Juana María. *Sexual Futures, Queer Gestures, and Other Latina Longings*. New York: New York University Press, 2014.
Roediger, David R. *The Wages of Whiteness: Race and the Making of the American Working Class*. New York: Verso, 1991.
Roybal, Karen R. *Archives of Dispossession: Recovering the Testimonios of Mexican American Herederas, 1848-1960*. Chapel Hill: University of North Carolina Press, 2017.
Ruiz, Julie. "Captive Identities: The Gendered Conquest of Mexico in *Who Would Have Thought It?*" In *María Amaparo Ruiz de Burton: Critical and Pedagogical Perspectives*,

ed. Amelia María de la Luz Montes and Anne Elizabeth Goldman. Lincoln: University of Nebraska Press, 2004.
Ruiz de Burton, María Amparo. *Conflicts of Interest: The Letters of María Amparo Ruiz de Burton*. Ed. Rosaura Sánchez and Beatrice Pita. Houston: Arte Público Press, 2001.
Ruiz de Burton, María Amparo. *Who Would Have Thought It?* Houston: Arte Publíco Press, 1995.
Salas, Miguel Tinker. *In the Shadow of the Eagles: Sonora and the Transformation of the Border during the Porfiriato*. Berkeley: University of California Press, 1997.
Saldaña-Portillo, Maria Josefina. "Adjudicating Exception: The Fate of the *Indio Bárbaro* in the US Courts (1869–1954)." *Indian Given: Racial Geographies across Mexico and the United States*. Durham, NC: Duke University Press, 2016.
Saldaña-Portillo, Maria Josefina. "Who's the Indian in Aztlán?" in *The Latin American Subaltern Studies Reader*, ed. Ileana Rodríguez. Durham, NC: Duke University Press, 2001.
Sánchez, Rosaura. *Telling Identities: The Californio Testimonios*. Minneapolis: University of Minessota Press, 1995.
Sánchez, Rosaura, and Beatrice Pita, eds. *Conflicts of Interest: The Letters of María Amparo Ruiz de Burton*. Houston, TX: Arte Público Press, 2001.
Sánchez, Rosaura, and Beatrice Pita. "Introduction." In *Who Would Have Thought It?* Houston, TX: Arte Público Press, 1995.
Sánchez Rosaura and Beatriz Pita. "(Shifting) Frames of Reference: Southwest by East." In *Conflicts of Interest: The Letters of Maria Amparo Ruiz de Burton*, ed. Rosaura Sánchez and Beatriz Pita. Houston: Arte Público Press, 2001.
San Patricio County District Court Records. Volume 2, Monday, October 5–Saturday, October 10, 1863.
Schneider, Gustav. Archive. Arizona Historical Society. MS 715 F.12 Box 1.
Scott, Joan. 1991. "The Evidence of Experience." *Questions of Evidence: Proof, Practice, and Persuasion across the Disciplines*. Chicago: University of Chicago Press.
Senate Concurrent Resolution 14. By Carlos F. Truan. June 13, 1985.
Sheridan, Thomas E. *Landscapes of Fraud: Mission Tumacácori, the Baca Float, and the Betrayal of the O'Odham*. Tucson: University of Arizona Press, 2006.
Sheridan, Thomas E. *Los Tucsoneses: The Mexican Community in Tucson, 1854–1941*. Tucson: University of Arizona Press, 1986.
"Situacion de Sonora y los Apaches." *La Estrella de Occidente*, June 26, 1868, column 1, page 3.
Skeggs, Beverly. "Context and Background: Pierre Bourdieu's Analysis of Class, Gender, and Sexuality." *The Editorial Board of the Sociological Review* 52, no. 2 (2004): 19–33.
Smalley, George. "Arizona Album: Pioneer Anecdotes—Fair, Fat, and Forty." *Tucson Daily Citizen* (Tucson, AZ), September 29, 1954.
Smith, Adam. *An Inquiry into the Nature and Causes of the Wealth of Nations*. 2 vols., 642–62. Indianapolis: Liberty Classics, 1981.
Smith-Rosenberg, Carroll. "The Hysterical Woman: Sex Roles and Role Conflict in 19th-Century America." *Social Research* 39, no. 4 (Winter 1972): 652–78.
Smylie, Vernon. *A Noose for Chipita*. Corpus Christi: Texas News Syndicate Press, 1970.
Standing, Guy. *The Precariat: The New Dangerous Class*. London: Bloomsbury Academic, 2011.

Streeby, Shelley. *American Sensations: Class, Empire, and the Production of Popular Culture.* Berkeley and Los Angeles: University of California Press, 2002.

Stren, Alexandra Minna. "Buildings, Boundaries, and Blood: Medicalization and Nation-Building on the U.S.-Mexico Border, 1910–1930." *The Hispanic American Historical Review* 79, no. 1 (1999): 41–81.

Taylor, Diane. *The Archive and the Repertoire: Performing Cultural Memory in the Archive.* Durham, NC: Duke University Press, 2003.

Thompson, Joseph A. *El Gran Capitán: José de la Guerra.* Los Angeles: Cabrera and Sons, 1961.

Tibesar, Antonine, ed. *Writings of Junipero Serra.* 4 vols. Washington, DC: Academy of American Franciscan History, 1955.

Tinnemeyer, Andrea. *Identity Politics of the Captivity Narrative after 1848.* Lincoln: University of Nebraska Press, 2008.

Tinnemeyer, Andrea. "Rescuing the Past: The Case of Olive Oatman and Lola Medina." In *María Amparo Ruiz de Burton: Critical & Pedagogical Perspective*, ed. Amelia María de la Luz Montes and Anne Elizabeth Goldman. Lincoln: University of Nebraska Press, 2004.

Tortorici, Zeb. *Sins against Nature: Sex and Archives in Colonial New Spain.* Durham, NC: Duke University Press, 2017.

Truett, Samuel. *Fugitive Landscapes: Forgotten History of the U.S.–Mexico Borderlands.* New Haven, CT: Yale University Press, 2006.

Turner, Frederick Jackson. "The Significance of the Frontier in American History." *Proceedings of the State Historical Society of Wisconsin* (1893).

Twinam, Ann. *Purchasing Whiteness: Pardos, Mulattos, and the Quest for Social Mobility in the Spanish Indies.* Stanford, CA: Stanford University Press, 2015.

Underwood, Marylyn. "Rodríguez, Josefa [Chipita]." *Handbook of Texas Online.* Accessed January 16, 2020. http://www.tshaonline.org/handbook/online/articles/fro50.

U.S. Congress, Senate, Hearings before the Subcommittee of the Committee on Territories on House Bill 12543, to Enable the People of Oklahoma, Arizona, and New Mexico to Form Constitutions and State Governments and Be Admitted into the Union on an Equal Footing with the Original States. *New Statehood Bill*, 57th Cong., 2nd sess., 1902.

Valencia, Sayak. *Gore Capitalism.* Cambridge: Massachusetts Institute of Technology Press, 2010.

Valerio-Jiménez, Omar S. *River of Hope: Forging Identity and Nation in the Rio Grande Borderlands.* Durham, NC: Duke University Press, 2013.

Vinson, Ben, III. *Before Mestizaje: The Frontiers of Race and Caste in Colonial Mexico.* New York: Cambridge University Press, 2018.

Weber, David J. *The Mexican Frontier, 1821–1846: The American Southwest under Mexico.* Albuquerque: University of New Mexico Press, 1982.

Weigman, Robyn. "The Anatomy of Lynching." *Journal of the History of Sexuality* 3, no. 3 (January 1993).

Weiner, Lawrence. *Chipita Rodríguez.* No publisher identified, 1982.

Wexler, Laura. *Tender Violence: Domestic Visions in an Age of U.S. Imperialism.* Chapel Hill: University of North Carolina Press, 2000.

"Wile of Mexican Girls." *El Paso Daily Times*, January 30, 1908.
Wilson, Bernard J., and Zaellotius A. Wilson. "From Maiden Lane to Gay Alley: Prostitutes and Prostitution in Tucson, 1880–1912." *The Journal of Arizona History* 55, no. 2 (Summer 2014): 167–86.
Wood, Ellen Meiksins. *Democracy against Capitalism: Renewing Historical Materialism.* Cambridge: Cambridge University Press, 2009.
Woosley, Anne I. *Early Tucson.* Charleston, SC: Arcadia Publishing, 2008.
Xenophon. *The Economist.* London: Macmillan, 1890.
Yung, Judy. *Chinese Women of America: A Pictorial History.* Seattle: University of Washington Press, 1986.
Zink, Amanda. *Fictions of Western American Domesticity: Indian, Mexican, and Anglo Women in Print Culture, 1850–1950.* Albuquerque: University of New Mexico Press, 2018.

Index

abstract labor, 20–21, 84, 89–90, 96, 98, 104
Acosta, Teresa Paloma, 80, 102–103
Adams, George E., 152
Adams, J.C., 155–156
African Americans, 17, 195n11. *See also* Blackness; Blacks
Afromestizos, 188n32
agriculture, 14, 138, 142, 145, 147, 200n32
Alarcón, Norma, 16
Albuquerque West Mesa murders, 1–3, 176–179, *180*, 181n3
Althusser, Louis, 184n74
American exceptionalism, 15, 49, 184n59
American Sensations (Streeby), 195n12
Anderson, Benedict, 40
Anthony, Susan B., 76
Apache, 70, 112
Aranda, José F., 54–55, 60
Arce, Christina, 63, 66
Aristotle, 28–31
Arizona, 140–141, 143–144, 146–147, 155–157, 199n11
autobiography, 34

Balibar, Etienne, 184n74
Bancroft, Hubert Howe, 33
Barela, Jamie, 1, 177
Batchen, Lou Sage, 196n37
Beecher, Henry Ward, 75–76
Bejarano, Cynthia, 2
Bernes, Jasper, 20
Biel, William, 165
Blackness, 51–52, 62–64, 66–68, 187n11
Blacks: in 19th century Mexico, 62–63
Bluntzer Hebet, Rachel, 80, 82–88
body(ies): as basis of economy, 27; in debt peonage, 117–126; focus on, 4; oiko-politic and, 33–40; in portraiture, 47; in racialized sexuality, 4–5; sexual capital and, 7; sexuality and, 19; surplus within, 40–44
borderlands: economics of, 6, 12–14, 143, 145–150; femininity and, 7; gendered racial formations in, economy of, 88–92; origin of term, 4; prostitution laws and, 145–150; racialization and, 8–9, 32; Ruiz de Burton and, 57–58; sexual capital and, 3; as shifting, 2
Bosch, Richard, 159
Bouchard, Hipólito, 35
Bourbon Reforms, 31–32
Bourdieu, Pierre, 181n10
Brooks, James, 112, 198n94
Buehman, Henry, 153
Burton, Henry S., 55

Cabeza de Baca, Fabiola, 107–108, 126–137
Cabeza de Baca, Luis María, 132
Cabezut, Manuel, 69–70, 74
Californianas, 9, 25–29, 33–40, 47, 106, 179, 185n5
California Recollections of Angustias de la Guerra Ord, 27, 34
Californio, 2, 7–10, 13, 18, 21–22, 25–34, 42, 44, 47–48, 55–57, 80, 108, 111, 142–143, 181n4, 185n5
Campbell, Randolph B., 192n19
Campt, Tina M., 144
Candelaria, Monica, 1, 177
Capital (Marx), 30
capitalism: abstract, 21; family and, 109; hegemony and, 171; monopoly, 18; racial, 5, 20–21, 184n59; transition to, 142. *See also* sexual capital
Captives and Cousins (Brooks), 198n94
Carillo, Leonardo, 80

Carrigan, William D., 94
Carrillo y Lugo, María Antonia, 32
Casarín, Manuel Jimeno, 33
casta system, 58, 188n32
Casteñeda, Antonia, 4, 17
castration, 95–96
cautiva, 53, 69–75
Cerritu, Henry, 27
Cerruti, Enrique, 43
Chavez, Victoria, 1, 177
Chávez-García, Miroslava, 41
Chevalier, Michel, 189n46
Chicana/o, 128–129, 177
Chinese immigrants, 6, 157, 161–162, 200n33
"Chipita" (Acosta), 80, 102–103
Chipita Rodríguez (opera), 80, 98–102
Cholula massacres, 16
citizenship, 7, 55, 72–73, 95, 114
Ciudad Juárez, 2, 181n5
civility, 7, 14–18, 23, 56, 108, 110, 179
Civil War (U.S.), 60, 89, 192n19
Clamor Público, El (newspaper), 53
class: capitalism and, 26; debt peonage and, 112, 115; femininity and, 42; gender and, 106; intersectionality and, 31; marriage and, 28; positionality, 136; prostitution and, 143, 163; race and, 58, 156–157; racialization and, 58–59; sexuality and, 19
Cloven, Virginia, 1, 177
Cocks, Catherine, 146
Coleman, A. D., 168
colonialism, 15, 21, 62, 106, 111, 128, 131, 135–137, 143, 177, 194n1
colorism, 23, 106
Comanche, 71, 112, 129, 132, 136
commodity, 182n21
Commons, John R., 157
communal land system, 6
Compromise of 1850, 113
Conner, J.E., 83
Cooke, Philip St. George, 114
Cornell, Charles, 158–161
Coronado, Raul, 48
Cortés, Hernán, 16
Cotton Trail, 79, 88–89, 91

Couto, José Bernardo, 51–52
criollos, 17, 55, 188n25, 188n32, 196n33

Dana, Richard Henry, 37
Davenport, James J., 117
Davis, Adrienne, 195n11
Day, Iyko, 5, 20–21
debt peonage, 6, 13–14, 22, 105–108, 111–126
de Jaramillo, Juan, 16
de la Cruz Romero, José, 115
de la Guerra, Pablo, 25
de la Guerra, Teresa, 10
de la Guerra Hartnell, Teresa, 27, 42–44
de la Guerra Ord, Angustias, 33–35, 43
de la Guerra Robinson, Anita, 25–26, 37–39, 43, 45
de la Guerra Robinson, Elena, 38–40
de la Guerra y Noriega, Don José, 10, 25–28, 31–33, 35–36, 42, 47, 185n28, 186n48
del Castillo, Adelaida, 16
Díaz, Porfirio, 148
domestication, 44
domesticity, 15, 41–42, 45–47, 183n39
Doña Marina. *See* La Malinche

Echeveste Reglamento, 41
Economic and Philosophic Manuscripts of 1844 (Marx), 5, 182n21
Edwards, Syllania, 1, 177
Elks, Cinnamon, 1, 177
Ely, Richard T., 157
encomienda, 111–112, 195n13
Eng, David, 95
Estrella de Occidente, La (newspaper), 52–53, 69–70
ethnocentrism, 106
eugenics, 157–158
exceptionalism, American, 15, 49, 184n59

family, 109–110, 131. *See also* kinship
Federal Writers' Project, 118
feminicides: Ciudad Juárez, 2, 181n5; West Mesa murders, 1–3, 176–179, *180*
femininity: borderlands and, 7; *indios* and, 71–72; nationalism and, 40–41;

normativity and, 41–42; Nuevomexicanas and, 107; proper, 7, 50; white, 15, 23, 41, 48–50, 54, 59, 64–68, 71, 73, 75–78, 150, 159, 200n32; in *Who Would Have Thought It?*, 50–51, 64–65, 67–68, 74–75
feminism, Marxist, 19, 109–110, 197n61
Fischer, Kristen, 195n11
Flynn, James, 156–157
Fortunati, Leopoldina, 109, 124–125
Foucault, Michel, 5, 144, 146, 165, 202n95
Fragoso, Julia Estela Monárrez, 2
France, 60–61
Freud, Sigmund, 95

Gadsden Purchase, 199n11
gender: class and, 106; defined, 4; imperialism and, 26; normativity, 126–137; racialized, 1–2, 4, 40–44, 88–92; use of term, 8. *See also* femininity
genízaro, 112
gente decente, 17
gente de razón, 17
Georges, Gusdorf, 34
Gilded Age, 152
Gilpin, John, 93
Gold Rush, 146
Gonzalez, Deena, 15, 28–29, 145
González de Noriega, Pedro, 31–32
Gramsci, Antonio, 171
Great Depression, 118
Guadalupe Vallejo, Mariano, 56
Guidotti-Hernández, Nicole, 3
Gurulé, José Librado, 107, 121–123
Guthrie, Keith, 80, 96–97

hacienda system, 6, 112, 135–136, 142
Hall, Stuart, 169
hanging, of Rodríguez, 93–97
Hartin, Henry, 156
Hartnell, William Edward Petty, 42–43
Hennessy, Rosemary, 169, 183n59, 184n74
Hesch Thorp, Annette, 196n37
Hewetson, James, 89
hierarchy, racial, 17, 49, 58–59, 188n25, 188n32

Hispana, 2, 9, 23, 107–108, 110, 135–137, 179, 181n4, 194n1
historical materialism, 47
Hughes, Josephine, 152–153, 200n44
Hughes, Louis, 200n44

imaginary, imperial, 49
Immigration Act of 1882, 149
Immigration Act of 1903, 149
Immigration Act of 1917, 140
imperial imaginary, 49
imperialism, 15, 26, 48–49, 56, 106, 126, 128
Indians, 17, 43–44, 61–62
Indigenous slavery, 112–114
indios, 69–75
individualism, 146, 152
industrialism, 138, 143, 145–146
industrialization, 13, 18–19
inequality, 17–19, 30
intersectionality, 2, 5, 9, 11, 13, 18–19, 21–22, 27, 29, 31, 58, 62, 73, 91, 96, 157, 168, 192n28
Irwin, Robert, 53

JanMohamed, Abdul R., 4–5
Jaremillo, Mariana, 114–115

Kandaswamy, Priya, 192n28
Kandiyoti, Deniz, 40
Kearney, Stephen W., 114
kinship, 118, 135. *See also* family
Kiser, William S., 112, 114, 117
Klein, Kerwin Lee, 134
Knight, Alan, 114
Kollontai, Alexandra, 19

labor: abstract, 20–21, 84, 89–90, 96, 98, 104; conditions of labor *vs.* labor, 13–14; performance and, 98; racialization and, 20; reproductive, 26, 28, 38–39, 90–91, 107–111, 124–125, 182n21; sexual, 5–7, 111; sexuality and, 19; time, 89–90; violence and, 6
La Llorona, 99–101, 103
La Malinche, 16–17, 53, 85, 100–101
La Mulata de Córdoba, 51–52, 61–63, 65–68

Land Act of 1851, 56
land grants, 10, 14, 42, 56–57, 89, 112, 119, 124
Langacker, Ronald, 123
Latour, Bruno, 18
Lazo, Rodrigo, 8
Legend of Chipita, The: The One Woman Hanged in Texas (Guthrie), 80, 96–97, 97
León, Molly, 169, 172–173, 174–175
Leonard, Thomas C., 147
Librado Gurulé, José, 119–121
Lomnitz-Adler, Claudio, 58
López, Marissa, 34
Lorenzo, Fileto, 160
Los Alamos National Laboratory, 127
Lowe, Lisa, 5, 20–21, 183n59
Luibhéid, Eithne, 150
lynching, 94–96

Magee, John E., 156–157
Malintzín. *See* La Malinche
Maltby, Henry Alonzo, 94
Manhattan Project, 127
Manifest Destiny, 15, 17–18, 40
Marcellina Bustamento v. Juana Analla, 13, 116–117, 121–122
Marcuse, Herbet, 19
Mariana Jaremillo v. José de la Cruz Romero, 107–108, 115–117
Marquez, Doreen, 1, 177
Márquez, Teresa, 118
marriage, 28–29, 32–33, 41, 133
Marx, Karl, 5–7, 20–21, 26, 28, 30–31, 89–90, 98, 109–110, 124, 178, 182n21, 184n74
Marxist feminism, 19
masculinity, 95–97, 105
materialism, historical, 47
Maya, 112
Maytorena, Jesús, 55
McClanahan, Annie, 20
McClintock, Anne, 131
McCullough, Hugh, 42
McCumber, Kate, 83, 85
McDonald, Brown, 141, 158, 161–162
McDonald, Immigrant Inspector, v. Siu Tak Sam, 161–162

McMullen, John, 89
McMullen-McGloin colony, 88–89
memory, 118, 134
men. *See* masculinity; patriarchy
Menchaca, Martha, 113, 188n25, 196n33
mercantilism, 13, 142
mestizaje, 53, 58, 72
mestizas/os, 15–17, 63, 100, 112, 115, 129, 137, 188n32
Mexicana: captivity and, 69–75; as term, 181n4; value of, 48; in *Who Would Have Thought It?*, 53–54. *See also* women
Mexican American: as term, 181n4, 194n1
Mexican-American War, 4, 25–26, 43, 55
mexicanidad, 48–49, 51–54, 58
Mitropoulos, Angela, 28, 30
mob violence, 94
Moden, E. B., 157
Monárrez Fragoso, Julia Estela, 178
monopoly capitalism, 18
Monroe Doctrine, 60
Montejano, Davis, 153
Moreno, Matías, 56
Morgan, Jennifer, 195n11
Mulata de Córdoba, 51–52, 61–63, 65–68
mulatas, 11, 23, 48, 51–54, 59, 62, 64–65, 115
Muñoz Martinez, Monica, 94–95
Murphy, Gretchen, 60

Napoleon III, 189n36
nationalism, 16, 34, 40–41, 106, 129, 131, 136, 157
National Origins Act, 147–148
nativism, 15, 106, 141, 148, 179, 199n7
Navajo, 112, 132
Neal, Benjamin F., 79, 87, 192n19
"new deal Modernism," 19
New Mexico: A Guide to the Colorful State, 121
Nieto, Julie, 1, 177
Noose for Chipita, A (Smylie), 80
normativity, 5, 7–9, 41–42, 126–136, 149, 171
nuclear bomb, 127
Nuevomexicanas, 7, 14, 23, 105–109, 117–126, 130–131, 133–134, 136–137, 142, 179, 181n4, 194n1, 195n3

Oatman, Mary, 61–62
oikonomia, 27–30
oikopolitic, 33–40, 44
Ord, James L., 33
Orvell, Miles, 165, 168
Otero, Miguel A., 114, 200n44
otherness, 51–52, 63, 66

Padilla, Genaro, 127–128
Page Act, 6, 150
"Panic of 1862, The" (Gurulé), 119–123
paternalism, 34–35, 136
patriarchy, 26, 40–41, 136, 171
patrones, 106, 110, 112, 114–115, 142, 195n3
Paz, Octavio, 16, 100
Perea, José Leandro, 119–122, 125–126
Pérez, Erika, 42
Pesqueira, Ignacio, 53
phallus, 95–96
photography, 44–47, 46, 163–175, 166–167, 170, 172–173
phrenology, 44
physiognomy, 44
Pita, Beatrice, 50, 54, 60, 188n24
portraiture, 45–47, 46, 164–165
Power, James, 89
print culture, 49–50
Progressive Era, 139–140, 147, 150, 152, 169, 199n7
property holding, 7, 30, 135
Prosser, Jay, 45
prostitution, 5–6; in Arizona, 139, 141, 143–144, 150–158, 163–164; laws, 145–150; in Mexico, 148–149, 160–161; moral reform and, 152–155; "national cleansing" and, 157–158; in Progressive Era, 139–140, 147, 169; race and, 158–162; technology of power and, 144, 162–175

race: class and, 58, 156–157; in racialized sexuality, 111; sex and, 158–162; sexual capital and, 2
racial capitalism, 5, 20–21, 184n59
racial hierarchy, 17, 49, 58–59, 188n25, 188n32

racialization, 1–2, 4–5, 7–8; civility and, 14–18; class and, 58–59; debt peonage and, 116–117; and dialectical relationship of gender and sex, 40–44; domesticity and, 45–47; gender and, 1–2, 4, 40–44, 88–92; labor and, 20; *mexicanidad* and, 58; normativity and, 8–9; reproductive labor and, 38–39; sexuality and, 1–2, 110–111; subjectivity and, 106
railroad, 49
Ramirez, Francisco, 53
Ramírez Aparicio, Manuel, 52
Ramos, Marisela Jiménez, 63
rape, 41, 95, 110, 149, 195n11
Rebolledo, Tey Diana, 112, 118, 121, 128
Reich, Wilhelm, 19
repartimiento, 111–112, 115, 195n13
reproductive labor, 26, 28, 38–39, 90–91, 107–111, 124–125, 182n21
respectability, 40–44
Riddel, Sosa, 16
Riva Palacio, Vicente, 52
Robinson, Alfred, 25–26, 37–38
Robinson, Cedric, 5, 20
Rodríguez, Josefa Chipita, 79–104, 97, 192n19
Rodríguez, Juana Maria, 177–178
Roediger, David, 183n59
Rogers, Richard T., 161
Romero, Veronica, 1, 177
Roosevelt, Franklin D., 118
Ross, Edward A., 157
Roybal, Karen, 130
Ruiz, Isabel, 55
Ruiz, Julie, 49, 55
Ruiz de Burton, María, 48–59

Salazar, Evelyn, 1, 177
Salazar, Manuel, 160
Saldaña-Portillo, María Josefina, 70–72
Sánchez, Rosaura, 34, 50, 54, 60, 106, 121, 189n46
Santa Fe Trail, 13–14, 125, 132
Savage, John, 79–80
Savage, Thomas, 33

scandals, sex, 75–78
Schneider, Gustav, 144, 162–175, *166–167*, *170*, *172–173*
Senkewicz, Robert M., 43
servantry, 34–35
sex, 18–21; debt peonage and, 111–117; materiality of, 107, 110; race and, 158–162; racialized, 40–44; sexuality and, 19, 183n59; as technology of power, 144, 162–175; use of term, 8
sex scandals, 75–78
sexual capital: bodies and, 7; in Bourdieu, 181n10; debt peonage and, 105–106; defined, 3; other uses of term, 5; race and, 2
sexuality: body and, 19; class and, 19; debt peonage and, 116–117; "foreignness" and, 158–162; imperialism and, 26; labor and, 19; La Malinche and, 16; materiality of, 110; otherness and, 51–52; racialized, 1–2, 4–5, 7–8, 109–111; sex and, 19, 183n59; use of term, 8
sexual labor, 5–7, 111
Shadow on the Nueces: The Story of Chipita Rodriguez (Herbet), 80, 82–88
Sheridan, Thomas E., 199n11
"Significance of the Frontier in American History, The" (Turner), 14–15
Silvera, Juan, 79, 81, 85–88
Singh, Nikhil Pal, 5
slavery, 30–31, 58, 105, 112–116, 195n11, 200n32
Smalley, George H., 139, 144
Smylie, Vernon, 80
social formation, 184n74
Soule, W. L. G., 156
Stanton, Elizabeth Cady, 76
Stowe, Harriett Beecher, 76
Streeby, Shelley, 114, 195n12
subjectivity, 4, 8, 20, 28, 34, 54, 56, 67, 83, 91, 93, 106, 110, 135–137, 146, 181n4, 184n59
Sullivan, Josephine, 83
surplus, 40–44
Szalay, Michael, 19

Tafolla, Carmen, 16
Taylor, Diana, 98
technology of power, 144, 162–175, 202n95
Tejana/o, 2, 4, 7–9, 13, 18, 89, 143, 153, 181n4, 191n1
temperance, 152–154
testimonios, 34, 121
Thirteenth Amendment, 116
Thompson, Alfred, 75–76
Tilton, Elizabeth, 76
time, labor, 89–90
Tinnemeyer, Andrea, 61
Treaty of Guadalupe Hidalgo, 55, 61
Truan, Carlos F., 103
Tucker, Karla Faye, 80, 103
Turner, Frederick Jackson, 14–15
Two Years before the Mast (Dana), 37

Uncle Tom's Cabin (Stowe), 76
U.S. Hispanic Literary Heritage Project, 118
Ute, 112

Valdez, Michelle, 1, 177
Valerio-Jiménez, Omar, 17
Villescas, Francisco, 160
violence: Chipita Rodríguez and, 97–103; economic context and, 178; labor and, 6; mob, 94; systematic patterns of, 3
Virgin of Guadalupe, 53

wealth, 30, 42, 108, 132–133
Webb, Clive, 94
Weber, David, 114
We Fed Them Cactus (Cabeza de Baca), 107–108, 126–137
Weigman, Robin, 95
Weiner, Lawrence, 80, 98–99
Welder, John, 86, 89
welfare state, 19
West Mesa murders, 1–3, 176–179, *180*, 181n2
Wexler, Laura, 44–45
white femininity, 15, 23, 41, 48–50, 54, 59, 66–68, 71, 73, 75, 77–78, 150, 159, 200n32
whiteness, 8, 15, 22, 41–42, 44, 49, 51, 55, 58–59, 64–68, 71, 91, 140, 147, 157

White Sands Proving Ground, 127
Who Would Have Though It? (Ruiz de Burton), 49–55, 59–68, 71–73, 76–78
Wilson, John, 80
women: economization of bodies of, 32; imperialism and, 26; Indigenous, 49; marriage and, 28–29. *See also* femininity; gender
Women's Tales from the New Mexico WPA: La Diabla a Pie, 118–126
Wood, Ellen, 184n74

Woodhull, Victoria C., 76
Works Progress Administration (WPA), 117–126
Works Projects Administration (WPA), 107
WPA. *See* Works Projects Administration (WPA)

Xenophon, 29

Zink, Amanda, 15, 41–42

www.ingramcontent.com/pod-product-compliance
Lightning Source LLC
Chambersburg PA
CBHW030646230426
43665CB00011B/982